The
Hour
of
Absinthe

Intoxicating Histories

SERIES EDITORS: VIRGINIA BERRIDGE AND ERIKA DYCK

Whether on the street, off the shelf, or over the pharmacy counter, interactions with drugs and alcohol are shaped by contested ideas about addiction, healing, pleasure, and vice and their social dimensions. Books in this series explore how people around the world have consumed, created, traded, and regulated psychoactive substances throughout history. The series connects research on legal and illegal drugs and alcohol with diverse areas of historical inquiry, including the histories of medicine, pharmacy, consumption, trade, law, social policy, and popular culture. Its reach is global and includes scholarship on all periods. Intoxicating Histories aims to link these different pasts as well as to inform the present by providing a firmer grasp on contemporary debates and policy issues. We welcome books, whether scholarly monographs or shorter texts for a broad audience focusing on a particular phenomenon or substance, that alter the state of knowledge.

NINA S. STUDER

The Hour of ABSINTHE

A Cultural
History
of
France's
Most
Notorious
Drink

McGill-Queen's University Press   Montreal & Kingston • London • Chicago

ISBN 978-0-2280-2220-6 (paper)
ISBN 978-0-2280-2221-3 (ePDF)
ISBN 978-0-2280-2222-0 (ePUB)

Legal deposit third quarter 2024
Bibliothèque nationale du Québec

Printed in Canada on acid-free paper that is 100% ancient forest free
(100% post-consumer recycled), processed chlorine free

McGill-Queen's University Press in Montreal is on land which long served
as a site of meeting and exchange amongst Indigenous Peoples, including
the Haudenosaunee and Anishinabeg nations. In Kingston it is situated on
the territory of the Haudenosaunee and Anishinaabek. We acknowledge
and thank the diverse Indigenous Peoples whose footsteps have marked
these territories on which peoples of the world now gather.

Library and Archives Canada Cataloguing in Publication

Title: The hour of absinthe : a cultural history of France's most notorious
    drink / Nina S. Studer
Names: Studer, Nina Salouâ, author.
Series: Intoxicating histories ; 11.
Description: Series statement: Intoxicating histories ; 11 | Includes biblio-
    graphical references and index.
Identifiers: Canadiana (print) 20240376447 | Canadiana (ebook)
    20240376471 | ISBN 9780228022206 (paper) | ISBN 9780228022213 (ePDF) |
    ISBN 9780228022220 (ePUB)
Subjects: LCSH: Absinthe—France—History—19th century. | LCSH:
    Absinthe—France—History—20th century.
Classification: LCC GT2898 .S78 2024 | DDC 394.1/30944—dc23

This book was designed and typeset by studio oneonone in Minion 11/14

Contents

Figures

Acknowledgments

I would like to start by thanking the anonymous reviewers of my book, whose input has been invaluable and much appreciated, as well as Richard Baggaley and Kathleen Fraser at McGill-Queen's University Press for their vital expertise, patience, and kindness, and Kathryn Simpson (of Minerva Writing Services) for their excellent feedback.

My fascination with absinthe started over a decade ago, based on the fact that both the drink and I share strong connections to Switzerland, France, and North Africa. Since then, I have had the opportunity to present and discuss North Africa's role in the history of absinthe at various conferences on drinks, medical history, and (North) African studies, such as the African Studies Association of the UK conference in Brighton, the Social History of Medicine conference in Oxford, the international congress of the Mediterranean Studies Association in 2014, the Drinking Studies Network conference in Leicester in 2015, the "Alcohol Flows across Cultures" symposium in Oxford in 2016, and more. I would like to thank everybody who asked incisive questions about my favourite topic and showed an interest in the colonial aspects of the historiography of absinthe at these conferences. Discussions with other historians of drinks, medicine, or North Africa have helped in shaping my understanding of the green fairy. I would also like to thank the students of three courses I have taught about the history of drinks, namely the "History of Drinks in Algeria" colloquium at the University of Bern in 2017, the "Colonial History of Consumption: Drinks in the Middle East and North Africa" seminar at the University of Zürich in 2020, and the "Alcohol in the North African Colonies: Crime, Sickness, and Civilisation" seminar at the University of Basel in 2021. Analyzing details of the history of alcohol in general and absinthe in particular with students was very productive, and their enthusiasm and insights gave me much joy. I would like to thank every one of my students.

Much appreciation to the magnificent staff members of various libraries and archives in Switzerland, France, and the UK who have helped me in finding even the most obscure of sources, often at short notice. We all know that without them no academic work would ever be written. Similarly, friends and colleagues have supported me through the various stages of my research, and I would like to thank Hanna Al-Taher, Fenna von Hirschheydt, Christopher Giganti, Patric O. Schaerer, Geraldine Probst, Zadia Zulfiqar, Filippo Petrucci, and Marie Hassler for their help. My thanks are also due to Marie-Claude Delahaye, founder of the Musée de l'Absinthe in Auvers-sur-Oise, who, while we have not yet met in person, was always willing to help a fellow absinthe enthusiast and whose passion for the subject has fuelled the research on absinthe over the past three decades.

I also want to take advantage of these pages to say that I am deeply grateful to many of my academic mentors, amongst them Gesine Krüger and Waltraud Ernst, who have shaped my interests, perspectives, and methods. I would also like to extend my thanks to Mohamed Ben-Madani and *The Maghreb Review* for their support over the past fifteen years. I am equally grateful to the late and much-missed Jan-Georg Deutsch. I often think about our last in-person discussion at his house in Oxford, where we chatted mostly about my fascination with the history of absinthe. Georg was attentive and supportive, asking just the right questions to make me question my assumptions and view the topic from a new perspective, as always.

I would further like to thank my parents, Christoph Studer, Monique Ruckstuhl-Créteur, and Marc Ruckstuhl, who provided me with Swiss absinthe chocolates throughout the past decade, and who visited the Val-de-Travers and the Maison de l'Absinthe in Môtiers back in 2014 with me, when I was still at the beginning of my absinthe journey. Without their love, this book would not have been possible. I also would like to express my thanks to my parents-in-law, Margaret and Alan Ross, for their constant support. Finally, I would like to express my deep gratitude to my husband, Darren Ross, for his never-ending, precious support. Listening to me expound on absinthe, discussing every detail of this book with me, and reading and rereading various drafts of my manuscript has turned my teetotal husband into an expert on absinthe! I dedicate this book to you, Darren.

The
Hour
of
Absinthe

Introduction

It is arguable whether there has ever been a drink as notorious as absinthe. A wormwood-based, anise-flavoured spirit, little different to any other highly alcoholic drink, has nevertheless generated a mystique that has endured from its creation in the late eighteenth century to the third decade of the twenty-first century. It is a story that encompasses art, sex, glamour, murder, insanity, racial "degeneration," and the very fate of nations and empire. This mythologizing led to the creation, and fabrication, of all kinds of modern folklore, much of it repeated with a growing plethora of inaccuracies. Understanding absinthe's story provides an insight into the glorification of wars, escalating fears of criminality, and the demonization of marginalized groups, especially in terms of race, gender, and class.

This book sets out to contextualize and deconstruct some of the numerous myths surrounding absinthe by undertaking a thorough examination of different sources, encompassing a wide range of authors, contexts, and media, in order to provide a clearer view of its general history. In particular, I intend to show how closely connected absinthe was – on a discursive level – to the institution and upkeep of France's colonial empire. Absinthe, which was documented in the Val-de-Travers in Switzerland from the 1760s onward, only gained popularity in France in the second half of the nineteenth century. As French soldiers during the military conquest of Algeria after 1830 were the first to take to absinthe, absinthe was, from the very beginning, associated with colonial "success" in the French consciousness. It was also in Algeria that, from the 1840s onward, the first alarms about the consequences of absinthe drinking were sounded.

I follow the most important phases of absinthe's rise and fall in this book, as detailed in medical publications, newspapers, the output of the French temperance movement, travel accounts, and memoirs of settlers in France's colonies. My overall focus is less on the actual consumption of absinthe and more on how absinthe was viewed, depicted, and mysticized by various groups of nineteenth- and early twentieth-century authors. Publications by medical and psychiatric experts, who used the diagnosis of "absinthism" from the 1860s onward to describe excessive absinthe consumption, form the basis of this book. These experts played an important part in the eventual downfall of absinthe, during which the medico-psychiatric discourse condemning the drink was taken up by the broader public. As absinthism was believed to be an enormous medical and societal issue, these medico-psychiatric sources depicted the consumption of absinthe in a mostly negative light, often exaggerating its effects and demonizing its consumers. These medico-psychiatric publications were, essentially, intended as a warning for the general public, and should therefore in no way be viewed as unbiased.

Absinthe's history developed over a period of over 250 years and spans, perhaps unexpectedly to some readers, a large geographic context. At the beginning of its popularity, the daily, ceremonial consumption of absinthe was mainly understood as being a provider of relaxation and joy. The phrase "l'heure de l'absinthe," "l'heure verte," or even, due to the green colour of both the drink and the bird, "l'heure du perroquet" – the hour of the parrot – designated the traditional time of day when French people took to cafés in the nineteenth and early twentieth centuries to drink one or several glasses of absinthe. It was also known more generally as "l'heure de l'apéritif."[1] This "hour" traditionally began somewhere between 4 and 5 p.m. and could end as late as 7 or 8 p.m. Absinthe was an aperitif, intended to give people an appetite before meals, which led to some sources, as well as twenty-first-century researchers, additionally defining the time between 11 a.m. and 1 p.m. as the "hour of absinthe."[2] In the context of this book, the phrase also includes the idea of the Belle Époque – understood here as the period between the 1870s and 1914 in French history, the peak of global absinthe consumption – being, metaphorically speaking, the "hour of absinthe." While the consumption of absinthe can be traced throughout France and the French Empire from the 1830s onwards, it took the drink a little while to catch on. Indeed, it only became France's drink of choice by the 1880s, a period when the phylloxera crisis – an insect infestation that destroyed grapevines and had first spread in the South of

France in the late 1860s[3] – caused a shortage of French wine.[4] At its height, absinthe was more popular and accessible than all other aperitifs.[5]

The 1860s saw the first wave of absinthe's popularity in France. The French author Charles Monselet dedicated a chapter of his 1865 book *From Montmartre to Sevilla* to the idea of a daily "hour of absinthe" dominating French lives. Monselet suggested that the "habit of absinthe" had only appeared in Paris in "the past several years."[6] From Monselet's perspective, the initial popularity of the hour of absinthe thus coincided roughly with a period in France in which licensing laws for drinking establishments were somewhat relaxed.[7] This came after the repressive period of the 1850s, in which the French government framed cafés as places "for political organization, for the transmission of news and dangerous ideas, and for the mobilization of popular protest," as the historian Susanna Barrows put it in her 1991 chapter "Parliaments of the People."[8] A 2010 study on absinthe led by the German toxicologist Dirk Lachenmeier explained that this easing of licensing laws in the 1860s led to an increase in "bars, cabarets and cafés," and that more than 30,000 such drinking establishments – *débits de boissons* in French – existed in Paris alone by 1869.[9] There were many nineteenth-century terms for these drinking establishments in France, depending on both the region and the clientele.[10] In the context of this book, I will, for simplicity's sake, designate them either as cafés or as débits/débits de boissons, unless I am quoting a source with a different term.

It was only during the 1870s that absinthe "began its meteoric career in the history of French social life," to use a formulation by the Canadian historian Michael Marrus.[11] Reports on the drink initially focused on the joy of a shared experience, leisure, and sociability.[12] In this, they mirrored wider contemporary conceptions of alcohol, which was, in the words of Howard Padwa in his 2012 book *Social Poison*, "in many respects the social substance of nineteenth-century Europe."[13] Yet while the last decades of the nineteenth century were absinthe's moment of glory, so to speak, they were also the "belle époque of anti-alcoholism," as the French historian Didier Nourrisson summarized it in his 1988 article about the "Origins of Anti-Alcoholism."[14] The meteoric popularity of absinthe was viewed as an alarming and potentially dangerous development by many, as spirits were understood to be more dangerous than the so-called "hygienic beverages" of wine, beer, and cider.[15] In 1900, wine was officially declared a hygienic drink and given tax benefits, while, in 1907, the tax on absinthe was raised.[16]

Amongst the non-hygienic alcoholic beverages, absinthe came to be understood as the most dangerous. By contrast, wine, even more than the other "hygienic beverages," was perceived as part and parcel of French identity, and drunkenness caused by wine as intrinsically "Gallic." Many nineteenth-century observers believed they were witnessing France turning away from wine, the French drink par excellence, in favour of absinthe. The well-known journalist Charles Mayet addressed this in his 1894 book *Wine in France*, stating: "The Gallic rooster, as I said, is a rooster that drinks wine." Yet, France was, according to Mayet, in the process of replacing the wine-drinking rooster with an absinthe-drinking one. By the 1890s, "from North to South, from the Alps to the Ocean, absinthe is queen. She sits enthroned in her green dress with her procession of various accessories."[17] This change in consumption was believed to have far-reaching consequences for both individuals and the nation itself. The French doctor Jules Rochard explained in an 1886 article on alcohol that the consumption of wine had outward signs, such as "illuminated faces" and "ruddy cheeks": "this was the cheerful and good-natured drunkenness; the Gallic drunkenness that all the poets have sung about and which differs from the frightening alcoholism of today, [just] as the noble wines of Burgundy and Bordeaux differ from the poison extracted from potatoes or beets."[18] The renowned Canadian historian of medicine Patricia Prestwich suggested in her 1988 book that people "intoxicated by industrial alcohol" – like absinthe – were "reputedly dull, somnolent, and brutish, presumably unnatural traits in a Frenchman."[19]

Once believed to be a beneficial drink and rumoured to have been distributed to French soldiers for health reasons in Algeria between the 1830s and the late 1840s, absinthe went on to become perhaps the most demonized drink in the world by 1915. By the beginning of the twentieth century, the narratives around absinthe no longer focused on the joys and conviviality of the hour of absinthe or on the art produced by those under its spell, but on the explicit dangers of the drink and those who had succumbed to it. Absinthe was the most toxic of aperitifs, the French doctor Georges-Alphonse-Hubert Lemoine assured his readers in 1911. This toxicity of absinthe made Lemoine despair over the increase in its consumption, which, according to him, had "quadrupled in twenty years. From 6,713 hectolitres in 1873, it rose to 49,335 hectolitres in 1884, to 192,699 [hectolitres] in 1897, [and] finally, in 1904, to 207,929 hectolitres. She [absinthe] tends to replace all other liquors in bars and cafés."[20] Absinthe consumption seems to have steadily increased during the last decades of the nineteenth century. This was in stark contrast with wine. While the yearly consumption of wine in France was at 141 litres per inhabitant during the 1870s, it fell to 96 litres during the 1880s, i.e., in the middle of the phylloxera crisis, before rising again to 101 litres during the 1890s.[21]

If Lemoine's numbers are correct, the consumption of absinthe indeed roughly quadrupled between 1884 and 1904, and it increased by more than thirty times between 1873 and 1904! Other sources presented far more bombastic numbers about absinthe to their readers. According to the French doctor Eugène Picard, for example, France consumed 750,000 hectolitres of absinthe in 1874 alone.[22] While Picard's numbers are unrealistic, he seems to have at least believed that his readership would find them shocking and representative. Numbers provided by the secondary literature, however, mirror Lemoine's claims, suggesting that by the beginning of the First World War both the consumption of absinthe and fears over its toxicity had reached their pinnacles. By 1910, France consumed 360,000 hectolitres of absinthe a year.[23] By comparison, in Switzerland, where absinthe was also perceived as a serious national threat at the time, 9,000 to 10,000 hectolitres of absinthe were apparently consumed per year, as claimed in an anti-absinthe pamphlet from 1907.[24] This frenzy of alcohol consumption in France, which was not limited to absinthe, prompted Marrus to describe the Belle Époque as "the great collective binge" in his seminal 1974 article "Social Drinking in the 'Belle Époque.'"[25]

While the amounts of absinthe consumed and the danger absinthe posed to these binging drinkers cannot be accurately measured, it is unquestionable that absinthe consumption increased massively during the second half of the nineteenth century, and that such a widely consumed and highly alcoholic drink did pose some danger to inveterate consumers. By the end of the nineteenth century, the practical experiences of most French medical and psychiatric experts, whether supportive of the temperance movement or not, seemed to prove that alcoholism rates were high – and rising. This was cause for concern. In 1905, the French doctor Louis Rénon, for example, directly linked the number of cabarets – i.e., venues selling alcohol – to the number of mental asylums: "you will see that there is a clear parallel between these two types of establishments. Everywhere where the number of cabarets is high, there are most lunatic asylums; everywhere where the number of cabarets is lower, there exist fewer lunatic asylums."[26] Faced with overcrowded mental asylums, limiting the number of drinking establishments must have seemed a logical solution to medico-psychiatric experts.

To circumvent issues of how best to measure an increase in consumption that contemporary observers found alarming, I take it for granted that there was some increase and choose to focus not on the actual danger posed by the drink, but on the myths that surrounded it and its perceived threat. It might be difficult for twenty-first-century readers to conceive of how alarmed some parts of the French population had become about absinthe during the Belle Époque. An example of the intense perceived threat of absinthe can be found in the 1897 dissertation by Robert Henri Hazemann on murders committed by people under its influence. Referring to the 1890 book *Insanity in Paris* by the French doctor Paul Garnier, Hazemann claimed that they were at a period in history that witnessed "drunkenness becom[ing] more and more aggressive; the alcoholic is more and more often a criminal."[27] It was feared that absinthe could turn ordinary people into violent criminals when under its Jekyll and Hyde influence.

These fears culminated in France's prohibition of absinthe on 16 March 1915, which was thus ahead of a September 1916 decree, the *Poisonous Substances Law*, that regulated drug possession in France.[28] Many have since suggested – for instance, Phil Baker in 2001 – that the French government strategically used absinthe as a scapegoat "for the national alcohol problem, and for the French army's unreadiness for the First World War."[29] However, it is important not to see the 1915 ban in a vacuum, but to include both the wider European context and France's colonial empire, as absinthe had been banned in some of France's colonies before it was banned in France. By 1915, absinthe had already been prohibited in the Congo Free State in 1898,[30] in Belgium in 1905,[31] in the French colony of the Ivory Coast[32] and Switzerland in 1908,[33] in Holland in 1910,[34] in the United States in 1911/1912,[35] in Italy in 1913,[36] and in the French protectorate of Morocco[37] and the French colony of Upper Senegal in 1914.[38] A prohibition in Germany followed in 1923.[39] Contextualizing the events of March 1915 with these earlier bans does not mean that absinthe was not used as a scapegoat by the French government; rather, it illustrates that the process of singling out absinthe as a particular danger had already been established at this point.

If one were to triangulate absinthe's intricate biography, one should look very closely at what happened to absinthe in Switzerland, France, and France's colonies, particularly in France's most important colony, Algeria. With a Swiss father and a French mother, and having been born in North Africa – in neighbouring Morocco – I feel a certain affinity with the drink. Throughout its history, absinthe not only underwent changes in moral and legal assessments, but also experienced clear changes in perceptions of nationality. Once plainly Swiss, it earned the "status of national drink" in France during the Belle

Époque, as the French historian Jacqueline Lalouette put it in her 1980 article on wine and alcohol consumption.[40] While absinthe became one of the "special marks of Paris" according to the US journalist Sterling Heilig in an 1894 article,[41] this idea of a dedicated "hour of absinthe," given over to enjoyment and sociability as much as to its consumption, spread from Paris to the rest of France[42] as well as to areas of French interest.[43] By 1884, for example, it had become "customary to offer vermouth, absinthe, or other refreshments to visitors" in Indochina, as reported by Charles Lemire.[44] Absinthe spread to even the most remote of the French colonies and territories,[45] and its popularity in the colonies lasted throughout the nineteenth and into the twentieth century. In his 1909 article "Alcoholism in French Colonies," Alexandre Kermorgant regretfully informed his readers about the widespread taste for absinthe in Indochina, Senegal, and Niger at that time.[46] While its history is inextricably bound to Switzerland, France, and Algeria, absinthe was a globally consumed substance. It was, at its height, a common drink in most of central Europe,[47] as well as "Francophile cities" like New Orleans.[48] Absinthe could also be found in perhaps slightly unexpected areas of the world. The French historian François Georgeon, for example, mentioned in his 2021 book on the history of raki that a wide variety of alcoholic drinks, amongst them absinthe, could be found in the large cities of the Ottoman empire in the last quarter of the nineteenth century.[49]

From the very beginning of France's second colonial empire, which started with the military conquest of the Algerian coast in 1830, absinthe was an established part of daily life in imperial France. Only one year before the French ban on absinthe was instituted, the Belgian author Léon Souguenet described his experiences of "the holy hour of the aperitif" while travelling through rural Algeria. He reported that the "small town exudes the subtle aroma of absinthe, social liquor if there ever was one; the terraces of the cafés flow over onto the roads."[50] In the colonies, absinthe was consumed by French soldiers, settlers, and travellers, as well as by parts of the colonized populations. Accounts such as Sougenet's show that the hour of absinthe not only shaped life in fashionable cafés in Paris, frequented by painters and poets, but even in small towns of France and the French Empire. Just like in France, European settlers in French colonies went to cafés not only to enjoy absinthe, but to exchange news and people watch, to relax and gossip. The hour of absinthe gave the French in the colonies a taste of home – while giving those in France a glimpse of the exotic. More than just a home comfort, absinthe was often regarded as a "necessity" for French people in the colonies. An article published in *The*

Times in 1861 explained in a clearly humorous way that Algeria imported "great quantities of Burgundy wines and absinth, and other absolute necessities to a Frenchman."[51]

The metropolitan French saw adverts and received postcards that depicted absinthe consumption in colonial contexts and read travel accounts in which people experienced life in the exoticized context of the colonies and consumed absinthe on their colonial "adventures." Surprisingly often, these adverts and postcards represented Muslims – in the cases of Fig. I.1 and Fig. I.2 Muslim women – posing with the drink. As a historian of France's colonial empire, I strongly believe that the history of absinthe and the history of French imperialism are indivisible. Absinthe should be understood as the drink of choice of the settlers in French colonies, just as much as of the bourgeoisie, the artists, and the working classes in Paris. Indeed, I would argue that absinthe's consumption by large numbers of French settlers in North Africa and France's other colonies had just as much of an impact on the portrayal and interpretation of the drink as its role as the famous muse of nineteenth-century artists.

Despite the globalization of the drink, absinthe remained a staunchly French product – and consequently a French problem – for many nineteenth- and early twentieth-century authors. Pierre Decroos wrote a legal dissertation on the regulation of absinthe in 1910, in which he acknowledged that, despite popular belief, France was not "the only country that consumes" absinthe. He added that "absinthism is not an exclusively French vice; but nowhere else does this scourge reach such frightening proportions as amongst us. France alone consumes as much absinthe as the [rest of the] world together."[52] Versions of this formulation of France being "the great absinthe drinker,"[53] or of drinking as much as, or more than, the rest of the world put together were fairly common. Éphrem Aubert claimed that by 1915 "*France* <u>alone</u> *consumed 2/3 of the absinthe produced in the whole world*,"[54] while in a 1910 paper on the question of "How to Stay Healthy" one can almost hear Paul Houdeville's dejected sigh: "And to think that France drinks on her own as much absinthe as the rest of the world together."[55]

Despite its status as one of France's "national drinks," absinthe was often framed – by opponents of the drink – as having invaded France and, worse, of somehow *un-Frenching* consumers. One expression of this notion can be found in an article by Paul Binsse or Bins, the Count of Saint-Victor, who was at the height of his fame between the 1860s and his death in 1881. In a humorous article about alcohol and national identities published in *La Presse* on 31 December 1860, he epitomized France as wine and England as beer: "It, this

Scènes et Types
13. HOURIA jouant El Kouitra

Figure I.1
Postcard showing an Algerian woman, playing the *kwitra*
(an Algerian lute), with a bottle of absinthe, an absinthe
glass, and a knocked-over empty bottle of alcohol.

heavy drink [i.e., beer], invaded France, which would have horrified our fathers; and in its wake came Absinthe, the horrible absinthe." According to Saint-Victor, the consumption of absinthe had severe consequences on the body of the drinker, who "seeks not the magical oblivion exhaled by the smoke of the vins généreux, but that toxic oblivion that weighs down the memory, stops the heart and freezes the brain."[56] *Vins généreux* is a French term that includes an idea of these wines being healthy and beneficial on the one hand and rich and abundant on the other.[57] "In the past, absinthe passed at most for a coarse aperitif, apt to whet the appetite crudely, as brutally as the knife opens the shell of an oyster," Saint-Victor added, but "now she has her drinkers, her orgies, her vault. Great minds are cited who have drowned themselves in her greenish dregs. It is the opium of the West, and it turns those who drink it into Chinese [people]."[58] In turn, opium, as Padwa explained, was similarly believed to "usher European users into states of Asian consciousness," altering their very blood into something foreign in the process.[59]

Figure I.2
Advert for Alfa: Absinthe Hygiénique Algérienne depicting an Algerian woman in traditional North African clothes and jewellery, before a mosque, holding up a full glass of absinthe.

Saint-Victor's punchy phrase of absinthe being the "opium of the West" soon entered the French consciousness. Only ten days after his article in *La Presse*, an article about local news for the newspaper *Journal du Cher* by a journalist of the name of G. Grandin professed to be compiling a "sad inventory of barbarism by pointing out the homicidal absinthe mania, which has already stupefied so many minds and extinguished so many lives." After this dire verdict on the effects of the drink, Grandin went on to quote Saint-Victor's passage about absinthe having forcibly invaded France, being the opium of the West and turning drinkers into the (Chinese) other.[60] To Paul de Saint-Victor and the various journalists taking up his phrase, it must have seemed concerning how popular absinthe – a drink relatively unknown in France before the 1830s – had become by 1861. To them, its popularity brought a sense of loss of national identity, with people being so intoxicated that they could no longer remember what it meant to be French.

While the severity of the consequences of absinthe consumption was often framed as being contingent on class, race, and gender, absinthe drinking itself was also presented as a habit that united all French people, in its sociability as much as in its dire consequences. The French doctor Witold Lemanski condemned the general popularity of alcohol amongst all classes in French colonies in his 1902 medical handbook with health advice for settlers in European colonies. "It is sad to say, but the most recent research and statistics show that drinking is everywhere, in the hovel as in the castle, in the most elegant dining rooms as around the white wooden tables of the farmhouse or canteen; people poisoned themselves at the Café de la Préfecture as well as at the Bar des Travailleurs or the Estaminet des Compagnons." Lemanksi, who himself lived in Tunisia at the time of the composition of his handbook, was not referring to specific cafés in either Tunisia or France here, but to various kinds of establishments, in which different classes met to socialize over a glass of absinthe. In the next passage of his lament, Lemanski made it clear that, while addressing drinking in general, he really meant the consumption of absinthe. "The worker, the anarchist, the socialist, as, alas! the most perfect gentleman, finds human equality in front of the greenish product of a great man of the century whose name – certainly! – is more famous than that of Pasteur himself."[61] While Lemanski did not mention the name of this "great man," the producer of the "greenish product" was probably Henri-Louis Pernod, who died in 1851, the founder – and namesake – of Pernod Fils, the most popular absinthe distillery of the time. Indeed, Pernod, his distillery and absinthe were, in the eyes of many around that time, inextricably linked.[62]

Like many other medical and psychiatric experts of the time, Lemanski strongly believed that France was living through an increase in the consumption of absinthe, and alcoholism in general, which, he feared, would lead to a corresponding increase in "criminality and madness, while birth rates, [this] counterpart to the degeneration of the race, so important for populating the colonies, are singularly lowering!"[63] This idea of absinthe leading to criminality, madness, and depopulation is part of wider Lamarckian narratives about degeneration, i.e., the idea that "acquired characteristics were hereditary."[64] Saint-Victor's suggestion, of absinthe transforming French drinkers into people who were decidedly not French, i.e., of acquiring un-French characteristics, also seems to be a very literal interpretation of these wider degeneration theories prevalent at the time. In his 1989 book *Faces of Degeneration*, the British historian Daniel Pick suggested that "crucially, degeneration in the second half of the nineteenth century served not only to characterise other races (for instance in the view that other races had degenerated from the ideal physique of the white races), but also to pose a vision of internal dangers and crises within Europe. Crime, suicide, alcoholism and prostitution were understood as 'social pathologies' endangering the European races, constituting a degenerative process within them."[65] Adapting Pick's vocabulary of "social pathologies" to Saint-Victor's article gives a deeper understanding of the motivation behind framing the "opium of the West" as un-Frenching absinthe drinkers: Saint-Victor compared French absinthe drinkers to people from a degenerate – within this deeply problematic nineteenth-century context – race, in order to address the internal dangers of degeneration posed to France by absinthe.

In France, fears about degeneration were linked with natalist ideas, as seen in Lemanski's quote, due to the fact that, in the second half of the nineteenth century, French birth rates were lower than those of other European nations.[66] These fears of depopulation were explicitly linked to alcohol from the 1870s – and France's defeat against Prussia – onwards. While it was generally believed that this slowing of French birth rates could be caused by a variety of substances and alcoholic drinks, absinthe was soon understood as being a chief culprit.[67] Women's absinthe consumption was often feared to have the most degenerative effects on future generations. In his 1894 book, Mayet claimed that, while the absinthe consumption of working-class men was alarming, that of women was worse: "Many women have, in fact, become accustomed to absinthe; any vendor you come across will tell you that men almost always mix it with water, while women very often drink it pure." Mayet and his contemporaries feared for the children of women who drank either absinthe specifically or alcohol in general. Children of alcoholics were believed to be "unbalanced, sometimes intelligent, but hot-tempered, tuberculous too, epileptic, often imbeciles, and without physical resistance."[68] Not surprisingly, Mayet and many of his contemporaries desperately wanted to put a stop to something that, they believed, had such wide-ranging effects.

While such fears of racial degeneration have been long forgotten, absinthe is still perceived as a scandalous and mysterious – and potentially dangerous – drink, with many twenty-first-century absinthe producers playing with these associations both in naming their products and in their chosen advertisements. Various myths around absinthe today are actively cultivated by the popular discourse on the drink and, to a lesser degree, by the literature on the topic. However, this enigmatic image of absinthe is nothing new: even during the global "hour of absinthe," absinthe was perceived as enticingly mysterious. Back in 1867, the journalist Henri Lierre authored a book entitled *The Question of Absinthe*, in which he addressed these very myths, albeit in a strangely sexualized way. "If we did not turn absinthe into a sort of terrible and fantastic monster, if we did not give it the charm of the forbidden fruit, the dizzying attraction of the abyss," fewer people would drink it, Lierre argued. "The noise would be less pronounced around the fairy with green eyes. I charge myself to undress her."[69] Both in the nineteenth century and today, absinthe manufacturers often represent absinthe – in adverts and labels on the bottles – as a fairy, dressed in green, due to the colour of the drink, often with red hair and green eyes.

To date, there have been very few historical studies solely dedicated to absinthe. The Swiss author Dorette Berthoud wrote a general article on absinthe's history in 1969,[70] while another Swiss historian, Charles Heimberg, studied the absinthe ban in Switzerland in the context of the labour movement in a 2000 article.[71] Finally, Patricia Prestwich wrote an excellent analysis of the medical history of absinthe in a 1979 article.[72] In contrast to this scarcity, there is solid academic secondary literature on specific aspects of absinthe, such as the chemical properties of the drink,[73] or its influence on art and poetry.[74] Recently, there have been a number of outstanding student theses on different aspects of the history of absinthe.[75] In addition, the general curiosity in this deeply mysterious drink has resulted in a series of books on the history of absinthe being published since the 1980s. The most prolific author on the history of absinthe is undoubtedly the founder of the Musée de l'Absinthe in Auvers-sur-Oise, Marie-Claude Delahaye, a biologist by training, who has written several books on various aspects of the history of absinthe, often specializing in the art and adverts of the drink.[76] Other monographs in French include the 1991 book by the Swiss politician, author, and former curator of the museum Maison de l'Absinthe in Môtiers Pierre-André Delachaux, *Absinthe: Aroma of the Apocalypse*, responding to the eightieth anniversary of the absinthe ban in Switzerland with late-twentieth-century local art,[77] and the French author and curator Benoît Noël's 2003 book *New Confidences on Absinthe*.[78] English-language publications range from the 1988 book *Absinthe: History in a Bottle* by the US author Barnaby Conrad, the book *Absinthe: The Cocaine of the Nineteenth Century* by the emerita professor of English Doris Lanier in 1995, and *The Dedalus Book of Absinthe* written by the British author Phil Baker in 2001 to, finally, the 2008 book *Hideous Absinthe: A History of the Devil in a Bottle* by the British historian and author Jad Adams. All these books, independent of the background of these authors, were written for a general audience.

This book focuses on facets of the history of absinthe that have traditionally been overlooked in the existing secondary literature, chief amongst them France's colonial empire. However, other important gaps in the historiography of absinthe must perforce be unaddressed in these pages. While a number of the sources used for this book were written by occasional or regular absinthe consumers – predominantly Swiss or French, male, middle-class – their descriptions of their own consumption are less examples of self-experimentation,[79] but were invariably employed by them either to establish their credentials in writing on the topic of absinthe or to present a quasi-anthropological approach to the rituals of drinking it.[80] Meanwhile, the medico-psychiatric sources that form the basis of my book describe the consumption of the "other." Searching for, compiling, and analyzing potential reactions to these descriptions by consumers – be it women, workers, and/or the colonized – should be an important next step in the historiography of absinthe, which, unfortunately, falls outside the scope of this book.

Chapter 1 serves as an introduction to the topic and is devoted to the origins of absinthe in Switzerland and its subsequent transplantation, both geographically and culturally, to the region around Pontarlier in neighbouring France. In short, chapter 1 addresses the questions of what absinthe is, where is comes from, and what was needed for a celebration of the "hour of absinthe." After an overview of the constituents of the drink, this chapter covers absinthe's history up to the establishment of the first absinthe distilleries in the early nineteenth century. While it is impossible to reconstruct an exact timeline for the origins of absinthe, this chapter delves into the myths that surround the beginnings of the drink. This is followed by an outline of the ritual of its consumption.

Chapter 2 focuses on the influence of France's empire on the spread of absinthe drinking, by examining the belief that an absinthe ration was distributed to French soldiers in Algeria during the initial military campaigns of the 1830s, 1840s, and 1850s. The title of this book alludes to the perceived glory days of absinthe consumption – when absinthe was understood to be the drink of the victorious French army after the brutal conquest of Algeria. This early popularity of absinthe was inextricably linked to a glorification of the "victorious" military, and, consequently, a celebration of a certain kind of masculinity and of the colonial mission. This chapter also examines how absinthe spread from these absinthe-filled French soldiers in Algeria to the French Métropole (i.e., metropolitan France, not Paris itself) and to other French colonies. The aim of this chapter is to centre the history of absinthe in a specific moment of military expansion after 1830 and in a deep imperial pride that pervaded France in the second half of the nineteenth century.

Chapter 3 gives an overview of how a drink strongly linked to the "glory" of the French military became the drink of both the bourgeoisie and the counter culture of artists between the 1830s and the 1870s. The emphasis of this chapter is on the joy associated with the ritual consumption of absinthe during this period. This chapter also looks at how absinthe was turned into a symbol of France, both at home and abroad, through advertising, presenting at once an image of a perceived respectability of the drink, as well as one of sociability, enjoyment, and sexual titillation. The secondary literature sometimes refers to the consumption of absinthe amongst the bourgeoisie during the early years of absinthe's popularity as almost a golden age – before absinthe became a medical issue. This mirrors certain nineteenth-century sources, in which bourgeois habits explicitly served to denigrate other groups that consumed the drink. As chapters 4 and 5 are dedicated to the absinthe consumption of these other groups – and to the question of an almost unique malleability of how absinthe was viewed depending on who consumed it – the aim of this chapter is to provide readers with a means of comparison. It should be added, however, that, while chapters 2 and 3 focus on a period in which absinthe was, according to the secondary literature, viewed overwhelmingly positively – as a symbol of enjoyment, creativity, and colonial success – these opinions are mostly absent from medical and psychiatric sources. Even this section of the book that focuses on the question of joy is thus coloured by the opinion of absinthe-critical sources that often mocked and judged the allegedly unanimous acceptance of absinthe during an earlier period.

Chapters 4, 5, and 6 trace absinthe's fall from grace, once it was described as the drink of marginalized groups. In many French accounts condemning the drink, class, race, and gender distinctions are clearly present: absinthe's toxicity partly seemed to depend on who consumed it, and not *every* absinthe drinker was believed to undergo a radical transformation. While there were, from the very beginning, voices that argued against the consumption of absinthe, they became stronger in the 1860s – supported by the French medical discourse – until they reached a clear tone of panic in the 1890s. While the overconsumption of absinthe was, technically, a problem for all layers of French society, it was framed as an uncontrollable issue when occurring in women, workers, settlers, and the colonized. Chapter 4 looks specifically at highly patronizing descriptions of absinthe-drinking women, which were intrinsically linked to contemporary theories of degeneration, as well as being used in attacks on the so-called *New Woman*. Chapter 5 focuses on absinthe turning into the drink of France's working classes and of the colonized, as well as on the narrative of an increased violent criminality among those who overconsumed it. Chapter 6 is dedicated to medico-psychiatric theories about absinthe in general and the diagnosis of absinthism in particular. In chapter 6, I also further explore the negative framing of absinthe as the "opium of the West," as well as the trope of absinthe as a killer of French people. I examine these two tropes to show the shift in the overall discourse around absinthe during the Belle Époque.

Finally, chapter 7 serves as both a conclusion to the book and an analysis of the absinthe bans in the early twentieth century. To bookend the history of absinthe in France and France's colonial empire, I will return to Switzerland. While I present the common narrative of the Swiss "absinthe murders" in 1905 as inspiring the various absinthe bans,[81] I also retrace how the situation in the colonies, the gendered fears of degeneration and declining birth rates, the fears of criminality committed by working-class absinthe drinkers, the pressure of the French wine-lobby, and the fashion in diagnosing absinthism led to the prohibition of absinthe in 1915.

In my overall analysis, I focus mainly on aspects of absinthe's alleged transformative powers, tracing what it was that different groups of people were believed to transform into – by both the medico-psychiatric professions and by other groups of authors – under the influence of this "enchanting" drink. Looking closely at the nature of this absinthe-induced transformation of drinkers provides insights into gender, racial, and class biases prevalent in these publications, mainly composed by white, French, middle-class male authors. Both sides of the absinthe discourse agreed that drinking absinthe changed a person. It inspired painters and poets and helped with the homesickness of French people living or travelling in the colonies, but it also made drinkers ill and turned them into something that was to be feared. In a 1907 article published in the English journal *The Economic Review*, the author H. Anet suggested that absinthe should be called "sorceress" rather than "green fairy," as its "witchcraft is bringing illness, ruin and dishonour to thousands of men, especially in the French-speaking lands. When people are bound by its spell, they become enslaved as perhaps by no other alcoholic drink." The idea of absinthe transforming its consumers continued in Anet's picturesque account, as he suggested that "absinthiated spirits must have been the magic beverages given by Circe to the companions of Ulysses, in order to metamorphose them into beasts."[82] This widespread belief in its special powers differentiated absinthe from other spirits of the time, making the drink appear closer to substances like opium and morphine. Tracing this discourse of transformation – from absinthe serving as a creative muse for artists to absinthe being a potion that metamorphosed drinkers into beasts – shows the deep malleability of what absinthe was believed to represent, which in turn allows insights into broader political, economic, and societal issues in Belle Époque France.

1

Absinthe's Mythical Origins in Switzerland's Val-de-Travers

This chapter serves as an introduction to the history of absinthe, providing information on what it consisted of, its disputed origins, and how it was – and still is – consumed. The chapter begins by examining fears of various dangerous ingredients being nefariously added to the drink, ranging from essential oils to copper sulphates. Disquiet about the specific ingredients of absinthe was one of the main explanations for its being singled out as a particularly toxic spirit. The second part of this chapter delves into nineteenth- and early twentieth-century accounts of absinthe's origins – by both French and Swiss, pro- and anti-absinthe authors – and shows how myths about its past were created and propagated in order to argue for or against the drink. This was not unique to absinthe, as can be seen, for example, in the American historian Kolleen M. Guy's study of the history of champagne in France, where she described the creation "of a 'mythic' past" of champagne as a means of adding "honor and respectability to a brand."[1] The final part of this chapter describes what was needed for its ritualistic consumption and analyzes what this says about consumers.

What Is Absinthe?

Due to its green colour, absinthe was often simply called "la verte," but there were also variations such as "the green fairy" and "the fairy with green eyes," or, pejoratively, "the green sorceress," "the green poison," or "the green peril." Before its consumption, absinthe is mixed with cold water, which makes it cloudy, milky, and white; it *louches*.[2] Despite it being famous for its greenness, there were also colourless versions called "la bleue," due to the blueish louche that formed when water was added,[3] or, for the same reason, "la blanche."[4] Due to the bitterness of the drink, sugar is commonly added, which masks its highly alcoholic nature. The fact that absinthe contained a high percentage of alcohol – higher than similar drinks – was well known in the Belle Époque. The French doctor Jules Arnould, for example, wrote in his 1902 book, *New Elements of Hygiene*, that absinthe – the "most common aperitif in France in our time, and also the most toxic" – contained between 50 and 75 per cent alcohol.[5]

Today, absinthe is divided into various categories: superior or "absinthe Suisse," which contains between 60 and 75 per cent alcohol; "absinthe demi-fine," which has up to 68 per cent alcohol content; and "absinthe ordinaire" with an alcohol content of up to 50 per cent.[6] "Absinthe Suisse" should not be understood as a geographic designation but as a means of defining both alcohol content and quality.[7] Not all of these categories were necessarily known or clearly defined to French authors writing in the nineteenth and early twentieth centuries. The French doctor Michel Lévy explained in 1862 that there were two distinct kinds of absinthe "that do not have the same energy of action." According to Lévy, "common absinthe" – "absinthe commune" in French, which seems to have been believed to be below "absinthe ordinaire" in quality – was made with "alcohol of 40°," while "absinthe Suisse" was made with "alcohol of 60, 70 and 72°."[8]

In the eyes of nineteenth-century absinthe opponents, it was not the high alcohol content of the drink that was the real danger, but what *else* was assumed to be in absinthe – essences, or essential oils, and nefarious additives to give it its green colour, to make the drink cloudy or to mask the foul taste of other ingredients.[9] The French doctor Joseph Saliège took part in a June 1920 discussion about a prohibition of anisettes in Algeria, in which he stated that "alcohol is harmful by itself, but it is infinitely more harmful when it is combined with essences, aniseed essence, wormwood essence, etc. All these essences have frightful effects on the nervous system. It is these essences, much more than alcohol, which make [people go] insane, [and] which encumber our hospitals wards." According to Saliège, the advent of absinthe on French tables had changed France's diagnostic landscape: "Before absinthe and anisette existed, we knew the good drunk; we did not know these people who become, imperceptibly, insane, who kill under the influence of drink, who are recruited into the army, every day more numerous, of street urchins and prostitutes."[10]

There are two ways of distilling absinthe, which are called the "hot" and "cold" methods. With the hot method, fresh herbs are added to already distilled alcohol, which is then distilled again, as described in the 1859 dissertation by Auguste Motet.[11] With the cold method, there is no second distillation.[12] An article in the *Indiana State Sentinel*,[13] published in April 1861, and partly based on Motet, explained that absinthe consisted of "the tops of the wormwood, flag root [Acorus calamus], anniseed [aniseed], angelica root, leaves of dittany (*origanum dictamnus*), and sweet marjoram. All these are placed in alcohol of very high proof, where they are allowed to remain eight days, when the mixture is distilled, and half an ounce of the essential oil of anise is then added to each three gallons of the liquor."[14] Amongst those plants it was believed that the common wormwood – *Artemisia absinthium* – bestowed upon absinthe the questionable honour of being on "the first rank among the dangerous liquors," to use a formulation by the French doctor Louis François Étienne Bergeret in his 1870 book on alcoholism.[15] The exact combination of plants used in the distillation process varied both according to geography and over time.[16] According to the 1886 edition of the *Treatise of Military Hygiene* by the French military doctor Georges Morache, absinthe had initially been exclusively "loaded with essential oils from the distillation of the buds, leaves and flowers of the plant *Artemisia absinthium*."[17] By the time absinthe became popular in France, fennel, mint, lemon balm, Acorus calamus, Cretan dittany, and common oregano were possible ingredients according to Motet, while also assuring his readers that "not all distillers have the same recipe."[18] Morache repeated several of these plants in his account, but also added cinnamon, cloves, star anise, "and 1 gram per litre of cumin."[19]

In the nineteenth century, concoctions made from plants were believed to have strong effects on both the bodies and the minds of consumers, as seen in the 1920 quote by Saliège above. Historically speaking, this effect had not always been interpreted negatively. Common wormwood, for example, was traditionally viewed as medicinal.[20] As components of alcohol, however, these plants were treated with suspicion. In his 1911 *Treatise of Military Hygiene*, Doctor Georges-Alphonse-Hubert Lemoine differentiated between two distinct kinds of herbal essences, which could be added to alcoholic beverages. Both groups had only negative effects on the bodies of consumers. According to Lemoine, those belonging to the first "induce epilepsy and convulsions, such as wormwood, fennel, hyssop," while those of the second group "are stupefying: angelica, oregano, lemon balm, mint, coriander." To this, Lemoine added that "absinthe is the most pernicious of all these liquors with essences," due to two reasons: first, it consisted of alcohol made from grain, which, Lemoine believed, had a "high toxicity," and second, it included "aniseed, wormwood, lemon grass, hyssop, angelica, fennel, star anise, and coriander."[21] Most French doctors of the time agreed with Lemoine's assessment of a "high toxicity" of alcohol distilled from grain – and also from potatoes, beets, and more – which they viewed as inferior to, and more dangerous than, that distilled from grapes. Absinthe had initially been made from *good alcohol*, that is, from grapes, but during the phylloxera crisis, absinthe manufacturers turned to *bad alcohol* or industrial alcohol, usually made from grain or beets.[22]

As discussed above, it was the inclusion of plant essences that was believed to be the main reason for absinthe's perniciousness. Independent of the alcohol used in it, Lemoine implied that, as the drink included plants from both groups of malicious essences mentioned above, absinthe could "induce epilepsy and convulsions" as well as "stupefy."[23] This belief in the toxicity of such herbal essences – and this dual effect of convulsion and stupefaction – did not end with the prohibition of absinthe in 1915, but was transferred to absinthe-like drinks. In his 1933 medical dissertation "Alcoholism amongst the Arabs of Algeria," Pierre Pinaud differentiated between "alcoholism" and "anisettism," i.e., the addiction to anisettes. This was clearly based on the distinction between alcoholism and absinthism, proposed in the mid-nineteenth century. According to Pinaud, "all the essences which may enter in the composition of absinthes or anisettes (wormwood, aniseed, star anise, fennel, mint, hyssop, angelica, coriander, lemon balm, wild thyme, thyme, oregano, rosemary, rue, lavender, sage) have very specific properties; they act on their own behalf and are at once epilepsy-inducing, narcotic, [and] soporific. They cause above all tremors, seizures, and troubles of the psychological sphere, even without the addition of alcohol. Sensorial excitation (sight and hearing), hallucinations, and clearly characterized delusions are also noted."[24] This statement about the effects of the essences in anisettes mirrors French anti-absinthe reports: Pinaud's description of the effects of the essences used in "absinthes and anisettes" as "epilepsy-inducing" and "soporific" directly ties in with Lemoine's 1911 portrayal of the perniciousness of absinthe.

These various plant essences were already dubious to many in the nineteenth century, but it was also widely believed that far more nefarious ingredients were added. Whereas the fragrant essences were believed to be added to mask the taste of *bad alcohol*, these ingredients were allegedly used to produce its distinctive appearance. The 1861 article in the *Indiana State Sentinel* suggested that, after the distillation of the drink, the manufacturers of absinthe tested both the colour of the drink and whether it became cloudy when water was added: "if it is lacking in these essentials it is brought up to the proper point with indigo, tincture of curcuma, hyssop, nettles, and sulphate of copper, (the ordinary 'blue vitriol')."[25] Both manufacturers and those selling absinthe in their débits de boissons were suspected of committing such falsifications.[26]

This idea of absinthe being fraudulently altered for aesthetic reasons – and that such alterations explained its particular perniciousness – was widespread. Morache suggested that "benzoin or other resins" were added to make absinthe cloudy and that its green colour came from "the leaves or the juice of celery, spinach, nettles, Alpine genepi [a form of wormwood], all substances that are not harmful, but also with *indigo, Gamboge* [a yellow pigment], *Malachite green,* [and] sometimes with *copper salts*."[27] Amongst these accusations, the most widespread was that unsavoury absinthe distillers added copper sulphates.[28] This was believed to have dangerous physical consequences for drinkers. In 1862, Louis Figuier wrote a medical analysis on the "Pernicious Effects of Absinthe" in which he referred to an 1860 report by the French psychiatrist Henri Legrand du Saulle. According to Figuier, Legrand du Saulle recounted that "in January 1860, a sort of epidemic, as it was called, prevailed in the 1st Regiment of Dragoons." Soldiers afflicted by this epidemic "felt violent colics, had diarrhoea, and some even vomited. On the invitation of the colonel, the doctors of the regiment undertook an investigation, which discovered the presence of copper sulphate in the absinthe in the canteens. A few days later, and in presence of the troops, the absinthe barrels seized in the canteens were smashed and thrown into the creek." This destruction of adulterated absinthe put an end to the epidemic and the soldiers quickly recovered their health.[29]

Particularly in the colonies, absinthe was believed to be heavily adulterated. Authors usually supposed that the consumers were duped and consumed a deeply harmful substance unknowingly. The French journalist and politician Jules Hayaux discussed this issue in February 1914 in an article called "Absinthe in Morocco: Interview with a Diplomat" for the daily newspaper *Le Rappel*. The unnamed French diplomat in question, who had stayed in Morocco, had explained to Hayaux that many people who consumed absinthe in Morocco "believe that it comes from France; they are mistaken. A large absinthe factory sends bottles, labels, and wormwood essence to Tangier, and prepares then on site an unnameable mixture, delivered to trade in bottles [which are] in all respects similar to those seen in France."[30] Absinthe producers completely rejected these claims. The distillery company Édouard Pernod officially stated in 1899 that all the absinthe sold under their name in France and in French colonies was "an impeccable product," produced exclusively, and using the same recipe, in Pontarlier.[31]

Hayaux continued by asserting that amongst the ingredients added to this "unnameable" absinthe, so the diplomat claimed, was sulphuric acid. "This poison contains such a dose of sulphuric acid that photographers routinely use absinthe" in the processes of preparing or colouring their plates.[32] While sulphuric acid was used by photographers in the nineteenth century,[33] this unlikely anecdote was probably intended to stoke fears amongst settlers and tourists about the quality of the absinthe they might drink, in the immediate lead-up to the absinthe ban in Morocco in April 1914.

In addition to these fears about adulteration, others worried that some absinthe was produced with different ingredients altogether. The understanding of wormwood being able to help with certain medical inconveniences led some doctors to wonder whether the wormwood used in absinthe differed from the *Artemisia absinthium* they knew medicinally. François-Joseph Cazin speculated in the second edition of his work *Practical and Reasoned Treatise of Native Medicinal Plants*, published in 1858, whether "absinthe Suisse" was "prepared with different artemisia, close to *genepi*, and especially with the Swiss or Alps absinthe (*Artemisia rupestris*)."[34] In Cazin's eyes, this supposed substitution of one wormwood for another seemed to be an explanation for the negative medical consequences of absinthe drinking. In the context of France's colonies similar claims of substitution can be found. Several authors insisted that, instead of wormwood, the root of the asphodel plant was used in the production of absinthe sold in Algeria. The English clergyman Joseph William Blakesley wrote in 1859 a book about his travels through Algeria, in which he explained the particular toxicity of absinthe in Algeria through this supposed substitution. According to him, "in an evil hour for the colony, it struck a French speculator that a spirit might be distilled from the root of the asphodel," which was local to Algeria. Blakesley continued: "He succeeded in his attempt; a vile poisonous liquor, dignified by the name of *absinthe d'Afrique*, was produced at a cheap rate, and acquired general popularity. The discoverer made a fortune, and his invention has slain more Europeans than the sword of Abd-el-Kader, and even according to high medical authority, than the malaria of the Metidja [i.e., the Mitidja plain in Northern Algeria]."[35] Some authors, conversely, believed this to be less toxic than absinthe produced with wormwood. In 1895 a Ch. Livon, for example, explained that this asphodel absinthe was drunk mostly by "the natives and the [French] soldiers" in Algeria, who "consume it in large quantity because of its low price." Livon speculated that this asphodel absinthe must have less marked effects than wormwood absinthe, "as the drinkers only experience the effects normally due to alcohol ingestion, while the officers who consume almost exclusively real absinthe feel the special disadvantages of it."[36] Due to the large amounts of absinthe consumed in Algeria, other authors reported that the absinthe drunk in the colony had to be weaker than the one commonly drunk in France, which seems not to have been the case.[37]

This claim of fraudulently labelled asphodel absinthe in Algeria was disputed during the colonial period and debunked by French doctors H. Triboulet and Félix Mathieu in their 1900 book *Alcohol and Alcoholism*: "It has been said that the Algerian absinthe was obtained with the help of an essence taken from asphodel bulbs, and that, through this origin, it [Algerian absinthe] could be *consumed in large quantities, without feeling untoward effects from it* (Laborde, Riche)."[38] While I could not reconstruct what exact publication by Laborde Triboulet and Mathieu alluded to here, Jean Laborde was a well-respected French doctor, who wrote an article about experiments conducted with alcohol for the *Gazette médicale de l'Algérie* in 1888.[39] Alfred Riche was a chemist, who regularly wrote about alcohol, and who was a contributor to Jules Rochard's 1890 *Encyclopedia of Public Hygiene and Medicine*. In that text, Algerian asphodel absinthe is discussed and Laborde is mentioned as never having been able to get the same epileptiform results from experiments with it, as others had obtained with normal absinthe.[40] This reference to Laborde's experiments does not necessarily mean that he had access to asphodel absinthe, as such animal experiments were conducted with essences from these plants, not the spirits made with the help of these essences.

Triboulet and Mathieu continued by stating that "'asphodel absinthe,' we regret [to say], is only a myth." They based their conclusion on information sent to them by a "very distinguished doctor from Philippeville, Dr Augier." This Doctor Augier informed them that "asphodel has never been used to manufacture absinthe for the reason that wormwood is the only plant that can be used for this. The absinthe that we drink here is provided by France and we find in the cafés, from Oran to Tunis, from Philippeville to the extreme South of our possession, only the brands sold in our cafés in Paris. In short, for the moment, asphodel is completely unused."[41] A Ch. Rivière similarly claimed in 1900 that asphodel had never been used for the production of alcohol in North Africa.[42]

While some of these nineteenth- and early twentieth-century claims of fraud and substitution seem exaggerated or even impossible – such as Hayaux's claim about absinthe and photographers[43] – the secondary literature suggests that adulteration of absinthe occurred fairly regularly. In his 2002 article "Myth, Reality and Absinthe," for example, Ian Hutton suggested that various harmful substances, such as cupric acetate and antimony trichloride, had indeed been added to cheap absinthes for aesthetic reasons.[44] Various chemical analyses were undertaken on absinthe that was believed to be adulterated in the nineteenth century – with varying results. A chemist with the name of Sébastien Choulette, for example, reported that he was asked in April 1855 to examine an absinthe sample in the Algerian city of Constantine. He found that the sample consisted of a "mix of eau-de-vie [alcohol distilled from fruit], volatile aniseed oil, absinthe infusion, and a decoction of prunes," which he – due to the presence of the "decoction of prunes"? – considered "a falsified drink."[45] Another analysis was described by an Er. Baudrimont in the 1882 edition of his *Dictionary of Alterations and Falsifications of Alimentary, Medicinal, and Commercial Substances*. According to him, it had "been claimed that *gamboge* has been found in an absinthe sold in Biskra (Algeria). Having had to examine this liquor, I recognized that it was free of any foreign product."[46]

While nineteenth-century authors suspected essential oils, *bad alcohol*, and falsifications when trying to explain the hallucinatory effects of absinthe described by many consumers over time, many twentieth- and twenty-first-century researchers have looked to thujone. Thujone is a "toxic, psychoactive ingredient in wormwood," in the words of Kima Cargill in 2008, which does have convulsant effects and was long believed to be hallucinogenic. Cargill further stated that research conducted on the composition of thujone showed that, "contrary to popular belief, thujone does not possess hallucinogenic properties."[47] Some researchers proposed that historic or pre-ban absinthe – unlike the contemporary absinthe consumed today – had a higher thujone content, which explained the negative effects ascribed to the drink.[48] Dirk Lachenmeier and David Nathan-Maister suggested, however, in a 2007 article, that this assumption was based on incorrect calculations.[49] In her 2020 chapter "Indeterminate Pharmacology of Absinthe," Vanessa Herrmann pointed out that the findings by different groups of twenty-first-century chemical researchers – represented by Hein et al. on the one hand and Lachenmeier and

various of his colleagues on the other – on the effects of thujone are contradictory and hotly debated, adding that this "reveals that the tension between
these two attitudes has not weakened even after more than 150 years."[50]

While it is possible that historic absinthe had occasionally been falsified for
a variety of aesthetic reasons – especially, apparently, in the colonies – none
of its regular components seems to have been particularly dangerous or, indeed, capable of causing the hallucinations experienced by drinkers: the
much-feared essential oils were essentially harmless, asphodel absinthe seems
to have been a myth, and the concentration of thujone was too low. The often-
described effects of the drink were, perhaps unsurprisingly, due to the high
alcohol content of the drink.[51] The high alcohol content, masked by sugar,
cold water, and pleasant company, seems to have been the main cause of the
various effects experienced by absinthe drinkers.

The "Discovery" of Absinthe

The majority of nineteenth- and early twentieth-century writers agreed that
absinthe had originated in Switzerland. There were, however, occasional al-
ternative claims. The French hygienist Ernest Monin was one of these dissenting voices. In his 1889 book, Monin connected absinthe with the Napoleonic
wars, claiming that, "ever since Bonaparte passed St Bernard [in 1800], the
Fairy with the green eyes acclimatized herself in France."[52] Similarly, the
French psychiatrist Paul-Lucien Wahl discussed absinthe in his 1910 study
Crime According to Science as a "convulsive poison" and argued that it had
"been introduced in France by the Italian army in 1796," adding that "its use
only became common [in France] after the wars in Algeria."[53]

Other dissenting sources suggested that absinthe had originally been an
"African," i.e., Algerian, drink. This point of view can be found in an article
from 1863, in which the author, Eugène Pelletan, asserted that absinthe, "born
in the scorching deserts of Africa, has become naturalized in Paris and is slowly
killing our young generation."[54] The author's assessment of absinthe's origins
might have been based on some accounts that claimed that a version of absinthe was traditionally consumed in Algeria by the Muslim population. Armand Pignel, who lived and worked in Algiers, claimed in 1836 that "to replace
the wine, the Moors drink a liquor that they make themselves, it is an excessively strong absinthe."[55] While I cannot reconstruct what specific drink Pignel
referred to, it might have been a version of the fig liquor *boukha*, a strongly

alcoholic spirit, consumed mainly in Tunisia, flavoured with aniseed and often mixed with water.[56]

Neither the theory of absinthe coming to France through the Napoleonic wars nor that of it being originally North African was the mainstream narrative; instead, most authors discussed how French or non-French the drink was. A journalist, whose name was given as A. Froemer, wrote an article in 1884 about the history of the family Pernod, in which he explained that "it is generally unknown that the first attempts at making *Swiss* absinthe were made by the French."[57] Such claims were possible because the facts surrounding the invention of the drink were, and still are, obscure.

Any attempt to present a coherent timeline of the contradictory nineteenth- and early twentieth-century accounts – and the twenty-first-century secondary literature based on them – would require so much oversimplification as to potentially mislead. I will instead introduce the various actors involved in absinthe's discovery in a manner not dissimilar to an Agatha Christie mystery, where the detective assembles the suspects in the drawing room at the climax of the book. After their introduction, I present the main strands of the various myths surrounding the so-called discovery of absinthe. The clearest examination of the perplexing origin story of absinthe, based on eighteenth- and nineteenth-century Swiss documents and reports, has been presented by Dorette Berthoud in her 1969 article "The Green Fairy," on whose findings I have heavily relied in this chapter.

The first characters in these retellings of the mythical origins of absinthe were the monks of the abbey of St-Benoît or Montbenoît in the city of Montbenoît, which can be found in the French department of Doubs, bordering Switzerland. These monks were believed by some to have discovered either absinthe or a precursor to absinthe.

The next suspect, so to speak, was a French doctor or surgeon of the name of Pierre Ordinaire, from the city of Quingey in the Franche-Comté,[58] who spent time in political exile in the small village of Couvet in the Val-de-Travers in Switzerland at the end of the eighteenth century.[59] Berthoud reported that Ordinaire moved to Couvet in 1771, where he lived in the Hôtel de l'Aigle. He later married Henriette Petitpierre, the daughter of the owner of the hotel. According to Berthoud, Ordinaire was a victim of anti-Huguenot laws that prohibited Huguenots from practising medicine in France.[60] Other accounts placed him in Couvet at a later date. Phil Baker explained that in some versions of this story Ordinaire fled to Couvet in 1792, escaping the French revolution as a monarchist.[61] Ordinaire's exact role in the invention of absinthe remains equally unclear: in some accounts, he concocted the first version of absinthe in Couvet as a "herbal remedy" for his patients,[62] while, in others, he merely imported the monks' idea from France or bought the recipe from a local Swiss woman, as will be discussed below. In a 2006 short entry on the "origins of absinthe," the Swiss editor Roger Liggenstorfer questioned, however, whether Ordinaire existed at all, or whether he was invented to give absinthe a more respectable – medical – background.[63]

A female member of Ordinaire's household – or possibly working at the Hôtel de l'Aigle – in Couvet also appears in some retellings of the myth. In various versions, she was either a servant or governess, sometimes unnamed and sometimes given the name of Mademoiselle Grand-Pierre[64] or Grand-pierre.[65] According to Berthoud, some sources suggested that Ordinaire had bequeathed his recipe to this Mademoiselle Grandpierre, while others doubted that she even existed.[66]

The next major suspects were Mère Henriette Henriod – or Henriot – and her daughters. They were believed to be the wife and daughters of a Lieutenant Henriod, who, however, seems to not have played a role in absinthe's origin story. Liggenstorfer also questioned whether the Demoiselles Henriod were really the daughters of Henriette Henriod, based on the fact that they were only five and eight years old at the time of Mère Henriod's death in 1797.[67] Independent of whether they were mother and daughters, they were treated as separate entities in these accounts. Mère Henriod and the Demoiselles Henriod lived in Couvet, and Mère Henriod – a "woman alchemist and a bit of a witch," according to Yves Chapuis – was believed by some to have been the true inventor of absinthe during the 1780s.[68] Jad Adams mentioned that, in some accounts, she was believed to be Ordinaire's housekeeper or even lover.[69] Reports that include her usually suggest that Mère Henriod either sold or voluntarily gave her recipe to Ordinaire. The Demoiselles Henriod, on the other hand, are described as having bought the recipe from either Ordinaire himself or from Mademoiselle Grandpierre,[70] before becoming the first absinthe manufacturers, using herbs from their own garden.[71]

Finally, there is Henri-Louis Pernod. There is a somewhat stronger consensus about his role: in practically all accounts, Pernod was described as the founder of the first absinthe distillery in Couvet in either 1797 or 1798.[72] There are, however, also versions that portray him as the inventor of the drink.[73] Pernod opened a second factory in Pontarlier, under the name of Pernod Fils,[74] across the French border, in 1805.[75]

In some versions, characters appear that cannot be found in the usual re-tellings – the red herrings in an Agatha Christie story, so to speak. The most important amongst them is, undoubtedly, Major Daniel-Henry Dubied, either a trader in the municipality of Boveresse in the Val-de-Travers,[76] or a French-man on vacation.[77] According to some, Dubied – the father-in-law of Pernod – bought the recipe from either Mère Henriod, the servant/governess of Ordinaire, or the Demoiselles Henriod,[78] possibly in 1797.[79] One of the other red herrings is a wigmaker of the name of Germain, who, according to Ber-thoud, was a friend of Ordinaire. Germain received the recipe from Mère Henriod and handed it over to Pernod. In some versions, a son of Ordinaire gave the recipe either directly to Dubied or to one of Dubied's employees.[80] Independent of whether any of these people were actually involved, they only occasionally made it into accounts of absinthe's discovery.

Belle Époque retellings of the origin story of the drink often have the feel of legends. This was something that these authors were aware of, and they regularly referred to obtaining their information directly from legends. The uncertainty of their information seems to not have bothered them much. Froemer explained in his 1884 article that his information was "according to a legend that we report as such, but which must contain some truth."[81] Froemer, and many of his contemporaries writing about the discovery of absinthe, thus believed in an essential truth contained within the many myths around the drink, and did not refrain from imparting them, without further proof, to their readers.

How these characters interacted, and what their exact roles were, differed in the various accounts. In 1894 an article was published in the scientific jour-nal *La Nature*, written by A.-M. Villon, a chemical engineer, who asserted that absinthe had, initially, been a "pharmaceutical preparation for use against gas-tric difficulties, against disorders of the digestive tract and the bladder." After this contextualization, Villon explained how absinthe had first been produced: "according to a book dating back almost a century, the invention of the ab-sinthe extract is due to a doctor named Ordinaire. According to a legend, the product was discovered by the monks of the abbey of Saint-Benoît (Mont-benoit)." Without giving further information about the unnamed book, Villon went on to clarify that "it could very well be that it was from the latter [the monks of Montbenoît] that Dr Ordinaire held the secret of the preparation of this liquor." According to Villon's version of this myth, Ordinaire had been "expelled from France for political reasons" and chose to settle in Couvet, "where he practiced the profession of doctor and pharmacist, which allowed him to work on his elixir."[82] Very similar accounts of Ordinaire's political flight from France and his central role in the history of absinthe – without the references to the abbey of Montbenoît, however – can also be found in some Swiss nineteenth-century accounts.[83] The Swiss journal *Le conteur vaudois*, however, in an article published in 1890, knew neither name nor nationality of this doctor involved in the discovery of absinthe, instead simply claiming that "towards the end of the last century, a doctor, whose name we have not been able to find, came to settle in Couvet to practice his art."[84]

In an article published in *Le Caviste* in January 1900, J. Guillemaud – similarly to Villon – explained that the "invention of Absinthe seems, says the legend, to be due to the monks of the abbey of St-Benoît." Ordinaire had learnt the "secret of making absinthe" from these monks and, upon being forced to flee France, settled in Couvet, where he produced it no longer as a "as a pharmaceutical preparation, but as an aperitif."[85] The same sequence of events can also be found in Froemer's 1884 version, which, like Villon, gave the honour of being the inventor to both the monks of Montbenoît and Ordinaire. Froemer introduced the topic by stating that "the creator of absinthe would be a French doctor by the name of Ordinaire," whom he further described, "going back to the legend," as practising "both medicine and pharmacy" and exiled to Switzerland for "political reasons." Yet further on, Froemer explained that "contrary to legend, it seems proven that the elixir of absinthe was born in France, a few leagues from Pontarlier, and that it would have been created by the monks of the abbey of Montbenoît; but nothing prevents us from supposing that Doctor Ordinaire, who probably belonged to this region, would have known the precious recipe from the monks."[86] In the three French versions, the origin of absinthe started in France itself – with the monks of Montbenoît – or with a Frenchman in his Swiss exile, while the Swiss journal *Le conteur vaudois* was not even aware of Ordinaire's French nationality.

Other accounts suggested that Mère Henriod had invented absinthe. In their 1913 book *Merchants of Madness*, the brothers Léon and Maurice Bonneff dedicated a subchapter to the history of absinthe, with the telling title "The source in Switzerland, the river in France." The brothers Bonneff, who were strict opponents of absinthe, acknowledged the quintessentially Swiss origins of the drink, stating that "the women and children martyred by Pontissalian alcoholism [i.e., alcoholism stemming from the French city of Pontarlier] ask when Parliament will decide to ban absinthe. It was in Switzerland that it was born, it was Switzerland that gave it to France, and, full of wisdom, Switzerland is in the process of getting rid of it." Their version of the discovery of absinthe started towards the end of the eighteenth century when "an old lady from Couvet (canton of Neuchatel), Mère Henriod, made home remedies and prepared a certain liquor that the people of the commune highly prized." After this introduction of Mère Henriod, as the inventor of the drink, Ordinaire, his servant – here a governess – and the Demoiselles Henriod appeared. The Bonneffs continued: "It is unfortunate that Mère Henriod knew a French exile, Doctor Pierre Ordinaire, that she left him the formula for absinthe, that he did not take this formula to the grave, that he had a governess, that she sold the recipe to the demoiselles Henriod, that these ladies began to manufacture and sell jugs of the 'extract' in the countryside."[87] Instead of Ordinaire inventing absinthe – after having learnt of it from the monks of the abbey of Montbenoît – the good doctor received a full recipe from Mère Henriod in the anti-absinthe account of the brothers Bonneff. Even though Mère Henriod did not entrust this original recipe to her supposed daughters, they still ended up with it, via Ordinaire and his governess.

According to Guillemaud, Ordinare himself – and not the Demoiselles Henriod – "was the first Absinthe manufacturer,"[88] while the versions proposed by Froemer and Villon agreed with the brothers Bonneff. Froemer suggested that, upon Ordinaire's death, "his secret, carefully guarded until then" ended up in the hands of his unnamed governess, who, in turn, "sold it to the daughters of Lieutenant Henriot."[89] This same sequence of events can also be found in the 1885 account of the Swiss journalist and author Franz August Stocker.[90] In Froemer, Villon, and Stocker's accounts, the Demoiselles Henriod went on to become the first manufacturers of absinthe, but the absinthe production of either the Henriod sisters or of Ordinaire himself was relatively modest.

The next important step in absinthe's story was the introduction of Henri-Louis Pernod in the last years of the eighteenth century. While Froemer did not explain how the recipe made its way from the Demoiselles Henriod to Pernod, he stated that, in 1797 – which was, according to Liggenstorfer, the year of Mère Henriod's death[91] – the "secret of the absinthe elixir" came into the hands of Henri-Louis Pernod. Pernod established a factory in Couvet shortly thereafter, before opening a second factory in Pontarlier in 1805, in order to circumvent French custom fees on Swiss products.[92]

While absinthe manufacture had started in Couvet – with Ordinaire, the Demoiselles Henriod, or Pernod – it was only with the relocation to France that the volume of production started to increase and spread abroad. By 1819, absinthe had made its way into adverts in England,[93] and by 1826 it could be consumed in New Orleans.[94] With this first expansion of its clientele, the demand for absinthe rose. This new demand was supplied by existing distilleries increasing their absinthe production, and through the foundation of new distilleries. On the centenary of the foundation of the Pernod Fils distillery in Pontarlier, in 1905, there were twenty-five separate distilleries in Pontarlier alone,[95] which employed, according to Lachenmeier et al., roughly 3,000 workers, and which produced ten million litres of absinthe per year.[96] The production of absinthe distilleries also increased. Each of Pernod's factories initially produced sixteen litres of absinthe per day, according to Villon, which rose to 450 litres in 1855. By the publication of his article in 1894, this daily production had further risen to several thousand litres.[97] Similar numbers can also be found in Froemer's account, who stated that by 1884, 8,600 litres of absinthe were produced each day in Pernod's factory in Pontarlier alone.[98]

Most Belle Époque publications retelling the legendary history of the origins of absinthe mentioned few, or no, specific names. A short notice in one of the daily newspapers in Oran, published in April 1901, for example, simply stated that it "was a French doctor, who took refuge in Switzerland in the eighteenth century who first used the elixir of absinthe, with which he made a point of curing all ailments." Even without the names of the French doctor and the exact place, it is clear that this short summary alludes to Ordinaire and Couvet. The author, critical of absinthe, believed Ordinaire to be the inventor of the drink and that it was nothing but a medicinal substance for him and those who inherited "his recipe" directly from him – probably Mademoiselle Grandpierre or the Demoiselles Henriod – "but at the beginning of the nineteenth century a distiller bought the mysterious recipe." The author further added that the unnamed distiller – Pernod, of course – made absinthe more harmful by increasing the alcohol content of the original recipe.[99]

The truth of any of these narratives is difficult to determine and does not seem to have been viewed as important by French absinthe drinkers, as was suggested by a British author with the name of H.P. Hugh in his 1896 article "The Absinthe Hour in Paris," in which he asked several questions about absinthe's origins: "Did Napoleon I. introduce absinthe into France? Did he serve it out to his soldiers in the marshes, and did they throw it away in disgust? Is it an old Swiss drink, with centuries of history?" While these questions seemed interesting to Hugh, he suggested that, if one puts "these and a dozen other questions to a Frenchman as he sips [his absinthe] gently," "he tells you that he does not know – that he is not interested." According to Hugh, this Frenchman "dislikes the idea that absinthe has a vulgar history," instead favouring "the idea that it came down directly from the gods."[100]

There is little doubt that Pierre Ordinaire was a real person and that he came into contact with absinthe in the little town of Couvet after he moved there in the 1770s, yet it seems likely that his role was not that of "discoverer." According to Liggenstorfer, absinthe was first publicly advertised in the canton of Neuchâtel in 1769 and 1777,[101] the former date preceding the earliest date, 1771, proposed for Ordinaire's flight from France. It is more probable that the drink had been traditionally produced and consumed in Switzerland for some time. Based on the nineteenth-century account of a Gustave Pierrepetit, Dorette Berthoud suggested that "absinthe was already known previously in the Val-de-Travers," i.e., before Ordinaire's arrival, where it was made by Mère Henriod.[102] Despite this claim by Pierrepetit, it is not possible to determine whether Mère Henriod invented absinthe or not. It might be more correct to assume that Mère Henriod herself was only one of several absinthe producers in the region in the late eighteenth century.[103]

These confusing and contradictory strands of the myth about absinthe's origins show that, for many French absinthe lovers, it was a thoroughly French product and its history was tweaked to make it more French and thus more worthy of nationalistic fervour. The prominent inclusion of Ordinaire – a medical expert – probably served to make the drink more respectable. Many Swiss authors, unsurprisingly, presented absinthe as a primarily Swiss drink. In a 1994 article for the *Journal de Genève*, the journalist and absinthe distiller Jean-Jacques Charrère described absinthe as having been invented by Mère Henriod and stated that in the "Val-de-Travers, everyone will tell you that absinthe is the (forbidden) fruit of their entrails." He understood that absinthe was viewed differently in France, adding that "in Pontarlier, on the contrary, you are guaranteed that a French doctor who took refuge in the Val-de-Travers, the Dr Ordinaire (! [sic]), invented the recipe to treat his patients."[104] The nationality of the drink thus seemed to have depended on the nationality of the authors. There was, however, an additional dimension to this, as French authors who viewed absinthe as a public danger that needed to be stopped also tended to present it as a Swiss drink.

Questions about absinthe's change of nationality were discussed at the time. After the prohibition of absinthe in Switzerland, the Swiss journal *Le conteur vaudois* published a note in 1908 with the title "The Nationality of Absinthe." The article discussed how, despite absinthe being prohibited in Switzerland, French absinthes were still often decorated with the Swiss flag: "Our excellent neighbour, France, so often eager to appropriate our literary, scientific, and other celebrities – every great man is French, it is agreed – does not adopt with the same enthusiasm our former little sins, if they are sins, which are also hers."[105] I am not the first to notice this malleability of the identity of absinthe, as this has been discussed by Charrère, as shown above, and by Jad Adams in his book *Hideous Absinthe*. Adams suggested that absinthe was able to adapt its nationality, its purpose, and the gender of its inventor, depending on the author's point of view: "Several cultural functions were served when Ordinaire and not Henriod was seen as the originator of modern absinthe: it meant the drink was a product of science rather than folk medicine; it became the creation of a man, not a woman; and if it had been made by a Frenchman, only staying in Switzerland then it could be claimed as French, not Swiss."[106]

As mentioned above, Kolleen M. Guy suggested that mythical origins were created for champagne in order to add "honor and respectability to a brand."[107] In the context of absinthe, the same mechanism was in place for both the whole drink and individual brands, in the person of Dr Ordinaire, who had wanted nothing but to cure his patients with his "elixir." This myth of discovery was, however, further complicated by the disputed nationality of the drink and by voices of absinthe opponents, who might have intended to add "dishonour and disrespectability" to absinthe, so to speak, with their retellings of its origins.

Ritualistic Consumption

As the "hour of absinthe" became an established time of the day in France and the French colonies, with men – and women – ordering their favourite brand of absinthe in their favourite cafés, the consumption of the green fairy slowly turned into a ritual, with a set time, tools, required knowledge, and, perhaps most importantly, it became somewhat unseemly without company. Part of absinthe's attraction seems to have been that it was often consumed outside. In his 2013 book, Didier Nourrisson explained that the formerly closed-up, inwards-oriented drinking spaces had opened up during the Belle Époque. These cafés extended onto the streets in what Nourrisson called the "time of the terraces."[108] Even though the focus of Belle Époque authors was on the public consumption of absinthe in these elegant cafés or glamorous salons, with all their ritualistic theatricality, or perhaps – in passing – on the habits of certain workers, who drank it far less glamorously at the counters of various débits, some absinthe was also consumed at home.[109] Sharing the "hour of absinthe" in a café with others was not always possible in the French countryside,[110] in colonial contexts,[111] or for women. In the cities, however, absinthe remained a drink that was consumed outside of the home, where working-class consumers especially could buy just one glass, if the price of a bottle proved to be too high for them.[112]

Absinthe was believed to be something of an acquired taste. "It is a strange drink," wrote H.P. Hugh in his 1896 article. "No one has ever tasted it for the first time without a shudder of disgust. With its strong medicated odour, its sickly taste and its uncanny colour, it suggests a nauseous drug more than a beverage." The second glass, however, was the dangerous one: "But do not drink it twice if you do not want to understand its fearful fascination: it is more deadly in the long run than opium, and [even Edgar Allan] Poe could not describe its domination when its victim is too weak to struggle."[113] Absinthe's pleasant taste could therefore only be recognized after this initial "shudder of disgust," but drinking more than one glass in one sitting was seen as poor taste.[114] As absinthe was drunk before meals, as an aperitif, it was necessarily consumed on an empty stomach. This, some French doctors feared, was dangerous,[115] which made it all the more important to stick to the one-glass rule. However, as Irmgard Bauer mentioned in a 2020 article, while drinkers were expected to limit themselves to one glass, "there was no rule against 'café-crawling.'"[116] Undoubtedly, some absinthe drinkers took advantage of this socially accepted loophole.

As the ritualistic nature of the "hour of absinthe" deepened, it became easier for the uninitiated to commit grave faux pas. Parisians "regard the drinking of their absinthe out of certain hours as a gross piece of ignorance and bad taste," wrote Heilig in 1894. "Few people in the smarter section of the city dare to brave the waiter's elevated eyebrows or their neighbors' looks of curious amusement which are sure to follow a demand for absinthe after luncheon or after dinner."[117] It was seen as equally poor taste – and dangerous to boot – to drink it neat, i.e., without the added water.[118] In her 2015 PhD thesis, Lauren Saxton suggested that the snobbery towards those who drank absinthe pure also showed different classes amongst absinthe drinkers, as the bourgeoisie was "likely to water absinth down far more than the working-class or the bohemians."[119] Richard Gasnier explained that workers "abstained" from letting water slowly drip into the glass, due to an absence of both tools and time.[120] Some women were also accused of preferring their absinthe neat.[121] Most consumers, however, added some water to their glass of absinthe. Once seated on a terrace, the 1864 article in *The Times* explained, the "waiter places before his customers a goblet and a decanter of water; into the former he pours from a black bottle about a liqueur glass of a dark green fluid, and then retires," at which point "the person thus supplied thereupon grasps the decanter, and proceeds to *faire son absinthe*. Slowly, drop by drop, and in small plashes, he lets the water fall into the tumbler."[122] Other consumers added other forms of alcohol or "gay-coloured syrups" to their absinthes.[123]

In order to prepare the drink to one's liking, i.e., to mix it with these other spirits or syrups, and to proficiently add the water and sugar, certain tools were required. While these might not have been involved from the very beginning,[124] spoon, sugar, and iced water soon became part of the often-described ritual of the "hour of absinthe" on the terraces of the cafés. The preparation of a glass of absinthe was something that had to be learnt. By 1865, Monselet explained that ordering a glass of absinthe could be complicated, as there were "a hundred ways to drink absinthe," by, for example, adding other drinks to it, as well as another hundred ways "to *make* it, that is to say to make it cloudy with water, to mix it, to beat it, to bind it." Monselet added that he had "known absinthe professors."[125] Despite the irony in Monselet's statement, this understanding – of the preparation of absinthe being an art or a science – was widely accepted in the nineteenth and early twentieth century.[126]

The ritualistic daily consumption of absinthe needed not only tools and knowledge, but also leisure, as can be seen in Fig. 1.1, in which a leisurely gentleman participating in the "hour of absinthe" was depicted as an elegant monkey. A French settler with the name of A. Villacrose explained in 1875 that he required both time and concentration when preparing his absinthe in Algeria. Pouring the water "drop by drop" was, according to Villacrose, "an operation that requires a quarter of an hour of work, a large amount of attention, after which I spent two quarters of an hour to absorb, by little sips, the liquid."[127] Due to the time needed for its preparation and consumption, celebrating the "hour of absinthe" on the terraces of cafés was the "stock exchange for the idle," Monselet clarified in 1865.[128] Just like the preference of drinking absinthe neat or diluted, and the inclusion of tools, this leisurely consumption also differentiated the classes of absinthe drinkers, as the "distinguished drinker shows that he does not take his absinthe like a worker who, hastily, on leaving the workshop" drinks a glass of absinthe at the counter, Nourrisson explained.[129] Devoting hours each day to leisure and idleness seemed, certainly to many French people in the nineteenth century, luxurious

Figure 1.1
Advert for a carpet and furniture store, Au Fil de la Vierge, by
Louis Legendre in Orléans, depicting the "hour of absinthe"
enjoyed by an elegantly dressed monkey who drinks and smokes.

and even exotic. In her 1983 book, Marie-Claude Delahaye, for example, explained that the "hour of absinthe" took place in a "climate of idleness," "a relaxed way of life," which reminded her of the consumption of another drink in France's former colonial empire: "Yes, the absinthe drinker takes his time … just like the Moroccan mint tea drinker."[130]

Most Belle Époque reports of the "hour of absinthe" described it being consumed both publicly and in company. Nourrisson explained that the consumption of absinthe was "eminently collective," it was "public alcoholization, a manifestation of sociability."[131] Absinthe drinking was social drinking par excellence for French people in the last decades of the nineteenth century, in the cafés and débits of the French cities as much as in colonial contexts. The ritual of sharing a drink quickly became a soothing experience for many in France. Two articles published in *The Times* show that the "hour of absinthe" was continued amongst the French even in moments of crisis. An article from a foreign correspondent, published in September 1870, reported that there were, at that time, 10,000 French prisoners of the Franco-Prussian War at Sedan, who, despite their circumstances, continued to "good humouredly" drink their absinthe every day in various cafés.[132] In an April 1871 letter to *The Times*, the author, given only as J.F. O., stated a few months after the end of the Paris siege, "Paris is itself and not itself. One street has a perfectly quiet and normal appearance, while, in the next, circulation is stopped; a detachment of the National Guard is ready to defend the approaches to a veritable fortress, and the cannon pokes its ugly muzzle through the barricades. In the meantime, the mitrailleuse rattles afar off, the ambulances keep coming in laden with the victims of the civil war; but the eternal *flâneur* looks calmly on and sips his absinthe at his little table outside the café on the Boulevard, in full view of the line of Garde Nationale extending across the Rue de la Paix."[133] The crises of 1870 and 1871 did not, therefore, stop the popularity of the "hour of absinthe," and potentially even increased it.[134]

As mentioned in the introduction, it was often suggested that sharing a glass of absinthe with other Europeans was the only moment of relaxation for French settlers and soldiers throughout France's empire. In his *Souvenirs of the Military Life in Algeria*, published in 1852, a Captain Pierre de Castellane described life garrisoned in Algeria, in a camp that was "far from being gay." He added that life was centred around a large tree, which he called "the *salon* of the camp": "There, while drinking absinthe, the favourite drink of the African army [i.e., the French army in Algeria]," it was possible to relax, "to share news, anecdotes, and also gossip."[135] In the colonies, absinthe provided comfort not only to French soldiers. The French doctor Witold Lemanski, who had lived and worked in Tunisia, wrote in his 1902 handbook for settlers in European colonies that, "on leaving the office, the shop, the bank, [or] the workshop, the employee, the worker, [and] the student are lured to the café. It is the irresistible attraction of that which glitters, the thrill of easy enthusiasm, the stupid and thoughtless camaraderie, the success of endless perorations at the counter, where, glass in hand, the brain is heated by alcohol fumes." While the "hour of absinthe" was thus reported as allowing European settlers of all classes to temporarily forget their miseries, Lemanski warned that once the café was left behind, this habit brought "larger despairs."[136] While Lemanski believed absinthe to be harmful for the drinker, future generations and France in general, he nonetheless acknowledged that sharing a daily glass brought French men "easy enthusiasm" and "thoughtless camaraderie." Not all agreed on this, however. Speaking about life in France, an author whose name was only given as Jean de Montmartre, in an 1898 newspaper article, contradicted authors believing absinthe drinking to be a social activity, as, according to him, "vermouth is the friend of repeated rounds, it is a sociable drink. Absinthe is rather solitary."[137] Similarly, the French journalist and historian Gustave Geffroy told the readers of the monthly temperance journal *L'Alcool* in 1896 that, while "the wine drinker is talkative, the absinthe drinker is silent."[138] Such statements hint at the fact that the French temperance movements often advocated not for abstinence but for the consumption of – hygienic! – French wine instead of spirits like absinthe.

Despite such contradictory claims, absinthe was commonly perceived, for better or worse, as being France's social glue during the Belle Époque – and some argued that no other drink could have fulfilled this specific role. The French doctor Jules-Michel Ferdinand Moreau, who was known as Ferdinand Moreau, wrote in his 1862 book that "the man of the world just like the ragman" had only one point of contact: "both, at the same time, take *their absinthe*."[139] According to Moreau, everyone – every man at least – drank their absinthe during the "hour of absinthe" in their respective café of choice, thus giving all French men a rare, shared experience. It should be added, however, that, while Lemanski, Moreau, and others made it appear as if practically every Frenchman took part in this daily ritual of celebrating the "hour of absinthe," this is an exaggeration.[140] This unifying component of absinthe, as a drink shared by all, was not a positive development in Moreau's eyes, as he added: "Let us assume that absinthe did not exist, do you think the man of the world would think of taking a glass of rum or cognac? Personally, I do not think so."[141] In contrast to others, who suggested that "it's no less the hour of absinthe," if one drank vermouth or madeira,[142] absinthe was, in Moreau's eyes, the essential component of the "hour of absinthe," without which it could not exist.

In nineteenth- and early twentieth-century accounts by both absinthe enthusiasts and opponents, absinthe takes on the role of a unifier of France during a particularly changeable moment in time. Yet while it is undoubtedly true that absinthe was, eventually, consumed across the class system in France, people stuck to establishments frequented by their own classes; most commonly, the only mixing that occurred during the "hour of absinthe" seems to have been that of adding "gay-coloured syrups" to one's absinthe.[143] Looking at the many ingredients that were commonly reported as required for this daily ritual – absinthe, iced water, sugar, an assortment of other liquors and syrups, spoons, and carafes, not to mention training, leisure, and companionship – shows that what was sipped on the terraces of (imperial) France's cities greatly differed from what was drunk at counters, neat, and quickly, sometimes without company, by "the employee, the worker, [and] the student," to use Lemanski's formulation,[144] on their way home.

2

Glorious Absinthe

It is commonly accepted that before the brutal military conquest of Algeria, which started in 1830, absinthe had been relatively unknown in France – a locally produced, comparatively unimportant drink. While the ritual of the "hour of absinthe" was probably first established on the terraces of the cafés of various French cities, the popularity of absinthe started in Algeria, where its presence dated, according to Casimir Frégier's 1863 study, "from the day after the Conquest."[1] This chapter addresses the crucial role that the conquest of Algeria played in explanations for the growing popularity of absinthe in France, by deconstructing both narratives around "absinthe rations" allegedly having been distributed by the French military and the idea of the French bourgeoisie only embracing absinthe as a means of celebrating the habits of returning French soldiers. The third part, finally, is dedicated to the importance of absinthe in the way of life of settlers in French colonies, as their enthusiastic celebration of the "hour of absinthe" soon became a point of attack against settler society in general, by authors in metropolitan France.

Absinthe Rations

The accepted narrative is that during the military conquest of Algeria between 1830 and 1847,[2] but particularly between 1844 and 1847,[3] French soldiers either decided to mix wormwood with their wine,[4] or were recommended or even allocated rations of absinthe for medical reasons.[5] Irmgard Bauer, for example, mentioned that during "the conquest of Algeria (from 1830) and the Franco-Moroccan War (1844–47), French soldiers were given absinthe as prophylaxis against malaria and other ills."[6] Phil Baker similarly suggested that the issuing of absinthe rations "was felt to work so well that it became a part of French army life, from Madagascar to Indo-China."[7] The secondary literature explains the use of absinthe by the army through military doctors – or the soldiers themselves – believing absinthe to be of help against various ills, such as dysentery,[8] fevers in general[9] and malaria in particular,[10] and dirty water.[11]

However, as I have already discussed in my 2015 article "The Green Fairy in the Maghreb,"[12] I have not come across a single source from the period of 1830 to 1847 – the year in which Emir Abd-el-Kader, the famous leader of Algerian resistance, surrendered to the French – or in the years immediately following the French victory that recommended or even discussed daily absinthe rations for French soldiers. Adolphe Armand wrote in 1854 that a ration of alcohol distilled from fruit was allocated to soldiers in Algerian "labour camps." As he had earlier in his book mentioned a prohibition of absinthe within the French army in Algeria, he clearly did not allude to an absinthe ration but to a ration of another distilled form of alcohol.[13] As daily coffee and wine rations were discussed by French military doctors from the 1850s onward, this absence is salient. Armand, for example, mentioned that French troops in Algeria were distributed wine and coffee rations alternately,[14] while Charles Viry described a daily wine ration in Algeria in his 1886 *Manual of Military Hygiene*.[15] In the course of my research, I have, by contrast, come across a series of absinthe *prohibitions* in the French army that predate France's 1915 absinthe ban by up to seventy years!

The earliest text discussing such a prohibition, that I have come across, can be found in the Francophone newspaper *Akhbar: Journal d'Algérie*, which acknowledged in December 1844 that four French officers had to be repatriated to France due to mental issues caused by their absinthe overconsumption. This note suggested that, at this point, absinthe had already been "prohibited at the outposts" of the French military in Algeria, without, however, providing further information on this ban.[16] By October and November 1845 several different newspapers published notes, which informed their readers about absinthe bans in the French army in Algeria with varying levels of detail. *L'Indépendant de la Moselle* noted on 29 October 1845 that a "decision by the Minister of War prohibits the use of absinthe in Algeria,"[17] while *L'Algérie* announced on 2 November 1845 that France's minister of war – Jean-de-Dieu Soult – had issued an order prohibiting the use of the "liqueur d'absinthe" amongst troops in Algeria and its sale in the camps.[18] A note in *La Semaine*, published in early November 1845, also notified its readers about the decision by the minister of war, before stating that the sale of absinthe was to be "prohibited in camps, canteens, and other places frequented by the military."[19] The 1857 *Elementary Treatise of Military Hygiene* by the French military doctor Jacques-François-Rémy-Stanislas Rossignol described these 1845 bans as being based on medical concerns: "One soon sees, effectively, especially when taken in an abusive way, the indications, under its influence, of excessively serious diseases, such as meningitis, encephalitis, cerebral softening, etc. In order to avoid these accidents, which always have a fatal termination, we must refrain from this pernicious beverage." The French government had come to the same conclusion, as "two ministerial decrees, from 27 September 1845 and 11 October of the same year, banned the use of absinthe by troops in Algeria, and the sale was prohibited in the camps, canteens, and other places frequented by the military."[20] Rossignol's use of the same formulation as the article published in November 1845 in *La Semaine* hints at both texts being based on an official announcement. The same two decrees were also discussed by others.[21]

These were not the first bans of an intoxicating substance within the French army in North Africa, as hashish had famously been banned by Jacques-François "Abdallah" Menou in October 1800 in Egypt, as described by the historian David Guba in his 2020 book *Taming Cannabis*.[22] Additionally, 1857, the year of the last of the absinthe bans in the French army in Algeria,[23] also saw a decree that was intended to regulate the sale and consumption of hashish in Algerian coffeehouses, i.e., aimed at the consumption of the colonized.[24] Both absinthe and hashish were thus presented as an issue, in Algeria, at the very same moment in time. Yet while the habit of consuming hashish was something that French soldiers picked up from contact with Egyptians – and, later, Algerians – these early bottles of absinthe were produced in Pontarlier and exported to Algeria by French merchants. Before the military conquest of Algeria, absinthe had been an insignificant drink in France's assortment of spirits and it had been initially marketed as medicinal. From this perspective, it can be said that absinthe was understood as only becoming dangerous on North African soil.

A reference to a further prohibition from the second half of the 1840s – i.e., the very period that the drink was allegedly officially distributed by the army – can be found in the 1848 second edition of a *Guide to the Traveller in Algeria* by E. Quetin, in which he discussed the "salubrious climate" of the region of Oran. Quetin believed that "sobriety, diet, and some aromatic plants are the only curative means" that most ills needed. Within this context of healthy living, Quetin mentioned a "recent decree (October 1848) [which] has prohibited in the army the sale of *absinthe*, a liquor whose immoderate use has deplorable effects on the health of the troops."[25] These bans apparently remained active throughout the nineteenth century, as Viry explained in 1886 that "since 1845, the sale of this liquor has been forbidden in the camps and canteens," adding that "this measure has not been repealed."[26] By 1861, knowledge of these prohibitions in the French army had spread across the Channel to England and even across the Atlantic, as, in this year, the English temperance advocate James Dawson Burns and the article in the *Indiana State Sentinel* both mentioned earlier prohibitions of absinthe in the French army and navy.[27]

Not all accounts credited Jean-de-Dieu Soult with originating this decree of prohibition. In 1854, Armand mentioned that, due to the effect the hot Algerian climate allegedly had on absinthe drinkers, Maréchal Thomas-Robert Bugeaud – governor-general of Algeria between 1841 and 1847 – had prohibited absinthe "as a poison." Armand did not agree with this decision, as he saw absinthe as "a liquor which, in a low dose and diluted by water, remains nevertheless, for the sober man, a very hygienic drink to quench the thirst which torments after an excessive fatigue."[28] Bugeaud's direct involvement in the prohibition seems plausible, as he was described as being repulsed by the omnipresence of absinthe in Algeria. Amédée Hennequin reported in an 1857 book on the new governor-general's "first reconnaissance' of the surroundings of Algiers in February 1841 that Bugeaud had 'noticed with pain that the European inhabitants of the villages Dely-Ibrahim and Douera dared not even go a few steps from their homes to cultivate the earth, and that colonization, thus paralyzed by terror, had hardly any other representatives than feverish publicans, selling absinthe to soldiers."[29] Bugeaud's frustration about French colonization being delegated to the hands of absinthe sellers was taken up by several outraged French authors of the time. "How is it that you only see French soldiers and Arabs on the roads, and that these villages are empty of settlers and only populated with adventurous speculators or absinthe sellers?" asked author Paul Varin in 1861.[30]

Abstinence from alcohol was not the goal of these bans. In order for these prohibitions of absinthe to be successful, it was believed they should best be accompanied by an improved access to hygienic alcoholic beverages. The French doctor Alphonse Laveran, for example, suggested in 1896 that, "in order for the soldier not to take the habit of absinthe in the regiment, we believe that wine, beer, or cider, whose quality can be monitored, should be made available for him, in the canteens." With these drinks – "healthy and at a very low price" – the soldier would be "less tempted by the cabarets in the neighbourhood of the barracks, in which he is served absinthe and eau-de-vie of very poor quality."[31] The French army in Algeria had thus singled out absinthe very early on – within fifteen years of its landing in North Africa – as a particular danger to the health and ability of its soldiers.

The fact that there were repeated prohibitions – two in 1845, one in 1848, as well as a later one in 1857 – seems to indicate that these bans were not entirely effective, though not everybody shared this point of view. Georges Morache discussed the prohibition of absinthe in his 1886 *Treatise of Military Hygiene*, in which he admitted that, for a period of twenty years – presumably 1830 to 1850 – absinthism had been an important factor in the life of the French army in Algeria. Yet Morache reassured his readers that the "number of soldiers of all ranks, who have let themselves be led [by absinthe], has never been as great as some people wanted to pretend." Despite this, the number was great enough for the leadership to act decisively, with the result that there "are few regiments today, where absinthe is tolerated among the liquors, which are sold in the canteens."[32] From Morache's point of view, the bans had been a success. This statement is somewhat contradicted by the fact that, due to the soldiers' pronounced taste for absinthe, new bans amongst the troops were introduced in other French colonies, such as Indochina, as we can infer from articles published in 1885,[33] i.e., the year before the publication of Morache's book.

While not directly addressing the bans, similar statements about the worst excesses of absinthe consumption in the French army having been quickly quelled can be found in other publications throughout the nineteenth century.[34] Henri Lierre, for example, explained in 1867 how, after French soldiers had discovered absinthe, "the taste for absinthe spread; the cafés in Algiers, Oran, Bougie, Constantine witnessed deplorable excesses." Yet Lierre claimed that these excesses were soon stopped: "Disapproval, which the press of metropolitan France echoed, caused a reform, and today, I dare say, no more absinthe is consumed in the garrisons of Africa than in those in France." When French colonial authors referred to "Africa," or the "African army," they usually meant Algeria and the French army in Algeria, contingent on the context. Lierre went on to say that cases of alcoholism, "which were never very numerous in Algeria, almost disappeared, and are only observed among some Maltese or Spaniards."[35] While settlers from Malta and Spain were usually included in France's conception of a "colonial society" in Algeria – in stark contrast to the local Jewish and Muslim populations – as discussed, for example, by the historians David Prochaska in 1990 and Ann Laura Stoler in 2002[36] – they were often depicted as inferior to the French.[37] Lierre's clearly fictional depiction of only them clinging to an overconsumption of alcohol in general and absinthe in particular – while French settlers had been moved to moderation – is coloured by this prejudice.

Other authors did not believe that these measures against absinthe had been effective – or at least not effective enough. The futility of absinthe bans in the French army was addressed by the French doctor Louis Figuier in an 1862 article about the "pernicious effects of absinthe," in which he mentioned a prohibition of the sale of absinthe "during the campaign of Kabylia in 1857," information that he had taken from a report by the psychiatrist Henri Legrand du Saulle. Showing that he was aware of the bans preceding this one, Figuier stated that "more than once, the selling of absinthe has been banned in our African army." According to him, "any interdiction remained powerless; the insatiable passion of the drinker, together with the interest of the manufacturers, were stronger than the goodwill of a tutelary administration." Figuier added that these prohibitions of absinthe had material consequences: "even though our memories are a bit vague in this regard, we have seen, in the city of Lunel, which was one of the main seats of the manufacture of absinthe, various factories stop production due to the prohibition instituted in Africa against the selling of absinthe."[38] An absinthe factory seems to only have been established in Lunel, in the department of Hérault, in 1850 by Édouard Pernod, one of Henri-Louis Pernod's sons. This would consequently have been after the prohibitions of the 1840s, but before the one in 1857.[39] While it is not impossible that the bans of the 1840s and 1850s had an effect on the growing absinthe production in France, Figuier's statement about an abrupt stop in Lunel should be taken with a grain of salt. As a clear opponent of the drink, his assertion seems to have been more wishful thinking than reality.

Despite these "tutelary" absinthe bans aimed at the troops in Algeria, the consumption of absinthe was also medically recommended during the same period. During the March 1832 cholera outbreak in Paris,[40] for example, official public instructions, approved by Comte Antoine Maurice Apollinaire d'Argout, the minister of commerce and public works, recommended that people should add absinthe to their water, suggesting that, "instead of drinking it [the water] pure, it will be better to mix in two tea-spoonsful of brandy or

absinthe to a pint."[41] Similarly, a doctor Jean-Pierre-Ferdinand Thévenot recommended absinthe as an effective prophylactic protection against fevers in
his *Treatise on the Diseases of Europeans in Hot Countries, Especially in Senegal,*
which was published in 1840.[42]

From the late 1860s onward, one can find the first sources openly stating
that, during the military conquest of the 1830s and 1840s, French soldiers in
Algeria had been advised by medical experts to add absinthe to their water.[43]
In a letter to the editor, published in *The Times* in 1907, an English author,
only identified as Whin-Hurst, was of the opinion that absinthe had once
been used by the French army in Algeria. If he remembered rightly, "it was at
one time recommended and used by the military authorities as a febrifuge
and specific against malaria in Algeria."[44] Some authors were convinced that
absinthe could be beneficial in making water drinkable,[45] or in fighting fevers.
Yet absinthe's benefits were believed to apply only when consumed moderately. In 1895, Charles Viry highlighted the positive effects of absinthe drinking, as absinthe "corrects the bitterness of a water of bad quality, and, in the
marches through Algeria, she has, when she has been used with an extreme
moderation, rendered some service." These beneficial effects of absinthe were,
according to Viry, counteracted by immoderation, as "unfortunately, the
abuse is very close to the use: he who begins with a few drops of absinthe [in
his water] ends up taking a daily dose of several glasses."[46] Variations on this
story – of absinthe being used for a reasonable medical end in the beginning,
but becoming dangerous through lack of moderation – can be found re-
peatedly in nineteenth- and early twentieth-century sources.[47]

Even the French temperance advocate Éphrem Aubert suggested in 1920
that absinthe could indeed help with the purification of unsafe water. He explained that "our expeditionary detachments [in Algeria] experienced more
difficulty in obtaining drinking water. The soldiers were then advised, by military doctors, to add to the impure water *some drops* of absinthe *per litre of
water,* in order to kill the pestilential microbes. The drink thus acquired a
pleasant flavour that brought men to gradually augment the dose of absinthe
to excess. *Consciously* avoiding the danger of fevers, they *unconsciously* delivered themselves to this other, much more redoubtable danger: *absinthism.*"[48]
Aubert did not criticize the soldiers' belief in absinthe's microbe-killing properties, but the fact that they did not agree with him on absinthe being more
dangerous than the polluted water. Aubert's reference to absinthe killing
"pestilential microbes" as a motivation in the 1830s and 1840s is anachronistic,

as the first steps of scientific germ theory were only made in the late 1850s by Louis Pasteur. Similar statements can be found in the secondary literature. Barnaby Conrad, for example, stated that between 1844 and 1847 the French troops in Algeria were issued absinthe rations, "as a fever preventative. Mixed with wine or water, absinthe was believed to kill microbes."[49] Similarly, Ian Hutton explained that in "1844 absinthe was issued to French legionnaires fighting in Algeria as it was believed to prevent fevers and kill bacteria in water."[50] The French military doctors potentially recommending the drink during the initial military conquest of Algeria were more likely to have explained its efficacy through the theory of miasmas. An article published in *The Times* in April 1872, which itself was based on an unspecified report in the *Pall Mall Gazette*, claimed that French troops struck with fever in Oran and Constantine during the initial conquest of Algeria were recommended to mix their customary white wine with absinthe, as "a preservative against miasmata, in lieu of quinine, which was by far too costly to be generally distributed."[51] Quinine was indeed not distributed on a wide scale in the French army in the nineteenth century, but this might have been due to a combination of its indeed initially very high price[52] and contemporary medical theories. As both the historians William B. Cohen and David Prochaska argued in their respective publications, French doctors in the nineteenth century had prescribed quinine after the onset of malarial fevers in Algeria. They viewed quinine as a curative drug and not as a prophylactic protection.[53]

The bans on the sale of absinthe to the troops within the army canteens were insufficient to put an end to the excessive consumption of the drink. As seen from the quote by Pierre de Castellane, who described a large tree, around which soldiers in Algeria gathered to drink absinthe, as "the *salon* of the camp" in 1852,[54] sociability played an important role in absinthe's popularity. It is certain that many began to consume it, because meeting to drink helped against their boredom.[55] Nineteenth-century sources additionally suggested that French soldiers turned to absinthe because they could not get their hands on other, more hygienic, alcoholic drinks that they were accustomed to. Victor Anselmier, who wrote a book in 1862 with the telling title *Poisoning by Absinthe*, described the introduction of absinthe into the life of the French army in Algeria through this absence of alternatives. For Anselmier, it was not rations issued by the army that introduced French soldiers to absinthe, but a mixture of hardship, necessity – due to the absence of other options – and the initial pleasantness of the drink. Once the soldiers had been introduced to the drink, the popularity of the green fairy took on a life of its own: "The arrival of so many consumers, placed in the same circumstances, gave to the manufacture of absinthe a great impulse; the use became customary in the expeditionary army. Each arriving regiment adopted this drink."[56]

Nineteenth-century accounts seem to agree that the popularity of absinthe was closely linked to the tastes of the French army in Algeria. It remains unclear, however, where the conviction came from that these French soldiers in Algeria had been issued a daily absinthe ration during the 1830s and 1840s. Was the idea of absinthe rations nothing but an explanation for the immediate and intense popularity of the drink in the French army? Was it based on certain medical voices that advocated, throughout the whole nineteenth century, for the advantages of absinthe in hot climates? Was it a justification by soldiers for their shared preference? Was it based on a misunderstanding of the military bans issued during the 1840s?

While it is likely that absinthe drinking in Algeria was never ordered from above by military doctors, it was, it appears, a form of self-medication for many soldiers. In nineteenth-century sources, French soldiers were regularly portrayed as trusting that absinthe offered them some protection against fevers, malaria, dysentery, and other medical issues connected, in their understanding, to unclean drinking water. There are many anecdotes, told in memoirs of French soldiers, travel reports, and more, that touch on the fact that these French soldiers in Algeria truly believed that absinthe somehow cleaned their drinking water. Gratia Blanc described in 1869 a meeting between officers in Algeria, before quoting one of them as having confidently said: "whatever people say, absinthe will never be condemned in this country where she is used to correct the bad taste of the detestable water that you are very often forced to drink."[57]

It seems that French soldiers actively looked for solutions to solve the problem posed by the consumption of water and that they believed absinthe to be a solution. Their turning towards absinthe was not irrational, as they followed the advice of some medical experts. In a book with the title *Hygiene for Everyone*, published in 1903, a doctor, Calixte Pagès, regretted that contemporary writings on absinthe only talked about "the evil that she [absinthe] does and never about the good." The advantage of absinthe was, in Pagès's view, apparent: the addition of absinthe allowed drinkers to consume "*a large quantity of water.*" In his opinion, no other drink achieved this as effectively as absinthe, as wine "removes the appetite" and cider and beer "make you sweat too much." In hot climates and for those whose profession included hard physical work – such as these soldiers in French colonies – Pagès recommended absinthe as useful.[58]

Independent of how they were introduced to the drink, French soldiers certainly developed a liking for the green fairy during the brutal initial conquest of Algeria. And once they had acquired a taste for absinthe – or for the sociability associated with it – absinthe was not difficult to procure. Indeed, "although absinthe is banned from military canteens, the soldiers are not cut off from it and can find it everywhere," wrote Eugène-François Ravenez, somewhat despairingly, in 1889.[59] The merchants that followed the army happily continued to sell absinthe to the masses of French soldiers in Algeria,[60] despite the bans and against medical recommendations.

Drinking Victoriously

The secondary literature on absinthe usually proposes that, upon their return to France from Algeria – or on medical leave during their service, as Lauren Saxton suggested[61] – these soldiers kept their taste for absinthe and continued to drink it publicly in cafés throughout France.[62] According to some nineteenth-century sources, absinthe spread from Marseille throughout France, which, considering these soldiers must have landed on France's Mediterranean coast on their way from Algeria, seems likely.[63] Absinthe thus became associated with the successful military conquest, "as the war-stained French hero sipped it, the jewel glints danced into his tired soul,"[64] explained Sterling Heilig rather poetically in his 1906 article on absinthe for US audiences.[65] In this narrative, the public consumption of French soldiers, sipping their glass of absinthe seated on the terraces of both fashionable and unfashionable cafés, a portrayal of which can be seen in an 1889–90 lithograph by Alphonse Loustaunau (Fig. 2.1), started the first wave of absinthe's popularity in France. It is unclear when this wave began exactly. In his 1996 book *The World of the Paris Café*, the historian Scott Haine traced the absinthe consumption of these French soldiers back to the 1830s,[66] while the French journalist and curator Benoît Noël placed the appearance of the first absinthe-drinking soldiers in French cafés in 1850.[67] If French soldiers started drinking absinthe in 1830 in Algeria, and drank so much of it that it had to be prohibited more than once during the 1840s, Noël's suggestion seems a little late.

Figure 2.1
Lithograph of a French soldier, returned from Algeria,
sitting on the terrace of a café in Paris, drinking a glass
of absinthe.

Upon their return to France, the taste for absinthe that these soldiers had developed in Algeria began to spread to the general population.[68] Having been invented in Switzerland and having become established in France in the early nineteenth century via the first Pernod Fils factory in Pontarlier, it was this moment of colonial success that ignited absinthe's success story in France. Doctor Ferdinand Moreau mapped absinthe's popularity in his 1863 book as following returning regiments: "Each regiment returning to France brought the taste for absinthe with it, which gradually became a daily use for almost all classes of society. Particularly during the past ten years [i.e., between 1853 and 1863], the fashion for it became so frantic that what once was an exception is now the rule."[69] It soon became lucrative for owners of débits de boissons in France to include absinthe in their range of drinks.

Mirroring Moreau's 1863 account, Victor Anselmier suggested in his 1862 book that absinthe had been associated "with our military successes" in Algeria since the 1830s. He added that "absinthe landed in France with the first regiments which returned, and, like a trophy, it followed the triumphal chariot." Absinthe became the "companion of the victorious soldiers," whose sight reminded French customers of "the conquered country, the sufferings and the joys of conquest." It was this very association of absinthe with the victory in Algeria that caused the popularity of the drink, Anselmier assured his readers: "Not much was needed in order for the African manners [i.e., of French soldiers in Algeria] to become fashionable in France in all the garrison towns."[70] This connection between France's colonial empire and absinthe was obvious to contemporary observers. An article published in the daily newspaper *Le Gaulois* in August 1885 stated proudly that "the history of absinthe, in Africa, is intimately linked to our victories and conquests under the sky and on the burning soils of Africa."[71] To the French, absinthe was "the sign of a glorious time in the African army," Anselmier explained, which made it a much-wanted product: "It was manufactured everywhere, it was sold to everybody."[72]

Soon, absinthe was consumed by more than just former soldiers in France. Its popularity spread first through Marseille and Paris, before reaching other cities and then the countryside.[73] Adverts appeared on the walls of small cities in France (Fig. 2.2). The secondary literature on absinthe followed this narrative and explained the popularity through French civilians – often belonging to the bourgeoisie – wanting to imitate the successful soldiers, home from France's brutal colonial war.[74] Once it had established itself in France as "King Absinthe," to use a formulation by Doctor Saliège in 1911,[75] the drink started

11 AUTUN. — *Tour de Clugny ou de l'Horloge* — LL.

Figure 2.2
Postcard showing the Marchaux or Clock Tower in Autun,
with a large advert for Absinthe Berger: Verte et Blanche.

its global journey. It first spread to France's colonial empire.[76] The same soldiers that had made the drink popular in France took their belief in the efficacy of absinthe in hot climates to other colonial stations, such as Indochina, Madagascar, and French Polynesia.[77] From France's colonies, absinthe spread further. A 1907 pamphlet arguing for a national ban of absinthe in Switzerland observed that the distilleries of the Val-de-Travers exported absinthe around the world, mentioning Italy, the United States, and South America.[78] Although the name of the author is not given in the text, it is generally accepted that it was composed by the well-known Swiss temperance advocate Robert Hercod, who was at the time secretary of the Bureau international contre l'alcoolisme in Lausanne.

While the secondary literature commonly identifies this initial spread of absinthe in France as the bourgeoisie glorifying the absinthe consumption of French soldiers, absinthe started to be viewed more and more negatively as the Belle Époque advanced. The initial perception of absinthe as the heroic symbol of France's colonial successes soon changed. Drinking absinthe came to be no longer viewed as sign of patriotism, though its origins were still deeply linked with France's experiences in Algeria. With this wave of absinthe frenzy, the first cases of a clear addiction to absinthe, with their severe physical and mental consequences, appeared in France, initially amongst the returning soldiers themselves. While there were plenty of civilians suffering from addiction to the drink in the last decades of the nineteenth century, symptoms of absinthism remained constant amongst soldiers returning from colonial endeavours throughout the nineteenth and early twentieth century. Indeed, Belle Époque sources on alcoholism often included case studies of French soldiers, returned from Algeria, who explained their alcoholism explicitly through their North African service. Doctor Joseph Roux, for example, discussed in 1881 the case of a thirty-eight-year-old French man, who had "contracted habits of alcoholism" as a soldier in Algeria. "*Several times a day he drank absinthe, and additionally abused eau-de-vie.* Back in France for eight years, he continued his alcoholic habits."[79] This man was introduced to absinthe in Algeria long after the bans of the 1840s and 1850s, which shows that these measures had not been as successful as many portrayed them to be. Indeed, dependency on absinthe remained a part of military life in Algeria into the twentieth century, as can be seen in a case study by Paul Dubuisson and Auguste Vigouroux in 1911. They described their patient as a twenty-seven-year-old man, "who did his military service in Algeria, [and who] has, like so many others, unfortunately, contracted the habit of absinthe there."[80] Both of these case studies, twenty years apart, used the term "contracted" to describe the initial contact of their patients with absinthe, as if absinthe – or alcoholism – was a contagious Algerian disease.

After the initial glorification of absinthe, the spread of the drink throughout France was indeed sometimes likened to a disease. One such comparison can be found in the 1886 book of Georges Morache. According to him, the French army in Algeria "was first affected [by absinthe], then, by the contagion of example, the habit was introduced in France."[81] In Morache's formulation, it remained unsaid who was responsible for this "contagion of example" – whether it was the French soldiers publicly drinking or those wanting to imitate their behaviour. As absinthe was believed to have been introduced into France by returning soldiers – even though it was an initially Swiss drink, now produced in both Switzerland and France – many authors held these soldiers directly responsible for the spread of absinthism in France. They were also blamed for contributing to the contagion in other French colonies.[82]

In summary, it can be said that the popularity of absinthe amongst the bourgeoisie in France was understood as being directly linked to the successes of the French army in the brutal military war of conquest in Algeria. As absinthe came to be viewed as more and more dangerous as the nineteenth century progressed, negative views were retrospectively applied to its introduction. The patriotic drink of France's colonial successes thus turned into an Algerian plague, in the eyes of absinthe opponents. Several nineteenth-century sources attributed nationalities to various substances and to the corresponding addictions stemming from their overconsumption. In these accounts, absinthism was firmly ascribed to the French in Algeria. In his 1888 study *Diseases of the Spirit*, for example, Georges Pichon explained that "in different countries, these unhealthy intoxications will thus don different forms, sometimes the most surprising." Amongst the different forms of intoxications, Pichon listed the "*opium eaters* of Turkey, the *opium smokers* of China; America has *teaists*, vanillism, Germany *cocainism*, Europe *morphinism*, Algeria *absinthism*, the Orientals *hashishism*. Alcoholism finally will spread its branches through the entire universe."[83]

Pichon's framing of alcoholism as a universal problem – affecting the French as much as everybody else – and of absinthism as an intoxication affecting mostly the French in Algeria, is indicative of how the problem of absinthe came to be understood by large parts of the French population. In this context, absinthism could be presented as a problem of French soldiers returning from Algeria – bolstered by case studies on their overconsumption in medical publications – and, as will be shown in the next part of this chapter, the colonies' settler population. This detachment of absinthism from mainland France served to absolve the habits of the absinthe-drinking French bourgeoisie, who had initially copied the behaviour of returning soldiers! For a large part of the nineteenth century, Pichon's loophole essentially allowed absinthism to be framed as not being a problem of mainland France itself.

The Drink of Settlers

It is very probable that before the first glass of absinthe was ordered in Marseille or Paris by one of these soldiers, returned from their military service in Algeria, French settlers in North Africa had already started to add absinthe to their water. "From the army, its use spread to the civilian population, from the colony it came to metropolitan France," reported the French lawyer Paul Griveau in 1906,[84] strongly suggesting that absinthe was established as a mainstay in Algeria, not only amongst soldiers but also civilian settlers, before it grew into the celebrated drink of the Parisian cafés.

At some point in the drink's history, Algeria was transformed into the land of absinthe in the French imagination, where every settler sat down for their daily glass. Throughout the last decades of the nineteenth century and the first decades of the twentieth, large adverts for absinthe dominated the streets of the coastal cities of colonial Algeria, either as posters glued onto buildings, kiosks, and trams, or as brand names directly painted onto walls, as can be seen in Fig. 2.3 and Fig. 2.4.[85] This interlinking between French settlers in Algeria and absinthe went so far that some French authors even suggested that the phrase "hour of absinthe" had first sprung up on the other side of the Mediterranean. In an 1888 account, based on a journey through Algeria, the author Camille Viré referred to the personal experiences of his travel companion, who had worked as a doctor in a hospital in the Mitidja plain and had claimed that there were French settlers in Algeria who "positively follow the religion of absinthe."[86] While the expression "hour of absinthe" was already established in France at that time, as shown by Monselet's detailed 1865 account,[87] this doctor seemed to have first heard of it in Algeria, as he informed his travel companion Viré that "there is even an expression in Algeria, passed into the language, which you find every day in the newspapers: At the blessed hour of absinthe."[88]

Figure 2.3
Postcard of the Rue Bab Azoun in Algiers, with adverts for Oxygénée
Cusenier Absinthe Recommandée and Absinthe Berger.

Figure 2.4
Postcard showing the former Boulevard National, today known as
the Boulevard Maata Mohamed El Habib, in Oran, with an advert
for Absinthe Rivoire on a tram, as well as adverts for the aperitif
Byrrh and Chocolat Menier on an advertising column.

The "blessed hour of absinthe" became part of daily life in Algeria, celebrated on the terraces of cafés,[89] but also at home, as can be gleaned from an image showing a French settler family in the town of Boufarik taking part in the "hour of absinthe" in 1855, reprinted in the newspaper *L'Afrique du Nord illustrée* in 1934.[90] From at least the 1850s onward, civilian life in Algeria seemed to have been fuelled by the "obligatory glass of absinthe," to use an 1855 formulation by Ch. Marcotte de Quivières.[91] Those who believed absinthe to be more harmful than other forms of alcohol condemned this love of the settlers for the drink. "Everywhere in Algeria, Europeans have the unfortunate habit of taking absinthe before meals, under the pretext of whetting their appetite," Charles Thierry-Mieg regretfully remarked in his 1861 travel account, adding that there had been, in the French army, "a crowd of victims, who die of *delirium tremens* or by spontaneous combustion."[92] This allusion to spontaneous combustion might be confusing to twenty-first-century readers. In his seminal 1968 article "Chronic Alcoholism in the First Half of the 19th Century," William Bynum explained that in the first half of the nineteenth century both delirium tremens and spontaneous combustion were recognized as "acute manifestations of alcoholism."[93]

In the metropolitan understanding of the situation, absinthe became so interlinked with the habits of European settlers in Algeria that its spread was often used as a metaphor for the colonization of North Africa itself. The French geographer Ernest Fallot, who was based in Tunis, described in 1887 how settler villages were first established following the initial military conquest between the 1830s and 1847 in Algeria. According to Fallot, these first settlements appeared in the trail of the French army. As these initial settlements became more established, "a few years later, if business is satisfactory, they build a stone house," by which Fallot meant a canteen, which sold food, drinks, and life necessities. This was done "in order to be more at ease and to return to civilized life. The combination of several of these cantiniers' houses gives birth to a village, and this is what has made [people] jokingly say that absinthe colonized Algeria."[94] A similar description of the initial establishment of these canteens can be found in an 1868 book entitled *Memories of Algeria, 1854–1855*, written by an anonymous doctor. His assessment was more pessimistic than that of Fallot, as he regretted the substantial presence of these cantiniers, who sold absinthe to both settlers and soldiers in Algeria and viewed it as a portent of failure. According to this doctor, "their presence does not reflect that civilization will be born in this country, but rather that it [civilization] comes here to die."[95]

People suggested that the spread of France's influence – both via settlers in its colonial empire and via emigrants in other countries – could reasonably be measured by the appearance of absinthe. In his 1901 book, the French doctor Émile Galtier-Boissière complained that, when it came to "absinthe, the most dangerous of all distilled drinks," France had "few imitators and the following sad observation has been made: 'The number of litres of absinthe drunk in foreign countries is proportional to the number of French people who live there.'"[96] The presence of crates of absinthe was thus believed to be an indication of the spread of French people and, in colonial contexts, of French civilization.[97]

Absinthe was the drink that French settlers – in Algeria and elsewhere – turned to, because they were convinced of the medical benefits of its consumption. The same medical reasons that had made such an impression on French soldiers, that had "converted the military to absinthe," Marie-Claude Delahaye pointed out, also worked on French settlers. According to Delahaye, this also led to the establishment of absinthe distilleries on Algerian soil,[98] yet Antoine-Léonard-Charles-Raphael Casanova specified in his 1885 medical thesis that "very little absinthe is fabricated in Algeria" and that most of the absinthe consumed in Algeria was imported from France.[99] A Mr Foix, director of a school in Algiers, further explained in 1899 that absinthe was no longer produced in Algiers, adding that "the long factory chimneys remain clear of smoke" and that the essential oils and the bottles of alcohol are left "in the mysterious corners of the estaminets."[100] While some absinthe seems to have been produced in Algeria in the nineteenth century, as both these quotes and Delahaye's decades-long research indicate, the majority of the absinthe consumed by settlers was imported from France.

Just like the soldiers, the French settlers in Algeria believed absinthe to be a form of self-medication, offering them protection from fevers, assisting in creating an appetite, and, most importantly, making water more palatable.[101] Those who recommended absinthe to French settlers often directly referred to the experiences of the soldiers. An author only given as J.-B. M. lauded absinthe to the readers of the *Gazette médicale de l'Algérie* in October 1889: "Without wanting in the least bit to be the defender of a habit, which has its dangers … I will note that absinthe has a veritable utility in hot countries, where the water is of suspect quality, disagreeable to drink, and even dangerous when it has not been boiled. How many times have not, in the distant expeditions of war, the advantages of absinthe been appreciated, which allows you, by its particular aroma, to use even brackish water without too much

disgut!"[102] In M.'s eyes, absinthe thus had a clear history of success that those
not living in "hot countries" might not be able to appreciate.

Another similarity between the absinthe consumption of French troops
and French settlers was that, just as within the army, absinthe was a social
drink amongst the civilian settlers in Algeria. Sharing a glass of absinthe gave
them the chance to meet, relax, and exchange news. "Absinthe, in Algeria, is
a meal, and they [i.e., French settlers] easily invite someone to take absinthe
with them like they invite [people] to lunch or dinner," explained François
Charvériat, who himself lived in Algiers, in 1889.[103] Unlike in France, however,
there was less of a dedicated time for absinthe. Drinking outside of the accepted periods was considered somewhat of a faux pas amongst the bourgeoisie in metropolitan France. One settler, A. Villacrose, in his 1875 book
Twenty Years in Algeria, described his fellow settlers as "for the vast majority,
people who only visit each other and talk to each other with a glass in hand."
Villacrose added that the settlers around him did "not understand that one
can sell wheat, hay, cows, or sheep, without toasting each other and closing
the deal over a glass of absinthe or champoreau."[104] Champoreau was another
very popular drink in Algeria and consisted of alcohol – often absinthe or an
anisette, but also sometimes wine – mixed with sugar, hot coffee, and, in some
cases, milk.[105] Villacrose thus painted a picture where absinthe – and champoreau – was consumed during certain social and financial interactions, independent of the time of day.

Civilian Algeria – as much as military Algeria in the years after 1830 – became a centre for absinthe consumption. Indeed, just as it was claimed that
France consumed more absinthe than the rest of the world put together, the
same statement was also applied to Algeria. Jean-Gabriel Cappot – under the
pseudonym of Capo de Feuillide – might have been the first to make this
claim in an 1854 article, in which he stated that, amongst settlers in Algeria,
"absinthe was the most commonly offered, just as its use was the most universally widespread. On its own, Algeria has consumed more of it than all the
other parts of the world combined."[106] Algeria thus seemed "to hold the record of alcoholization," as doctors H. Triboulet and Félix Mathieu regretfully
stated in 1900.[107] In this assessment Triboulet and Mathieu relied on information collected by the French doctor Pierre Rouby, who had claimed in 1895
that a quarter of all settlers in Algeria were alcoholics.[108] While these claims
were certainly exaggerated, the consumption of individual settlers was described as shockingly high. "Many of our patients say that they have only been
drinking [absinthe] since their arrival in Algeria," explained the French doctor

Lucien Raynaud, while discussing cases of excessive alcohol consumption amongst French settlers in Algeria in an 1896 article, "for 10, 15, 20 years, they have taken 2 to 4 absinthes a day, not counting the glasses of cognac in the morning, the 2 litres of wine with meals, not counting the extras." A specific case study of Raynaud's concerned a mason who had been living in Algeria for sixteen years and who had since then "been drinking 4 to 5 absinthes a day; on Sundays he takes 14, 15 or 20 [glasses of absinthe]; often he drinks it neat. On getting up, he swallows 1 to 4 small glasses of eau-de-vie or pure anisette. At each meal half a litre of wine."[109] As discussed above, absinthism came to be framed as a diagnosis that could be found in France, but that was a particular problem amongst both French soldiers and European settlers in Algeria. For the French doctor François Eugène Baufumé in his 1871 monograph, both the civilian and military absinthe consumption in Algeria was proof of a failure of character, as they – steeped in French civilization – should have known better: "In Algeria, our settlers and our soldiers, which a more advanced civilization and bitter experience should preserve, find, in the abuse of strong liquors and especially in absinthe, a no less terrible cause of destruction than the action of an inhospitable climate."[110] This failure of character, in turn, was believed to put France's colonial mission at risk.

While the absinthe consumption of French soldiers was sometimes viewed as a regrettable mistake – ordered from above or based on incorrect information provided to them by army doctors – that of French settlers was often framed as a weakness of character, for which they were bitterly condemned. Commenting on the immoderate absinthe consumption of the French settlers in Algeria became a staple of both French and non-French travel literature.[111] In metropolitan France it was believed that this predilection of French settlers for absinthe had negative effects on their bodies as well as on France's colonial project, that the drink had turned into a stumbling block for the French colonization of Algeria.[112] Continuing down this path of blaming absinthe for the failures of French colonialism, Pierre Rouby explained, in his 1895 paper "Alcoholism in France and in Algeria," that this development was especially dangerous in Algeria, where absinthe-drinking French settlers were surrounded by Muslims, whom he believed to be strictly abstinent. While "the Arabs" drank water, "the settlers all drink absinthe and alcohol," Rouby explained.[113] He believed that these settlers who "poison themselves with absinthe and alcohols, degrade themselves, weaken, make degenerate children, and are extinguished at the third or fourth generation" put France's colonial mission at a disadvantage. Without constant "new blood" from "neighbouring countries" and those few settlers who drank moderately, "Algeria could come back without battles to its former masters, the victors disappearing faster by alcoholism than if they were killed with gunshots."[114] The argument was that France needed physically and mentally capable French citizens in order to successfully colonize. People under the influence of absinthe could not fulfil this role. "Algeria needs arms to colonize," Lucien Raynaud explained to the readers of the temperance newspaper *L'Alcool* in 1896,[115] and the arms of alcoholics were not reliable tools. This belief in absinthe hindering France's colonial mission was also adopted by non-French writers. In 1860, for example, the British lawyer and historian George Wingrove Cooke discussed the process of the French conquest of Algeria, which he deemed to be somewhat unsuccessful, as it had not conquered enough arable land. According to Cooke, France's presence in Algeria only manifested itself in "splendid roads and bridges," "smart towns," and France's "*fainéant*, absinthe-drinking, and billiard-playing urban populations."[116]

Settlers were criticized for their conviction about the essential usefulness of absinthe and depicted, by those in metropolitan France in general, and by medical experts in particular, as somewhat irrational.[117] In turn, these settlers defended their absinthe habit by repeating their contention that absinthe was the healthiest drink for the Algerian climate. In 1895, an article about "the Algerian settler" was published in the newspaper *Le Petit Bouira*, written by a settler, whose name was given as W. Nick, who stated that absinthe drinking was "the alleged great failure of the Algerian settler." Nick did not deny the fact that French settlers in Algeria drank absinthe, stating: "Yes, it is true: the settler drinks absinthe. He drinks a lot of it and several times a day, at the edge of a well, near his potato field, at home before meals and sometimes afterwards." But, according to the author, this choice of absinthe – instead of the hygienic alternatives of wine, beer, or cider – was for a reason, as "we must remember that absinthe is the drink that suits our country best. She is healthy and refreshing and, by her strong dose of alcohol, she kills the germs of the generally poor and poisoned water. We drink a lot of absinthe in Algeria, because we have realized that she is the most wholesome of drinks for the inhabitants of this country and several doctors have shared this view."[118] It is difficult not to read this passage as a repudiation of metropolitan interference!

The belief that absinthe drinking was a vice particular to French settlers in Algeria – and that this was detrimental to France's imperial interests – was perhaps best represented by a quote attributed to Charles Ferry. Ferry was a French politician and younger brother of Jules Ferry, twice president of the

Council of Ministers of France. Charles Ferry's alleged description in 1883 of the whole population of French settlers in Algeria as "profiteers" and "absinthe drinkers" had greatly outraged settlers, who saw this as proof "of how little Algerians [i.e., French settlers in Algeria] are thought of in high places."[119] The French historian Charles-Robert Ageron explained in 1979 that the French settlers in Algeria believed themselves to be, in general, misunderstood in France: "To believe them, all of the French would have presented the [European] men of Algeria as politicians of the cafés, absinthe drinkers, profiteers, or slavers."[120] While Ageron did not directly refer to Ferry's quote, his chosen vocabulary of "absinthe drinkers" and "profiteers" shows that either he or the sources he based this assessment on were influenced by Ferry's alleged claim.

In an 1890 book, inspired by the representation of Algeria at the Exposition universelle de Paris in 1889, Raoul Bergot defended the French settlers in Algeria. Bergot admitted that "those who live there, the settlers in Africa, treated by Charles Ferry, as absinthe drinkers and profiteers, have among them a certain amount of black sheep," yet he believed that it was unfair to judge all settlers by this minority: "We must therefore judge the settlers from their work; the work of Algerians [i.e., French settlers in Algeria], already so strong, will become great. Like an army, they spread across this land, [which had been] for ten centuries barbarian, uncultivated, covered in ruins, whose soil has been invaded by giant thistles and scrubs; they conquered this Africa, with the pick, with the plough. They are the pioneers of civilization and well deserving of their Fatherland; because, every field they clear, every tree they plant, is the soil of France which grows and gets richer."[121] This narrative of North African decay is a common trope in Orientalist writing,[122] and used here by Bergot to defend the white sheep amongst the settlers from Ferry's attack as well as to justify their absinthe consumption through these allusions to pioneering hardship.

That Ferry's insult hit a nerve amongst settlers is further proven by the fact that over ten years later, French settlers still referred back to it and evidently still felt the need to defend themselves. A French settler, who called himself Jean de Blida, wrote a letter on the absinthe consumption of French settlers in Algeria to a local newspaper, *La Tafna*, which was published in May 1894: "You would laugh, therefore, if I told you that the Algerians disdain or hate absinthe. They have made it, on the contrary, their drink of choice. But, from there to say that they have dedicated a cult to her [absinthe], that they use and abuse her, that they deserve, in a word, the epithet bestowed upon them by the politician Charles Ferry, is a big step, a very big step." While French settlers in Algeria loudly defended themselves against Ferry's accusation of being profiteers and absinthe drinkers, Jean de Blida's statement (and W. Nick's above) shows that not many of them would have denied that settlers did, indeed, consume large amounts of absinthe. Yet Jean de Blida also added that, in his opinion, the French in metropolitan France drank more absinthe than those in Algeria. According to him, the settlers in Algeria drank absinthe for the leisure and sociability the hour of absinthe offered them. They "go to the café less to drink than to breathe in, at the same time as the elixir of the emerald colour, the freshness of the morning, the gaiety of the street, the sight of the pretty woman who passes by. In France, the weather, less favourable, does not allow stations on terraces, they drink absinthe in the café, inside; they drink more than here."[123] Interestingly, Jean de Blida's defence of settler habits also shows the widely shared conviction that if absinthe were consumed inside, hidden from the view of passers-by, everybody would consume more. He thus clearly interpreted the public sociability of the "hour of absinthe" in Algeria as a protection mechanism against overuse.[124]

It was not only settlers in Algeria that took to drinking absinthe. Settlers from all French colonies felt that they desperately needed moments of home comfort. A doctor by the name of Georges Treille discussed in an 1899 book, *Principles of Colonial Hygiene*, the "melancholy" and "sadness" that many European settlers felt in their new colonial contexts. Amongst the reasons for these emotions, he numbered "the increasing bitterness felt by the remoteness, the detachment from all superior interest, and, conversely, the instability, the envy, all these enervating passions that only colonials [i.e., European settlers in colonies] know so well." Alcohol in general and absinthe in particular served as a distraction, and helped them forget their sadness. Even though he was of the opinion that this quasi-dependence on absinthe as an anti-melancholic was a thoroughly negative development, Treille believed that, for European settlers in colonies, "the only moment of comfort, the only hour when everything is forgotten, is the hour of absinthe."[125] Treille's statement shows the belief that everyday life in the colonies was harder than in mainland France – due to the distance from French civilization – and that certain concessions had to be made for those willing to make that sacrifice. In his 1907 book *The European in the Tropics*, the French doctor Adolphe Bonain referred to this passage in Treille's book, and added: "These are the true reasons that push a large part of the white population to frequent cafés, the danger is all the greater as they [the cafés] answer on the one hand to a physiological need; and on the other we must recognize that it is one of the most legitimate aspirations of the civilized man, the instinct of sociability, which creates the occasion."[126]

The idea of an excessive consumption by European settlers was adapted from Algeria to other French colonies. In April 1872, an article published in *The Times* discussed how popular absinthe had become in all French territories: "Absinthe then crossed the ocean, and established itself supreme in French colonies. Deleterious as the free use of absinthe may be in France, it is not to be compared with the lamentable results of its consumption in Cayenne [the capital of French Guiana], New Caledonia, and Port Said."[127] Port Said was not a French colony, but under control of the Suez Canal Company, which in turn had been founded by Ferdinand de Lesseps.[128] The article continued by stating that in Cayenne, New Caledonia, and Port Said, the settlers drank absinthe "in excessive quantities and the consequence is a frightful increase in death statistics."[129] Some authors believed that the French government should have stepped in to solve this problem. Joseph Saliège expressed in 1911 his frustration about the high rates of settler alcoholism in Algeria, which he claimed had increased in thirty-five years from 260 to 1,228 cases. According to him, "our role is all mapped out; the duty is clear": "We have to protect, like an attentive mother, the young Algero-European race that has just been born to public life," by which he meant the "race" of European settlers in Algeria. Saliège believed that it was France's duty to "prevent [these] beautiful boys," from turning "into madmen, into the sickly, the hysterical; we have to build a dam against the rising tide of street urchins and prostitutes, fruit picked from the absinthe plant."[130]

In conclusion, it can be said that it was widely agreed, in the nineteenth and early twentieth century, that French settlers enthusiastically took to drinking absinthe, largely for the same reasons that had made the drink popular amongst French soldiers, i.e., a mix of medical concerns and an "instinct for sociability," to use Bonain's formulation.[131] In metropolitan France, French settlers were framed both as living idly and as living harder lives due to their isolation and distance from French civilization and culture. Both sides of this coin were represented by their consumption of absinthe: those who viewed French settlers as lazy and as putting France's colonies at risk saw proof of their idleness in their absinthe consumption, while those who depicted French settlers as isolated and suffering hardships believed that settlers could only find relief in their shared celebration of the hour of absinthe. The intense malleability of absinthe – and of what the hour of absinthe was believed to represent – allowed for both interpretations to coexist.

3

"The Cult of the Aperitif"

This chapter is dedicated to the absinthe consumption of both the bourgeoisie and the bohème in the nineteenth century, as well as to the depiction of absinthe in advertising. The secondary literature often frames the absinthe consumption of the bourgeoisie and the bohème as two opposing extremes – with one being viewed as respectable and the other as inherently immoral. In the context of this book, the consumption of both groups is treated as the third phase in the popularity of absinthe. The first phase began with the "discovery" of absinthe in Switzerland and ended with the transplantation of absinthe to France in 1805, while the second phase included the consumption of French soldiers and settlers after 1830. This third phase – absinthe's first wave of popularity in France – was defined by three points: 1) absinthe was still new and immensely fashionable; 2) absinthe was consumed by a relatively small group of people; and 3) absinthe drinkers were looking for either joy or inspiration. While the medico-psychiatric sources analyzed in this book were typically critical towards all excessive absinthe consumption, they mostly described this phase as one defined by pleasure and sociability. By contrast, the phases following the consumption of the bourgeoisie and the bohème were dominated by the absinthe consumption of various groups of "undesirables," with the sources focusing far less on choice and enjoyment.

The Joy of Absinthe

Alcohol was omnipresent in Belle Époque France. In a newspaper article written in 1898 by Jean de Montmartre, the "hour of aperitifs" was described as a "national custom," and the author assured his readers that aperitifs were only consumed in France.[1] This claim was, of course, incorrect. Indeed, the custom of the aperitif might have been established in Italy before it spread to France in the mid-nineteenth century, as the literary scholar Gretchen Schultz argued in a 2017 article.[2] While it is beyond the scope of this book to determine the origins and spread of the custom, at the time of Jean de Montmartre's publication at end of the nineteenth century, the leisurely consumption of aperitifs was firmly established in Italy.[3]

Nevertheless, within France, the celebration of the hour of aperitifs was viewed very much as a national achievement. For Jean de Montmartre, drinking an aperitif was quintessentially French. He claimed that one glass of his aperitif of choice "is enough" for a Frenchman. "He savours it peacefully, he savours it with bliss; but very seldom does he double it. The aperitif is a rest, a recreation, a break, and not a debauchery. It is especially the bourgeois workers, who rarely drink between meals, that we see [being] faithful to the cult of the aperitif."[4] Chief amongst these aperitifs was absinthe, which became the "icon" of the Belle Époque,[5] a symbol for this moment of leisure and enjoyment.

This ritualistic daily absinthe consumption was initially celebrated, not condemned. "Moderate levels of intoxication were acceptable and even encouraged," suggested Lauren Saxton. "Many argued that this low level of impairment allowed their thoughts and wit to flow more freely, and that so long as they were drinking wine, champagne, or heavily watered down absinth, they became the best versions of themselves in these moments."[6] While the French bourgeoisie appreciated absinthe all year round, it was particularly welcome in summer due to its refreshing nature,[7] when people could comfortably sit on the terraces of the cafés, which is reminiscent of narratives about the positive effects of absinthe under the Algerian heat, propagated by French soldiers and settlers alike.

It is difficult to pinpoint exactly when France's hour of absinthe began. An article published in the *Figaro* by the French journalist and author Alfred Delvaud in August 1862 claimed that, "in the past, in 1821, absinthe was drunk only by lackeys; today everyone drinks it, artists and poets, lorettes [i.e., courtesans] and scholarship holders."[8] A similar statement can also be found in an article published in *The Times* on 4 May 1868, which seems to have been based on Delvaud's. In this article, the unnamed author stated that a "quarter of a century ago absinthe was the drink of French coachmen, grooms, and footmen, and people of the lowest class; to-day, its most ardent lovers are to be found among educated and well-to-do Parisians. Literary men, professors, artists, actors, musicians, financiers, speculators, shopkeepers, even women, yield themselves up to its seductive influence."[9] The year 1821 would have been before the French military conquest of Algeria; a quarter of a century before 1868 would have been 1843, i.e., potentially at a moment when the first regiments of soldiers returning from Algeria had already ordered their absinthe in cafés in Marseille or Paris. I have not come across other sources claiming that, before the French military conquest of Algeria and its subsequent moment of glory amongst the French bourgeoisie, absinthe had been a lower-class drink in France.

Michael Marrus suggested in 1974 that in the early 1860s absinthe was still "a fairly exotic drink in France."[10] While the height of France's absinthe craze can be safely placed between the 1870s and 1890s, Marrus's assessment seems to be contradicted by some of the source material. Charles Monselet dedicated a subchapter of his book to a detailed report on the hour of absinthe in 1865,[11] and the phrase "absinthe professors" – a humorous designation of somebody who had made a science of their absinthe consumption – was current at this time, especially amongst writers and novelists. The earliest mention of absinthe professors found in the research for this book comes from a June 1859 article by Angelo de Sorr, which was the pseudonym of the French author Ludovic Sclafer.[12] Similarly, an 1868 article in *The Times* described the hour of absinthe in Paris as an already well-established practice and not as a new development.[13]

While Delvaud's claim, Monselet's 1865 book, and the popularity of the phrase "absinthe professors" prove some familiarity with absinthe in French life in the early 1860s, it is undoubtedly true that its popularity increased from this point on. In the early 1860s, absinthe had only started on its path to "a favourite drink, a fashionable drink," as absinthe ended up being described in an article in the daily newspaper *La Dépêche* in 1895.[14] Expressions for the "hour of absinthe" became bywords for leisure during the early evening hours in the Francophone world, as can be seen in Fig. 3.1, a postcard that showed French men and women in the garden of a restaurant in Saint-Avertin, with absinthe glasses, bottles, and water carafes on the tables next to them. By 1879, absinthe had "become so fashionable amongst certain groups that it has given its name to part of the day: we say *the hour of absinthe*, as we say the hour of dinner," explained one author by the name of Jules Frey.[15] While being still relatively new when Monselet described the habit in 1865, drinking absinthe – in groups, publicly and leisurely, in cafés in the early evening – had truly become part of everyday French life by 1879. This popularity was further reinforced by advertising campaigns for different absinthe brands.

4. - SAINT-AVERTIN. - Restaurant Fouqueux. - *H. B.*

Figure 3.1
Postcard showing groups of elegant men and women in the
garden of the Restaurant Fouqueux in Saint-Avertin, with absinthe
glasses, bottles, and water carafes placed on some of the tables.

Sipping one glass of absinthe, sweetened with sugar and strongly diluted
with iced water, before a meal in the company of both friends and strangers,
became a "respectable and almost universal bourgeois habit" in France.[16] In
this phase of absinthe's popularity, it was a habit that was mostly reserved for
France's "moneyed class,"[17] for the "elite of France, including the idle rich,"[18]
as, before the phylloxera crisis, absinthe – still produced with grape alcohol
– was relatively costly.[19] Contrary to the financial strains that a glass of absinthe
represented before the 1870s, however, Alfred Delvaud was of the opinion that,
by 1862, everybody drank absinthe in Paris. He suggested that his readers
should "one summer day, around five o'clock," travel across the city, "and you
will see all of Paris, seated at the door of the cafés, drinking absinthe." Walking
around all quarters of the city, "you will see workers, students, soldiers, employees, idlers, ragpickers, people of good and bad looks, of good and bad life,
busy 'making their absinthe.'"[20]

    While usually defined as the drink of the bourgeoisie during this early wave
of popularity in France, i.e., of the elites and the middle classes, this quote by
Delvaud suggests that it was, even at this point, consumed by wider groups of

people in search of enjoyment. The French psychiatrist Henri Legrand du Saulle clarified in 1877 that absinthe should better be viewed as the drink of the lower middle classes and the *déclassés* only – i.e., those fallen from their social ranks. While he did not discuss the absinthe consumption of France's elites, his claim was based on him disagreeing with those framing absinthe as a problem of the working classes. According to him, absinthe was "sought above all by low-level employees, non-commissioned officers in sedentary corps, clerks," as well as foremen, representatives of trading houses, sex workers, and low-level artists. Legrand du Saulle further suggested that the "déclassés from most professions," "the irregulars in the stock market, the press, the theatres, and in gallantry, the malcontents with problematic existences, the misunderstood philosophers and poets, the adventurers and swindlers," all turned to absinthe. Despite this long list of professions and temperaments given to absinthe-drinking, Legrand du Saulle reassured his readers that, put together, they amounted to a "fortunately very low" number, which was due, in his opinion, to the working classes "only consum[ing] red wine."[21]

While the consumption of absinthe was, for some, a question of belonging to a certain class, others presented the joys of drinking absinthe as something that united all of France's social classes, as can be seen in Delvaud's 1862 claim above. According to Sterling Heilig, both working and upper classes, both "master and man," celebrated the hour of absinthe both before lunch and before dinner in Paris in 1894. Heilig suggested that the search for a pause in the working day, dedicated solely to enjoyment, was the motivation for all. Drinking absinthe was a much-needed moment of relaxation for all Parisians, with both absinthe and the break itself providing them with new energy. "By slow degrees they feel their poor, tired backbone strengthen and their brains grow clearer, and they feel a touch of happiness. It is so pleasant to sit looking at the street and all the pretty ladies passing by." The daily habit of drinking absinthe together brought these – male! – consumers a deep feeling of comfort, Heilig claimed: "All the world grows brighter. Memory, imagination, hope, and courage find a gentle stimulation."[22] Just as they were for the French soldiers in Algeria and settlers in France's colonies, these cafés became spaces of predominantly male sociability during the "hour of absinthe," places to relax, gossip and people watch, and also where one could gather information and conduct business.[23]

France in general, and Paris in particular, became known for the elaborate and elegant celebration of the hour of absinthe, as can be seen in articles written in newspapers published outside of France.[24] A letter printed on the front page of the newspaper *Le Rappel algérien* in September 1909 inverts the pattern of French travellers writing shocked reports about the high absinthe consumption in Algeria. The author, only given as Jean, recommended to the readers of the newspaper a journey to Paris, independent of their financial means: "You will savour there for nothing, some of the most appreciated human joys: joy of the eyes, joy of the ears, joy of the heart." One of these joys was the "hour of absinthe" and Jean told his readers to "sit down, around five o'clock in the evening, on the terrace of [the cafés] Mazarin, Madrid, or Pousset." In these cafés, "for 40 cents you will contemplate a spectacle unique in the world."[25] A "unique spectacle" – even though very similar descriptions of the "hour of absinthe" can be found in many travel reports about Algeria![26]

For Jean, it seems to have been the grandeur and glamour of the hour of absinthe in Paris that stunned him. "This spectacle of the Grands Boulevards at the hour of absinthe, I give up trying to describe it to you," Jean added.[27] Accounts such as this suggest that taking part in the Parisian hour of absinthe was high on the to-do list for tourists during the Belle Époque, precisely because it was perceived to be a glamorous – and very French – affair. Just as the French middle classes might have been inspired to drink absinthe following the example of French soldiers returned from Algeria, tourists – both from other countries and from France's provinces and colonial empire – might have wished to experience true Frenchness by tasting a glass of absinthe in the company of the masses partaking in the hour of absinthe. This did not necessarily end with the 1915 absinthe ban. An article published in the *New York Times* in 1925, focusing on the increase in alcohol consumption in France after the First World War, proposed the idea that highly alcoholic drinks – such as "absinthe in disguised form" – were often consumed in France by the non-French. According to the unnamed author, "it is a notorious fact that in Parisian cafés and bars frequented by Americans the quantity of alcohol consumed is proportionately far greater than that disposed of in cafés patronized largely by natives."[28]

Despite this perception of absinthe drinking being particularly Parisian, it was not only Paris that celebrated the hour of absinthe. V.-S. Lucienne explained in 1899 that, while absinthe had been introduced and made "fashionable in Paris and in the great cities" by the soldiers returning from Algeria, absinthe was now commonly consumed before dinner, when "in Paris, as in most great cities by the way, the cafés are invaded by absinthe drinkers."[29]

While it is not clear whether Lucienne meant that absinthe was consumed in "most great cities" within the context of France or whether he included cities in other countries too, the absinthe consumption outside of France was directly addressed by other authors. An article published in the *Journal de Genève* in June 1908 – i.e., only a month before the ban on absinthe was decided on in Switzerland – argued that absinthe's strong seductive effect on people was partly due to the time of the day it was consumed: "It is upon leaving the factory, the workshop, or the office, after the morning's or the day's work; the comrades, before returning home, stop at the café. One meets there, friendship flows to the full, the most joyful words are exchanged, the street is lively, the hour is cheerful."[30] While absinthe became a global drink during the Belle Époque, this joyful and leisurely celebration of the "hour of absinthe" was a particularly Francophone habit. This can be seen, for example, in the fact that, even though absinthe was a very popular drink in the French-speaking part of Switzerland, it never truly conquered the German-speaking cantons, as can be seen in debates preceding the national 1908 ban.[31]

This description of absinthe consumption in Geneva in the early twentieth century is very similar to those of the hour of absinthe in Paris or Algeria, focusing on the same experiences of relief and sociability at the end of the working day. Yet despite such reports of absinthe traditions outside of France – be it in Switzerland or in France's colonies – absinthe appeared deeply French to foreign observers. In an 1896 article for the monthly London-focused magazine *The Ludgate*, H.P. Hugh described the hour of absinthe in Paris as uniting both factory workers and business owners, adding that "the drink and the hour are part and parcel of the French character."[32]

The joys of absinthe did not solely come from this daily moment of leisure. People simply enjoyed its refreshing taste. Writing after the change from grape alcohol to industrial alcohol in absinthe's production, the article in the *Journal de Genève* stated that, in addition to the attractiveness of the part of the day dedicated to the drink, absinthe was both cheap and tasty: "It weighs less on the wallet than vermouth, cognac, chartreuse, white wine, or beer. Above all, it [absinthe] is much better. The smell is already attractive. It is a pleasure to inhale it, while one proceeds on the delicate operation of preparing the enchanting beverage." The unnamed author's conclusion was that "absinthe is delicious."[33] It should be added that, as with every aspect of the drink, not all found the perfume of absinthe to be attractive. In his 1897 dissertation, Robert Hazemann – strongly opposed to absinthe – complained that "in some places, on summer evenings, the consumption on the terraces of the cafés is so great that the boulevard 'stinks of absinthe.'"[34]

While there were many authors, especially amongst the doctors and psychiatrists, who were deeply critical towards all absinthe consumption, drinkers in the Belle Époque generally believed absinthe to be innocuous, when keeping to the bourgeois rules: absinthe was harmless when one consumed it only during the hour of absinthe before meals, when one limited oneself to one glass, and when one did not take it neat.[35] While breaking these rules was considered a faux pas amongst members of the bourgeoisie, the disregard of these rules was also used to vilify the absinthe consumption of women, the working classes, settlers, and the colonized. His personal experiences with the drink led Sterling Heilig in 1894 to the conclusion that the dangers of absinthe had been vastly exaggerated: "It is with great diffidence that I give my own opinion about absinthe. So many of my friends drink it, seemingly without a shade of danger, that I feel tempted to suspect, along with the great mass of Parisians, that the doctors make a bogie of it, confounding the ill effects of alcohol with those of absinthe. The fact that absinthe must regularly be drunk (even by fiends) diluted with at least three times its weight in water, and that it affords no pleasure but a stomach ache, heartburn, and headache when taken after meals makes it appear to be a safer tipple than our whiskey." He also explained that, when it came of the dire warnings about absinthism by French doctors, the "great bulk of the public here in Paris do not take much stock in them."[36]

Many of those who partook in the hour of absinthe believed that the ill effects of the drink could be kept at bay by the virtue of moderation and constraint, which, in turn, some authors framed as a very French characteristic. Moderation seems to have been understood as one of the key factors in whether absinthe drinking was deemed acceptable or not. Heilig himself based his belief about the essential harmlessness of absinthe on his experiences with French "restraint,"[37] and compared the downfall of the son of an English noble, whom he called Richard, through his uncontrolled consumption of Amer Picon – not absinthe – with the normal aperitif consumption of French men.[38] Amer Picon, a bitter with a quinine basis, is yet another French aperitif with strong links to North Africa, as its inventor, Gaéton Picon, apparently came up with the recipe in 1837 while suffering from malaria during his military service in Algeria.[39] According to Heilig, this Richard had "abused a subtle drink through inexperience. Frenchmen do not. Those who take three goblets have worked up by slow degrees from one." He further explained that this daily consumption of aperitifs by French men was condoned by their wives, as, through their "habitual self-control," they returned home to "their dinner in a state of mild expansion. Their wives find them kindly, optimistic, and make small objection."[40]

This restraint of the French when it came to the consumption of aperitifs that Heilig portrayed in his articles was, some nineteenth-century sources suggested, less characteristic of French people as a whole than specifically of the bourgeoisie, meaning that, while absinthe might have been consumed by all classes, it became particularly unsafe in the hands of the poorer classes, who might not possess this virtue of moderation. An article published in the *New York Times* in 1887 represented this clear class bias, explaining that "absinthe is used by nearly all moderate drinkers in this capital [i.e., in Paris] as an appetizer before dinner," before warning: "but its immoderate use is productive of untold evil, as the chronicles of the hospitals can vouch for, and its slaves are becoming more numerous every day, particularly among the poorer classes, who fly to it because it is cheap and soon intoxicates."[41] While the unnamed author mentioned that after the phylloxera crisis, the low price of absinthe tempted the "poorer classes" to drink too much absinthe, their overindulgence in the drink was often framed as a failure common to their class – a lack of moderation.

The French doctor Pierre Rouby explicitly discussed this alleged moderation of the upper classes in his 1895 comparison of alcoholism in France and in Algeria: "I believe I am not far from the truth in saying that a quarter of the [European] population [in Algeria] suffers from dipsomania, under the influence of absinthe, of the Algerian anisette" and "another quarter, without being yet dipsomaniac, drinks more than is reasonable." With half the population either alcoholic or drinking unreasonably, the state of the French settler colony was dire, Rouby warned: "To save the situation, there remains one half of the population that uses absinthe, alcohol, and wine moderately. It is among this half, I must say, that the people of the upper classes can be found, while the alcoholics are recruited from the lower classes of society; but there are many exceptions [to this rule] that have to be noted."[42] From Rouby's perspective, no French settlers in Algeria lived abstinently, as the half of the population that he put the hopes of the colony on still consumed "absinthe, alcohol, and wine moderately." It was, therefore, not abstinence from the joys of the hour of absinthe that was desirable – as this would have meant a voluntary exclusion from sociability – but moderation.

Yet even as absinthe was perceived as the fashionable drink of the French middle and upper classes, some people were deeply suspicious of the joys it lent to its wealthy consumers. There were even conspiracy theories connected to the upper-class consumption of absinthe. In his 1862 article, for example, Alfred Delvaud introduced his readers to the idea of so-called "absinthe clubs." According to Delvaud, this *"Club des absintheurs"* consisted "of twenty irremovable members: death alone is responsible for renewing the personnel." Delvaud added that "all have sworn solemnly," with their hand on a glass of absinthe, to "never drink anything else, never get tipsy with something else, never love anything else. And, strange thing! – strange as the honesty of thieves among themselves – it is the only oath they do not break."[43] The goals of this "absinthe club," beyond the pleasure of its members, were not discussed by Delvaud. An 1868 article in *The Times* repeated Delvaud's claims, without directly referring to him, before suggesting that these club members "assemble daily at some appointed place of rendezvous at a certain hour, and proceed to dissipate their energies and their centimes in draughts of that fatal poison which fills the public and private madhouses of Paris."[44] What the article in *The Times* described was groups of French men taking part in the daily hour of absinthe, yet in this context of an ominous conspiracy the hour of absinthe suddenly appears sinister.

Thus descriptions of absinthe consumption were intensely class-based. While refined enjoyment was the main characteristic of descriptions of middle- and upper-class consumers, discussions of the habits of the working classes, settlers, women and the colonized, focused on their overindulgence and their lack of moderation and etiquette. Despite absinthe being viewed more and more negatively throughout the Belle Époque, the bourgeois version of France's hour of absinthe – with its focus on social interactions, relaxation, and pleasures – lasted well into the twentieth century. Neither the diagnosis of absinthism nor conspiracy theories about bizarre absinthe clubs discouraged middle-class people from taking a break from life while enjoying their glass of absinthe on the terraces of their favourite cafés. In 1893, the French journalist and novelist Émile Goudeau explained that, despite medical objections to the drink, absinthe "still has its adorers: it remains the aperitif par excellence, and at five o'clock its cult starts everywhere."[45] Because it was so much more than just a simple drink, absinthe remained, through it all, the icon of the Belle Époque.

In Search of Inspiration

Soon after the fashion for absinthe had been ignited amongst France's middle classes by returning soldiers, enjoyment of the drink also came to be seen as a sign of bohemianism.[46] Although it was still an integral part of the daily schedules of the bourgeoisie, absinthe was adopted as the drink of choice of poets and painters, who inserted the green fairy into their works of art.[47] While the secondary literature strictly divides the consumption habits of the bourgeoisie from those of these decadent artists, some late nineteenth- and early twentieth-century sources viewed these artists as belonging to the wider bourgeoisie. In his 1910 dissertation on absinthe, for example, Pierre Decroos stated that a "very characteristic phenomenon occurred at the end of the last century: absinthe drinkers were no longer recruited from the same social categories. Until 1875 or 1880, absinthe was only consumed by the bourgeois." The change that Decroos described was absinthe's discovery by the working classes, once the prices fell. Before that moment, Decroos explained, "in the Parisian circles, writers and artists indulged in the 'verte' with a passion, seeking, said Dr Boissier, 'to increase their mental activity, to make their thoughts faster and more original, to experience and suggest newer and more exquisite impressions.'"[48] While I could not find the exact publication Decroos mentioned here, the Dr Boissier he referred to in this passage was presumably Émile Galtier-Boissière, who was part of France's temperance movement.[49] Decroos continued by informing his readers that "Maupassant, Musset, Edgar Poe, Verlaine were among the victims of the seductress liquor."[50]

Decroos did not further explain why he counted writers and artists as being part of the wider bourgeoisie – presumably because Guy de Maupassant and Paul Verlaine, for example, came from clearly bourgeois families. However, while they might have been born into the French middle and upper classes, these artists did not belong to the traditional bourgeoisie. Indeed, the literary scholar Katharina Niemeyer described these absinthe-drinking writers and painters in her 2009 article as "representatives of a decidedly anti-bourgeois avant-garde in art and literature."[51] The cafés frequented by these artists were different from the ones in which the bourgeoisie observed the hour of absinthe[52] – as well as from those that the working classes flowed to after work. French painters not only went there to drink, but also to work. Unemployed women "who wanted to be models, waited in front of a glass [of absinthe], hoping to be noticed," suggested Marie-Claude Delahaye, adding that they were often paid for their services with a glass of absinthe.[53]

From the 1850s onwards, one can find accounts of people belonging to bohemian Paris enjoying their absinthe.[54] Yet some "bohemians, dandies, and artists" had started to drink absinthe in the 1830s, i.e., upon the return of the first soldiers from Algeria, Marnin Young suggested.[55] In an 1866 play by the French dramatist Charles Narrey, a scene is set in Paris at the hour of absinthe: "We know that this little strip of asphalt [in front of the cafés] belongs by right of conquest to a hundred and fifty idle people," who chose to have their absinthe there. This innocent description conjures up, whether it was intended or not, images of colonization and occupation, again actively placing absinthe consumers in the role of conquerors, yet the specific idlers that Narrey had in mind were not veteran soldiers, returned from the colonial war in North Africa, nor were they members of the traditional bourgeoisie. They were "irregulars," "wanderers," who would consume their absinthe while "smoking, chatting, [and] dreaming."[56]

It was with these customers that absinthe gained a new connotation. The "hour of absinthe" came to be perceived as conducive to creativity. While the middle classes took to drinking absinthe to connect to the colonial achievements of the French army – and to have a socially acceptable break from work – bohemian absinthe drinkers were in search of inspiration. In his 1864 book on *Madness before the Courts*, Henri Legrand du Saulle explained that "men of letters and artists pay the highest tithe to absinthe," as they believed they needed it to stimulate their creativity.[57] Amongst the artists described by the secondary literature as enthusiastic consumers of absinthe were Edgar Degas, Henri de Toulouse-Lautrec, Édouard Manet, Charles Baudelaire, Paul Verlaine, Arthur Rimbaud, Pablo Picasso,[58] Paul Gauguin,[59] Oscar Wilde,[60] Alfred Jarry,[61] Edgar Allan Poe,[62] Joris-Karl Huysmans,[63] and Ernest Dowson.[64] Vincent van Gogh's relationship with absinthe especially has been dissected by the secondary literature.[65]

These artists turned to absinthe in search of inspiration, "in search of new pleasures capable of increasing their sensitivity and their power of creation," to use a formulation from the 1988 article of Marie-Claude Delahaye,[66] similar to how they also used opium and hashish during the same time period.[67] It was framed as distinct from other "new pleasures," and other substances, with the historian David Earle pointing out in his 2003 article that the relationship that artists – especially writers – were believed to have with absinthe was different from the one they had with alcohol in general, because of absinthe's "cohesive fashion" – i.e., the complicated rituals of the hour of absinthe – and "its mythic ability to transport the artist."[68] The latter – the hallucinations so often associated with the consumption of absinthe – was what attracted artists to the drink.

This inspiration was believed to come from absinthe's direct action on the brains of drinkers. The French doctor Auguste Motet – who is credited as first describing absinthism as a separate diagnosis – reported in his 1859 dissertation that absinthe had "irresistible attractions," especially to creative people. According to Motet, "from the first sips an indefinable sensation invades the whole being: it seems that a new activity is imprinted on the whole organism; a world of ideas arises, rushes, overflows: the imagination creates its enchanting chimeras, and often, under the influence of this stimulus, the most ravishing creations of literature and the arts are born." Soon, however, Motet warned, "the brain acquires the habit of no longer giving birth to anything without it [absinthe]."[69] Similar statements about this specific action of absinthe on the brains of creative people can be found in many nineteenth- and early twentieth-century sources.[70]

This idea of absinthe's direct influence on the brains of drinkers lasted throughout all of absinthe's reign, as can be seen in the seminal 1912 book *Alcohol* by the engineer and temperance advocate Louis Jacquet. Having asked himself how absinthe managed to spread "so quickly and in such notable proportions," Jacquet explained this by absinthe's "particular attraction, a powerful seduction, which is not found to the same degree in other alcohols." Referring to Étienne Lancereaux's research – who was one of the earliest critics of absinthe and advocated for its complete prohibition[71] – Jacquet added that absinthe "has, it has been said, the property of *soaking the brain*," similar to "morphine, opium, and certain brain poisons."[72] Once they had started to drink absinthe in search of inspiration, these artists were believed to have fallen for its particular – and deleterious – pull. In this, a distinct form of agency was attributed to the drink. Ernest Monin stated in 1889 that absinthe had "claimed" people like the writers Alfred de Musset (1810–1857) and Gérard de Nerval (1808–1855) as well as the journalist Alexandre Privat d'Anglemont (1815–1859). Monin further added that "almost everyone (it must be said) who becomes absinthic [i.e., suffering from absinthism], in Paris, belongs commonly to the vast tribe of the déclassés. But absinthe chooses, preferably, *fairly intellectual* victims (if one may say so), to make them more easily descend, drop after drop, to the lowest social levels."[73] Amongst these *déclassé* victims of absinthe, some, it was suggested, had enjoyed a certain amount of academic success, as can be seen in an 1889 article by a doctor Daviller, who explained that he had seen absinthe drinkers on an evening in Paris, "almost all of them failures or strays, generally from very good families and most of them with diplomas and university titles."[74] Monin further explained that this idea of absinthe choosing "*fairly intellectual* victims" was not limited to bohemian – and potentially Daviller's failed academic – circles of Paris, as in Algeria it was mainly officers and "men of letters," who "profess the liveliest taste for this drink."[75]

All the artists mentioned above were well-known absinthe drinkers, but Alfred de Musset came to be particularly identified through his love for absinthe. The French journalist Maxime Rude described Musset in 1877 as having spent half his life in Parisian cafés, "smoking packets of cigarettes there every day, drowning their drying ardor in absinthe, which spoiled the man and the poet at the same time."[76] After his early death in 1857, Musset was believed to have died from his absinthe overconsumption,[77] his heart failure being attributed to either alcoholism in general or absinthism in particular. He was not the only artist believed to have died from his love for the drink, as many of the artists who were famous for having searched for inspiration in a glass of absinthe died prematurely.[78] In his 1906 article, however, Sterling Heilig contradicted this narrative of artists dying of absinthe. "There are French geniuses who turned to the green drink for inspiration and ruin. Some found inspiration. Some found inspiration and ruin. Some found ruin only. Of the middle category Alfred de Musset and George Sand have been the archetypes in bourgeois traditions, but his [Musset's] old housekeeper, Adele Colot, who still lives, affirms that Alfred stuck to champagne, like a gentleman." Heilig also did not believe that George Sand had died of her absinthe consumption, as he had himself heard, the summer before, "from the now aged son of her faithful farmer and factotum that the Lady of Nohant 'died of cigarettes.'"[79] While there are uncertainties about Sand's death, she seems to have died from intestinal issues.[80]

Based on this personal knowledge available to him concerning both the deaths of Musset and Sand – which he seems to have accepted unquestioningly – Heilig was critical of absinthe's deadly reputation and wary of potential claims of other people having died from it. Nevertheless, Heilig still believed that the overconsumption of absinthe was harmful. These "decadent poets," he claimed, had gone "in powerfully for this opalescent inspiration. Young men twelve or fifteen years ago, where are they now? The artist Ricardo Flores has drawn one of them in these late days. It is his 'Portrait of a Friend at Charenton Asylum.'"[81] This idea of absinthe being the purveyor of hospices, asylums, and cemeteries – chief amongst them the psychiatric hospital in Charenton – was often mentioned in nineteenth-century sources.[82]

Throughout the Belle Époque, the narrative started to establish itself that France had lost a whole generation of creative and intellectually gifted minds, who had turned to absinthe to spur their creativity and who had then been unable to withstand its malicious pull. In his 1898 article on the "National Aperitif" for the daily political newspaper Le Radical, Jean de Montmartre explained that "from time immemorial, there has been a distressing picture of the disorders and miseries of the bohemian absinthe drinker. Tragic examples have been cited; the victims of the green goddess have been shown [to be] as lamentable as the yellow opium-smokers of the Far East."[83] The tone of accounts about the bohème immoderately consuming absinthe was often one of tragedy, of talented people – in their endless search for inspiration – willingly risking an early death. The French doctor Émile Galtier-Boissière lamented in 1901 that there were "scholars, officers, who were presaged the most brilliant future, whose intelligence has thus disappeared, smothered by absinthe or eau-de-vie."[84] The fear of this loss of national brain mass, so to speak, was also voiced both in Switzerland[85] and in France's colonial contexts. An article published in La Presse in 1921 with the telling title "How Alcohol Can Kill a People" regretfully stated: "Alas! We experienced in France the scourge of absinthe and, especially in the colonies and in North Africa, we know how many brilliant minds have sunk to the bottom of glasses filled with this poison."[86]

The status of absinthe as the drink of choice of France's bohème further increased the general popularity of the drink. With artists turning to absinthe, the "hour of absinthe" became even more of an occasion to people watch. An article by the French journalist and author Lucien Victor-Meunier in the daily newspaper Le Rappel, published in December 1897, framed the "green" hour as a "truly Parisian hour when the pavements, from the Opera to the Faubourg Montmartre, are crowded with well-known faces."[87] It is also possible that the publicly staged consumption of artists and poets inspired a new group of consumers – admirers of these artists or of their unconventional lifestyle – to turn to absinthe.[88]

In summary, it can be said that accounts of artists consuming absinthe depicted the green fairy as a unique drink, different from other spirits due to its alleged hallucinogenic properties. This can be observed in both accounts of its positive action as a muse and reports about the high fatality rates amongst its consumers. It should also be added that, while the absinthe consumption of the bohème was often depicted differently from that of the traditional bourgeoisie, it was regularly compared to that of *"fairly intellectual* victims," to repeat Monin's formulation.[89] Absinthe was believed to act directly on the brains of consumers, which, while condemned by the medico-psychiatric professions, was not always perceived negatively by consumers. The motivation behind the absinthe consumption of artists was thus the same as that of creative people of all kinds,[90] of "men of letters,"[91] and of men with "diplomas and university titles,"[92] i.e., of people, who belonged to the bourgeoisie. It was the green fairy's reputation as a uniquely powerful hallucinogenic that moved artists, and, presumably, these *"fairly intellectual* victims" to turn to absinthe in their search for inspiration.

Advertising, Patriotism, Sex, and Hygiene

In her 2008 article, the historian Sarah Howard explained that, due to innovations in lithography and photography, "Belle Époque Paris was saturated with images, particularly advertising posters,"[93] and that the Belle Époque had "shaped, and been shaped by, the distilled alcohol industry, particularly the production and advertising of aperitifs."[94] The enormous popularity of absinthe from the 1870s onward was thus partly due to these new forms of advertisements, as the height of its fame coincided with the "golden age" of alcohol advertising in France, which Didier Nourrisson defined as the period between the 1880s and 1940s.[95]

Absinthe distilleries soon discovered that they could use these new forms of advertising to their advantage. Barnaby Conrad noted that, upon the return of the absinthe-drinking French soldiers from Algeria, "the custom quickly pervaded French society, aided by the Pernod brother's business acumen and advertising."[96] As the consumption of absinthe grew, so did the competition. Howard explained that, in this competitive market, it was not unusual for some alcohol producers to spend "one quarter or even one third of its outgoings on publicity."[97] These adverts often depicted the absinthe consumption of the bourgeoisie in a positive way, i.e., as elegant, glamorous, and healthy.[98] However, this was also the period when temperance campaigns first started to use posters arguing against the consumption of alcohol.[99] Strolling through French and also colonial cities, one might be confronted with posters for absinthe and against it.

Absinthe adverts usually took the form of posters. In a 2004 article, the French historian Myriam Tsikounas suggested that there was a curious absence of absinthe adverts in the French press: "while its prohibition only occurred in March 1915, absinthe, very present in posters, was non-existent in the press. Did the absinthe manufacturers bet everything on posters or did the newspapers refuse to welcome a poorly regarded drink?"[100] While posters were undoubtedly absinthe's preferred advertising medium, Paul-Maurice Legrain, doctor of the Ville-Evrard asylum and one of France's main temperance advocates,[101] contradicted Tsikounas's perception of the situation in a 1906 article. According to Legrain, there were occasionally articles in newspapers "which pass as Puritan," praising the medical properties of certain wines: "This fact in itself is vulgar," he stated. He was repulsed by the hypocrisy of this double standard, adding: "We are accustomed to seeing on the front page a diatribe against absinthe, and on the fourth [page] the most honest ad for such-and-such Absinthe."[102] This attack on the hypocrisy of newspapers in Legrain's article seems to be based on Robert Hazemann's 1897 thesis, who had himself been an intern at the Ville-Evrard asylum. In his thesis, Hazemann suggested that "the newspapers complacently report, with all details, how such-and-such, seized by madness brought on by repeated libations of absinthe, killed his comrade, his wife, etc. Some journalists even dare to raise their voices against absinthe in this regard; and on the fourth page of the same newspapers, we see spread out in large letters; absinthe X is beneficial. Only take absinthe Z it is recommended by your doctor. Absinthe Y oxygenated is necessary for [your] health, other newspapers respond in chorus."[103]

While Legrain and Hazemann intended to point out the hypocrisy of newspapers that both advocated for temperance and profited from the money absinthe distilleries spent on advertising, their statements clearly show that some absinthe adverts could be found in newspapers. Similarly, in the context of the North African colonies, many examples of very simple absinthe adverts – most often in the form of little plaques containing only a name and, occasionally, a slogan, and an address – can be found in colonial newspapers. The newspaper *L'Afrique du Nord illustrée*, for example, displayed adverts for Absinthe Bresson,[104] Absinthe d'Élite,[105] and La Gorgette[106] in 1912, as well as for Absinthe Déchanet in 1913.[107]

Various débits de boissons also mentioned absinthe in their own signs, and used posters provided to them by absinthe manufacturers. "Do not the retailers themselves strive to invent enticing signs, to vary their appearance according to the districts, to flatter the political preferences of some, the artistic or literary [preference] of others?" asked Charles Mayet in his 1894 article, about the role played by absinthe sellers in the representation of the drink.[108] Owners of drinking establishments – aware of their clientele's preference for absinthe in general or a specific brand of absinthe – might choose to advertise its availability in their débit.

Despite this, the main force of advertising was in the hands of the manufacturers, who tried to highlight the "individual identities" of their brands, according to Howard. Adverts linked them to "the exoticism, health, seduction, and regional traditions that consumers craved."[109] Amongst these different topics, Patricia Prestwich identified three main focuses of absinthe advertisements: patriotism – "bottles were bedecked with tricolours and entitled *Patriot* or *Equality*" – as well as sex and hygiene.[110] Indeed, while soldiers and settlers in the French colonies were belittled in metropolitan France for their belief in absinthe's medicinal properties, throughout the Belle Époque many absinthe brands chose to depict their products in advertisements as having "hygienic benefits."[111]

When it came to brands using sex to sell absinthe, Prestwich referred to the aforementioned article by Charles Mayet, which he had written in February 1894 for *Le Temps*. In it, Mayet described a specific advert in detail, stating that there was an "absinthe manufacturer who, in a large chromolithograph given free to retailers, represents a demi-mondaine in a ball gown, gloved up to her shoulders, holding a glass of absinthe in one hand and [who], smiling, shows it [the glass] with her other hand to passers-by, saying: 'Absinthe is my sweet sin.'"[112] There were, in fact several adverts for the brand Absinthe Terminus in the 1890s – for one example, see Fig. 3.2 – which depicted elegant women with this specific slogan.[113] But it was not only the sexual attraction of female customers that was used in adverts. As absinthe itself was traditionally identified as a woman – it was the green fairy after all – many brands used sexualized representations of absinthe in their advertising campaigns in order to attract male customers. Absinthe brands chose to present their product as beautiful – often only partially clothed – seductresses, which was in line with other adverts of the time. Marcin Skibicki suggested in a 2019 article on women in French adverts that alcohol posters in general were "extremely feminized" during the Belle Époque.[114] This identification of absinthe with women was not only apparent in advertisements, but also in written sources. This sexualization of absinthe is, for example, obvious in a 1908 article in the

Figure 3.2
Lithograph showing an elegant French woman with a glass of absinthe in her hand, with the slogan "Absinthe Terminus – it is my sweet sin!"

Journal de Genève on the consumption of absinthe in Switzerland. According to the unnamed journalist, green fairy "is the nickname that popular experience has given to her. Almighty, but wicked fairy. Irresistible mermaid. High priestess of alcoholism. Purveyor of hospices and cemeteries."[115]

As Prestwich suggested, absinthe brands also liked to wear their patriotism on their sleeves, but while there was deep, patriotic sentiment in many absinthe adverts, other adverts played with exoticism. Amongst these are the famous Orientalized adverts for Blanqui, which Delahaye described as bringing customers "the pleasures of the Orient,"[116] coinciding with a general fashion for Orientalism during the Belle Époque.[117] These adverts tried to tempt customers by uniting sex with exoticism. Other absinthe brands chose to depict other "exotic" contexts, such as those produced for Absinthe chinoise in the 1860s (Fig. 3.3).[118]

There were, however, also absinthe adverts that eschewed patriotism, sex, or hygiene, but instead focused on absinthe's transformative power. One particular advert depicted the whole world as unified by its shared consumption of Absinthe Rivoire. This advert, seen in Fig. 3.4, was called "Future Monument of Peace" and was published in 1905. In it, the artist Marcellin Auzolle (1862–1942) chose to depict a statue, bearing the word "Pax." The statue, which is roughly fountain-shaped, has a bottle of absinthe and a winged woman at the top holding up a branch. The winged woman is reminiscent of Nike, the Greek goddess of victory, who often carries a laurel wreath. The branch here, however, seems to consist of common wormwood, absinthe's most famous and most feared ingredient. Below the bottle, Auzolle's monument consists of three different levels, with groups of men happily drinking absinthe together. The figures on all three levels are caricatures of specific political figures of the nineteenth century, but some of the non-European men have been depicted using clearly racist stereotypes. These men were at some point the political leaders of the nations they represent in the advert – nations that had been in conflict with each other at some point in the nineteenth century. Absinthe Rivoire thus chose to sell its product by representing a global network of former enemies, transformed by absinthe, and now peacefully drinking together.

At the topmost level, one can recognize Edward VII, king of Great Britain and Northern Ireland, pouring a glass of absinthe for Paul Kruger, state president of South Africa. Edward VII puts his left arm companionably around Kruger's shoulders, as a Black man – presumably Cetshwayo kaMpande, king of the Zulu Kingdom – drinks a glass of absinthe to their left. Auzolle possibly

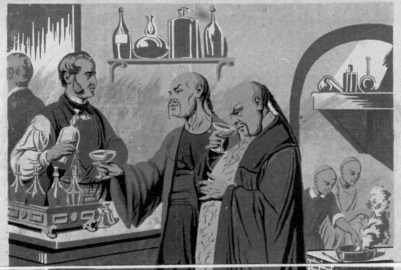

Figure 3.3
Advert for Absinthe Chinoise depicting two Chinese men in
ornate and stereotypically "Oriental" clothes standing at the
counter of a *débit de boisson*, drinking glasses of absinthe.

Figure 3.4
Advert for Absinthe Rivoire with the title "The Future
Monument of Peace," by the artist Marcellin Auzolle,
depicting a fountain-shaped statue with groups of men
of different nations drinking absinthe together.

portrayed Dost Mohammad Khan, emir of Afghanistan, as looking on from the right. While Dost Mohammad Khan was Muslim, he is nonetheless shown with a glass of absinthe in his hand. The conflict, to whose end Edward VII and Paul Kruger were presumably drinking, was the Second Boer War, which lasted from 1899 to 1902. Not all the conflicts depicted in the advert were that recent, however, as the Anglo-Zulu War took place in 1879, while the conflict between Edward VII and Dost Mohammad Khan might have been the First Anglo-Afghan War, which lasted from 1838 to 1842.

On the second level, below these first figures, viewers can recognize the German emperor Wilhelm II at the very left, talking to Émile Loubet, who was the French president in 1905. Wilhelm II and Loubet are toasting each other, with Wilhelm II's hand cordially on Loubet's shoulder. For French consumers – surely the main audience of Auzolle's advert for Absinthe Rivoire – the 1870–71 Franco-Prussian War must have still felt recent. In the middle of this second level is Franz Joseph I, emperor of Austria, leaning on Victor-Emmanuel III, king of Italy, who pours three glasses of absinthe. The conflict between Austria and Italy alluded to in the advert might be the Third Italian War of Independence of 1866. To their right is Menelik II, emperor of Ethiopia, holding a pipe, with his right hand on Victor-Emmanuel III's shoulder. Their two nations had been at war in the First Italo-Ethiopian War of 1895. To the right of this group, finally, is Tsar Nicholas II of Russia, with his left arm around an unidentified man in uniform, potentially Emperor Meiji of Japan, in which case they are toasting the end of the Russo-Japanese War of 1904–05, barely finished at the time of completion of this advert!

On the lowest level of the statue, on the very left, are five people grouped around the figure of Uncle Sam. To his left are two unidentified Native Americans, one of whom might be Sitting Bull, while to Uncle Sam's right are an unidentified young Black boy and Black man, as well as an unidentified monarch in a crown and an ermine coat. Uncle Sam holds a bottle of absinthe in his hand and seems to offer a glass to the adult Black man. Auzolle depicted the Black boy as drinking absinthe. All of these figures seem to represent various conflicts between the US government and groups both within the United States and outside – in the form of the unidentified monarch – of the nineteenth century. To their right, Auzolle depicts another group of six men, standing around a little table. These have been identified by Marie-Claude Delahaye in 2002 as George I of Greece (on the very left) and Peter I of Serbia (next to him), leaning on Abdul Hamid II, sultan of the Ottoman empire. Delahaye further suggested that Ferdinand I of Bulgaria is also depicted in the image,[119] but I could not identify him. On the right side of the table Emir Abd-el-Kader, France's main opponent in Algeria, is shown, pouring a glass of absinthe, even though by 1905 he had been dead for twenty-two years. On the right of Abd-el-Kader are two more unidentified men. While the group on the left shows various US conflicts, this group seems to focus on conflicts of the Ottoman Empire, such as the Greco-Turkish War of 1897, the Serbian–Ottoman Wars of the mid-1870s, and, potentially, the end of Algeria's history as part of the Ottoman empire in 1830. It should be noted that this group includes at least two Muslim men – Abdul Hamid II and Abd-el-Kader – happily toasting peace with a glass of Absinthe Rivoire.

The moral of this advert is clear – all former conflicts were forgotten when people drank Absinthe Rivoire. In line with the arguments of this book, many of the conflicts depicted as solved through absinthe by Auzolle were colonial wars. While this poster paints an idyllic picture of life under absinthe's rule, so to speak, not all commentators viewed the presence of advertisements positively at the time. In 1906, Paul-Maurice Legrain viewed the presence of advertisements in Paris at the turn of the century as a means of seducing gullible people. According to Legrain, people in Paris were living through "the golden age of advertising," during which "simpletons and credulous" people were tempted by the "streams of multicoloured lights" used in adverts.[120] Given Legrain's focus on fighting all forms of alcohol, it is clear that he believed customers who might otherwise abstain were being seduced by adverts for alcohol, absinthe in particular.

Both absinthe opponents and advertisers agreed on one point: absinthe was a drink apart from all the others. It had properties that differentiated it from other drinks and it had a unique impact on its consumers. While opponents feared that the absinthe drinking of consumers could "metamorphose them into beasts,"[121] advertisers promised their (male) customers that the consumption of absinthe would show their patriotism, help their health, and make them more successful in their interactions with women. While the majority of doctors and psychiatrists, whose publications form the basis of this book, depicted absinthe negatively, this chapter introduced more positive representations of the drink that were prevalent in the nineteenth and early twentieth century. Absinthe took the form of a respectable habit amongst the bourgeois, of a muse amongst artists and members of the intelligentsia, and of a patriotic, healthy, seductive, and even pacifying drink in advertising. While these different interpretations reinforce this idea of a deep malleability of what absinthe could be interpreted as, it is important to point out that all of these more positive representations of the green fairy included notions of sociability, of an experience shared with others, of leisure and enjoyment. While still present in some accounts, these concepts are less likely to be found in descriptions of the absinthe consumption of women, the working classes, and the colonized.

4

The Green Fairy's Seduction of Women

Up to this point, I have focused almost exclusively on the absinthe consumption of men. This exclusion of women is based on the medical and psychiatric source material dedicating very little space to the absinthe consumption of women. Women were depicted both as non-consumers of alcohol in general and absinthe in particular, and as partly to blame for its popularity during the Belle Époque, which, as discussed in the introduction, Michael Marrus defined as a moment of a "great collective binge" in France.[1] Based on an analysis of reports collected at the Préfecture in Besançon, John Borja explained in his 2021 thesis, "Absinthe, Alcoholism, and the Asylum in France, 1870–1918," that "although few in number compared to men as far as rates of alcoholism go in the early twentieth century, women nonetheless received much of the blame for passing on and exacerbating the social problem of alcoholism in France."[2] Women were thus blamed both for their own absinthe consumption and for not preventing others – particularly their husbands and children – from drinking.

In the course of my research, I have not come across sources by nineteenth- or early twentieth-century women that openly discussed how they took part in France's "hour of absinthe." Consequently, the male-centric medico-psychiatric discourse cannot be counterweighed in this chapter. Instead, explanations for the absinthe consumption of women offered in these sources will be considered as a sign of the prejudice that women faced during the Belle Époque rather than faithful representations of the drinking habits of individual women. This chapter will first discuss the three ways that women were understood as coming into contact with absinthe – as victims, paragons, or guilty women – before looking more specifically at fears about sinking birth rates and the degeneration of France, and, finally, the question of absinthe in the context of the emerging New Woman.

Victims, Paragons, and Guilty Women

In his 2015 chapter on alcoholism and temperance movements in France in the nineteenth and twentieth century, Thierry Fillaut suggested that it is productive to divide reports on French women and alcohol into three groups: reports about the victim, reports about the guilty woman (who drank or who enticed others to drink), and those about the exemplary woman, who abstained from alcohol and whom I will call paragons in the context of this chapter.[3] Indeed, women in nineteenth-century sources were most commonly depicted as victims of the absinthe-drinking men in their lives, be it financially,[4] physically,[5] or through the early deaths of their husbands, fathers, and sons.[6] While the tone of reports focusing on women as victims was overall one of pity, Fillaut suggested that the French temperance movements framed these victims as partially responsible for their own fates, as they had not been able to keep the men in their lives from drinking.[7]

Reports about "guilty women," i.e., those who liked the taste of absinthe, were, before the 1880s, mostly defined by expressions of surprise and shock.[8] Up to this point in France's history, French women had been understood as drinking little in general, or even, as Patricia Prestwich put it, as being "inherently abstemious."[9] Due to this abstemiousness, the large majority of alcoholics interned in French psychiatric institutions in the nineteenth century were men.[10] Examples of sources that framed alcoholism as a male issue can be found throughout the nineteenth and early twentieth century. The famous French pacifist Théodore Ruyssen, for example, discussed in a 1913 article the high consumption of alcohol in France, regretting that "France occupies the first rank of the alcoholized nations." Yet he also believed "that there are, even in France, abstinent people, that children hardly drink, that women, the elderly, and the sick, the insane, the soldiers and the sailors drink little."[11] Similarly, a 1907 pamphlet, composed by absinthe opponents in Switzerland, claimed that, as women – and children – did not consume absinthe, it was an exclusively male problem.[12] This assumption that women were one of the main groups that drank little in France – and Switzerland[13] – was widespread. Consequently, the appearance of alcoholism amongst French women was "a new and shocking phenomenon for contemporaries at the end of the nineteenth century."[14] When it came to this "new" consumption of alcohol by women, not all drinks were viewed equally. Prestwich explained that, even though "prejudices against drunkenness in women were deeply entrenched in French culture," this did not generally apply to a moderate consumption of wine.[15] The turning to absinthe by French women – in public spaces, no less – was thus perceived as a momentous change.

While some "ladies of high families are reported to have yielded to its [i.e., absinthe's] fascination," according to the *Indiana State Sentinel*,[16] and while "many ladies of distinction have fallen victims to its use,"[17] to use a formulation from *Scientific American*, both published in 1861, it was believed that this "new" phenomenon of female alcoholism affected mostly women from the working classes. Doctor Paul Garnier portrayed this connection between working-class women and alcoholism as almost self-evident in his 1890 book *Insanity in Paris*: "In a huge urban agglomeration like Paris, within the working classes which form, it should be noted, the ordinary clientele of the service of the special Infirmary [of which Garnier was the chief doctor], the woman tends more and more to imitate the man in his way of life." Garnier believed that women copied men's excessive behaviours and spent less time at home, having to leave the house "for occupations born of new conditions or social necessities," which made them more vulnerable. Now having similar opportunities as men, this symbolic working-class woman, Garnier warned, "comes to commit the same abuses" of alcohol.[18] In contrast to Garnier's claim that it was, above all, working-class women who turned to alcohol, some twentieth- and twenty-first-century researchers, such as Marie-Claude Delahaye, have suggested that women of all classes began to take part in the hour of absinthe.[19]

In their absinthe consumption, women were ascribed very little agency: it was generally agreed that they were seduced by the drinks consumed in their proximity, so to speak. It was commonly suggested in the nineteenth century that the growing absinthe consumption of men somehow infected women. In an 1897 article, a Doctor L. – probably the aforementioned Paul-Maurice Legrain – worried about the "growing cult of absinthe in our country." According to him, there was a clear hierarchical progress to absinthe drinking: "From the bourgeois, the contagion spread to the worker, from man to woman, from woman to child. No woman blushes now to sit at a table outside of cabarets in front of a glass of absinthe."[20] This idea of contagion – specifically of absinthe spreading from a man to a woman – can already be found

Figure 4.1

Drawing showing a newlywed couple on their wedding day, with the husband preparing a glass of absinthe for his bride under the watchful eyes of the other guests.

in Henri Balesta's 1860 monograph on absinthe.[21] In Doctor L.'s interpretation, absinthe drinking spread through those higher on the hierarchy setting a bad example, and those lower on it imitating their behaviour, potentially gaining in peril the further it progressed downwards.

Yet despite a general outrage over women's discovery of absinthe, some nineteenth-century accounts mentioning women's consumption painted a picture of general enjoyment. Émile Goudeau's 1893 book on eating and drinking habits in Paris included a drawing of a newlywed couple by the artist Pierre Vidal (Fig. 4.1), in which the husband prepares a glass of absinthe for his wife. Goudeau described this new tradition of the "aperitif of the bride" as "characteristic" behaviour. In the middle of the day, "one has laughed too much, played too much, joked too much. One feels the fatigue of the morning ceremonies. Good! Then the aperitif intervenes like a whiplash of pleasure, which will restore to the muscles and nerves of the guests the vigour required for the rest of the party, for the end of the wedding. This is probably the new bride's first absinthe with sugar. What a ceremony! What a baptism!" Goudeau further explained that the wife's bridal absinthe was prepared with "infinite precautions" by the new husband.[22] As described by Goudeau, this "first absinthe with sugar" of the bride was a joyful moment for both the couple and their guests. Connecting this happy moment to theories about the spread of absinthe amongst women, this was not an account of a woman copying the behaviour of a man, nor going to a café or a débit before her meals, to drink, enjoy herself and be sociable, but an exceptional moment in her life – and thus more acceptable.

An example of joyous, every day female absinthe consumption can be found in an article in the temperance newspaper *L'Alcool* published in September 1897, in which the French journalist Gustave Geffroy described his experiences of the hour of absinthe. This is one of these quasi-anthropological approaches to the topic mentioned in the introduction. According to Geffroy, the streets had been full of people who had just finished their work. Some were tired, but the majority "had an aspect of strength and joy." He observed "supple and strong men" in these crowds of people, but also "women with courageous faces, these girls with slender waists, these garlands of children, everything expressed the joy of living, of owning the street, the trees, the pink sky, the heat and clarity of summer."[23] It is implied that these women, on the way to their glass of absinthe, had just left work, together with the men in their company.[24]

According to Geffroy, these people – men, women, and children – congregated in different cafés to sit down for their absinthe, which they were apparently handed by the waiters without even having to order. Despite being against absinthe, Geffroy admitted: "The spectacle, despite everything, kept its sweetness, its charm, its blooming life. These were not the gloomy types, the rows of fools I often observed, standing before the counter, or seated on high chairs, staring at the bewitching liquor, mechanically stirring the spoon in the murky opal [liquid]." Certain groups of working-class men were usually described as taking their absinthe at the counter, which makes it apparent that Geffroy's comment was criticism aimed at them. The workers he observed on that specific day, however, "kept a vivacity, a conversation, a laugh." He further noted that "they were not isolated, [nor] absinthe maniacs; they were undoubtedly beginning their apprenticeship of the poison; they found there the charming flavour, the delicious bait." While Geffroy suggested a chronological progress of absinthe drinking, with the groups representing the beginning, and the "fools" drinking alone a stage towards the end, another important difference between these two categories of absinthe drinkers – the gloomy, solitary drinkers standing at the counters and the joyful groups seated around tables – was the presence of women, in Geffroy's eyes. These women actively, eagerly, participated in this "hour of absinthe," as Geffroy described two of them as "delicately, pouring the water drop by drop, melting a piece of sugar above the glass." As the preparation of absinthe needed practice and knowledge, this seems not to have been the first time they had taken part in the hour of absinthe. According to Geffroy, women were, overall, "numerous, and all drank their little absinthe, like the men. Some had slight hesitations, simpering as [they would] around a forbidden fruit. They pushed their lips forward, tasted [their absinthe] as gourmand cats, and their beautiful eyes shone lovingly."[25] This bizarre sexualization of female absinthe consumers in Geffroy's account is in line with the depiction of both the green fairy and women in absinthe adverts.

Sterling Heilig similarly depended on his intimate knowledge of the boulevards for his 1894 article about the consumption of absinthe in Paris, which led him to the conclusion that not only had women started to drink absinthe, but they had a particular propensity towards it: "the truth is that they [women] take to absinthe as ducks take to the water." While Heilig based his assessment on his own observations, he also relied on reports of "trustworthy observers," whose authority seems to have consisted of simply being male participants in the hour of absinthe. "Women seem to have a special taste for all these medicated drinks. There are trustworthy observers who declare that anyone who takes a look through the cafés at the special hour of 5 p.m., no matter in what quarter of the capital, will find that women have accustomed themselves, almost universally, to drinking absinthe."[26] The reference to absinthe as a "medicated drink" – and thus more attractive to women – was based on absinthe brands portraying their products in adverts as hygienic and healthy, as well as on tales about the mythical origins of absinthe as initially having been nothing but the elixir of Dr Ordinaire.

Pinpointing the exact moment when French women started to drink absinthe proves to be difficult. While some working-class women had been drinking in cafés from the late eighteenth century, as discussed by Scott Haine in *The World of the Paris Café*,[27] the same was not true for bourgeois women. Marrus explained that it was only in the 1880s that "public drinking was beginning to involve women with some claim to gentility" and that "the world of the cabaret had hitherto been an almost exclusively male sanctuary."[28] By the time of Heilig's 1894 report, women from the bourgeoisie seem to have fully broken into these sanctuaries, as he explained to his US audience: "It must be borne in mind that here in France the wife or mistress goes with her husband always as an equal to the café and the restaurant." Details of Heilig's description of these women place them in the bourgeoisie: "I think that the American will be surprised to find how many decent, sober women, self-respectful, *gentille*, well dressed and nice mannered, frequent the cafés and the saloons and drink absinthe, Amer Picon, and vermouth without offence and to the great advantage of good order and a proper atmosphere."[29] Heilig's description of the consumption of these bourgeois women mirrored – in its focus on order and conviviality – that of bourgeois men.

Working-class women, on the other hand, were described as mostly absent from many of these débits de boissons during the Belle Époque. Jacqueline Lalouette explained that, in contrast to both luxury establishments and the lowest, rowdiest ones, the clientele of these working-class establishments was "essentially masculine." A woman "incurred too much reprobation if she entered the cabaret and in principle, she did not even risk it on pay nights to 'retrieve' her husband."[30] Indeed, women who went to cafés on their own risked being mistaken for sex workers.[31] Lalouette acknowledged, however, that some larger establishments proved to be an exception to this general disapproval aimed at female working-class customers: "large cafés with popular clientele but copying bourgeois appearances where the worker, having learned to dress up, goes on Sundays with his family."[32]

Beyond these discussions of the gendered spaces of these débits de boissons, it should be noted that both before and after the 1880s, some women consumed absinthe at private gatherings, both in their own houses and, in the case of the upper classes, in salons. Doctor L. – as mentioned, probably doctor Paul-Maurice Legrain, who regularly wrote for the monthly temperance journal *L'Alcool* – discussed a switch from tea to absinthe in his 1897 article. According to him, "one of my colleagues, practising in Besançon, tells me about a singular habit. In the salons, at the so tasteful hour of five o'clock, it is no longer tea that is served, it is absinthe," which was, he added, consumed by "our beautiful ladies" as well as by their husbands.[33] This substitution of tea for absinthe could also be found amongst other classes, apparently, as V.-S. Lucienne regretted in an 1899 quote that "it is no longer only the rich who poison themselves with absinthe, but the whole working population that makes use of this beverage. Even women drink it openly, and, in some family reunions, it is no longer tea that is served, but the 'green poison.'"[34]

While nineteenth-century authors often presented a narrative of women being tempted to drink absinthe by the men in their lives, another factor had a strong influence especially on middle- and upper-class women turning to absinthe: absinthe adverts aimed specifically at them. Katharina Niemeyer specified that "targeted advertising" tempted women consumers from the bourgeoisie during the Belle Époque, who were now "addressed separately as a target group in advertising posters and advertising postcards."[35] These targeted adverts were discussed by Marie-Claude Delahaye in a booklet published in 2007, in which she collected images from both advertising and art that depicted female absinthe consumption under the title *Absinthe au féminin*. Adverts depicted absinthe as a thoroughly modern drink, consumed by fashionable bourgeoises. These adverts of absinthe-drinking women, Delahaye suggested, portrayed both the drinkers and the drink as chic, healthy, and modern.[36]

Humorous postcards of the time, gently or not so gently mocking the modern woman, also took up the question of clothes and regularly depicted absinthe-drinking women in trousers, as shown in Fig. 4.2. The height of absinthe's popularity was a time in which certain women claimed more rights, which, as Delahaye clarified, caused a backlash. As a consequence of this, these women were often depicted by French caricaturists as "women dressed in eccentric fashion, smoking and drinking absinthe."[37] Humorous postcards followed this, as can be seen in Fig. 4.3 and Fig. 4.4. Absinthe drinking was thus understood, both by some women themselves and by some of their critics, as an expression of the so-called New Woman, who started to demand more freedoms. In this context one should remember, as Thierry Fillaut suggested, that it was often during moments of change in the status of women that "denunciations of the rise in alcoholism and alcoholism among women increase."[38] Criticism of the New Woman also intersected with fears about France's declining birth rates in the late nineteenth century, as discussed by Daniel Pick.[39] As alcoholism in general, and absinthe in particular, were understood as contributory reasons for France's depopulation, the consumption of absinthe by the New Woman must have seemed particularly objectionable to people preoccupied with theories of degeneration.

This new woman of the Belle Époque was understood and depicted as "flouting convention in her love life, profession, dress sense or sporting ambitions," Felicia Gordon explained in 2006.[40] For this she was attacked, with criticisms often focusing on her alleged absinthe consumption, which, it was

Figure 4.2
Drawing depicting a woman in trousers, sitting on a table,
smoking, and pouring herself a glass of absinthe.

Les Femmes de l'Avenir

20. - Député

Figure 4.3
One of a series of postcards depicting the "Women of the
Future." It shows a photograph of a woman politician with
a glass of absinthe in front of her.

Figure 4.4
One of a series of postcards depicting "The Emancipated Woman." It shows
a photograph of a woman preparing a glass of absinthe for herself.

feared, led her to neglect her duties as mother and wife.[41] A similar development could also be observed in the late nineteenth century in the United
States, according to the historian Weldon Clark Terril, who suggested in his
2022 article that absinthe-drinking women in the United States were attacked
for, allegedly, turning away from motherhood.[42]

Women were not only absinthe consumers. Many of the débits selling absinthe and other forms of alcohol in rural France were in the names of men
but run by their wives.[43] Other establishments were run by single women or
widows in the 1880s,[44] which in turn encouraged more women to attend these
establishments.[45] Additionally, débits often employed female serving staff, as
this was believed to attract a larger male clientele,[46] in France as well as in the
colonies.[47] Between 1873 and 1880, the employment of waitresses had been
forbidden in France. A law instituted on 23 January 1873 – a backlash against
both the Paris Commune and the loss against Prussia in 1870–71[48] – prohibited public drunkenness,[49] women waitresses, music, and other things associated with café culture, and instituted a strict surveillance of working-class
cafés.[50] The prohibition of waitresses was rescinded in 1880, together with a
wave of relaxation of regulations, which the temperance movement viewed
as disastrous.[51] In his 2015 article, Andrew Ross pointed out that drinking establishments that employed waitresses were called "brasseries à femmes" –
women's brasseries – showing that their presence was an attraction in itself.[52]
Even if these women did not consume absinthe themselves, they fell into Fillaut's category of "guilty women," as it included those who encouraged others
to drink.[53]

It was not only the presence of waitresses which attracted a male clientele.
Nineteenth- and early twentieth-century sources regularly mentioned women
as a form of entertainment for the men sitting in cafés, as they were either
drinking their own absinthe at neighbouring tables, or even just walking – or
bicycling! – past, as shown in a sketch by Leon Rosé, published in the weekly
journal La Vie en culotte rouge in 1911.[54] Descriptions of the beauty of women
as an integral part of the male enjoyment of the hour of absinthe can be found
for both France[55] and the colonies.[56] In this context, it should also be mentioned that absinthe was, according to the secondary literature, believed by
some to be an aphrodisiac.[57] This was, however, contested at the time, with
the French hygienist Ernest Monin stating in his 1889 study of alcoholism that,
on the contrary, one symptom of high absinthe consumption was that "the
genital power, the sexual desires weaken and then disappear early on."[58] Absinthe's power as an aphrodisiac has since been definitively disproved.[59]

The women understood to be most at risk of becoming absinthic were those working with the green fairy – a direct contamination from contact with the drink, so to speak. This pertained mostly to those employed by absinthe distilleries, but it is possible that women working in spaces that sold absinthe were also believed to be at risk. "I will cite from memory a [female] owner of a hospitable house in the upper town [of Algiers]," wrote the French doctor Lucien Raynaud in 1896, "who was not happy if she had not finished her half-litre of absinthe each day."[60] Mostly, however, these fears concerned women working in various absinthe distilleries, which can be observed in Fig 4.5 for Pernod Fils. In their 1912 book *Merchants of Madness*, the brothers Léon and Maurice Bonneff mentioned that, in Pontarlier, "many of the women who work at the [absinthe] distilleries are absinthics. In the small factories, the staff are given absinthe at will. It is a salary in kind. [Similarly,] bakers are entitled to a loaf of bread. In large establishments the management does not allow the expensive drink to be gulped down [by their workers]. Some male and female workers do [drink] without the employer's authorization. The poison tastes good and its smell encourages consumption."[61] Fears of women's addiction to absinthe might have led to a curtailment of this free source of

Figure 4.5
Postcard showing a bottling site of Maison Pernod Fils in Pontarlier, with predominantly female workers.

absinthe, as, according to Delahaye, women employed by Pernod Fils in Pontarlier were given a daily glass of wine, whereas male workers were given a glass of absinthe.[62]

Fillaut's final category of women was that of the paragons, who abstained from alcohol and could potentially make others reconsider their alcohol consumption.[63] Bourgeois women were active in the French temperance movement, whose goal in the nineteenth century was, above all others, the prohibition of absinthe. The historian Victoria Afansyeva suggested that within the Association contre l'abus du tabac – which also joined the fight against alcoholism in the late 1860s – the members were made up of 74 women and 546 men in 1872, while the Société française de tempérance, founded in 1871, counted only 5 women in 1872 amongst about 400 members.[64] The Union française antialcoolique, which was founded in 1894, had a stronger participation of women,[65] as they made up 22 per cent of its membership in 1896.[66] Existing upper-class women's movements also adopted the topic of alcoholism as one of their causes.[67]

In 1895, the Union des femmes pour la tempérance was founded, under the leadership of a Maria Legrain. Afansyeva added that, while being active in the fight against alcoholism in France in her own right, she was most often viewed as simply the wife of Paul-Maurice Legrain.[68] The women engaged in these different temperance movements – just like their male counterparts – actively tried to reach women, not only to curb the alcohol consumption of women, but also because it was believed that women's influence could moderate drinking in men. The temperance brochures and posters were heavily gendered, limiting the role of a woman to being a good mother and wife, with the added dimension of preventing her husband from consuming too much alcohol, "thus protecting her children as much as herself from this scourge which is decimating families and the entire Nation."[69]

As demonstrated, it was not only the absinthe drinking of women but, more generally, their alcohol consumption that was understood as a frightening new development in the Belle Époque. In the sources, women were judged according to their means of contact with absinthe, and Fillaut's categorization of how French women interacted with alcohol in general – as victims, paragons, and guilty women – also applies to their relation to absinthe. Additionally, women of all three categories were assessed by whether they conformed to contemporary notions of femininity or not: Victims were blamed because they had not prevented their husbands from drinking; paragons, on the other hand, were those who attempted to temper the absinthe consumption of both other women and their husbands, thus protecting both women and their children. Guilty women, i.e., those who either drank or sold absinthe, were often described as fashionable and enticing, but also as failing their primary duty, i.e., the birthing and raising of healthy and strong French children.

The Degeneration of France

While female absinthe drinkers were depicted in advertisements as attractive, glamorous, and seductive, the consumption by women of alcohol, and absinthe in particular, was, in general, viewed deeply negatively, and was often linked to questions of both degeneration and class. "What the doctors fear the most is from the women drinking," Sterling Heilig put it simply in his 1894 article on absinthe. Doctors singled out the absinthe consumption of women as having consequences not only on their personal health – and the lives of their families – but also on the very future of the nation. "Alcoholism in general (and absinthism in particular) creates a special race, both from the point of view of the intellectual faculties and physical characteristics. This race, say the doctors, may very well continue for a limited time, with all its physical infirmities and vicious tendencies, for several generations. But, exposed to every sort of accident and malady, the race soon disappears. The family dies out."[70]

To nineteenth- and early twentieth-century readers steeped in these fears of racial degeneration – who equated women's consumption of absinthe, consciously or subconsciously, with reduced birthrates, unhealthy children, and the disappearance of their race – the rising numbers of female absinthe drinkers must have seemed a frightening prospect. Yet despite such dire warnings, psychiatric institutions were not suddenly overrun by women once they had started to drink. Émile Galtier-Boissière's 1901 statement about such institutions starting to admit "a number of women who have lost their minds through absinthe," is somewhat of an exception.[71] Further, once institutionalized, these absinthic – or, more generally speaking, alcoholic – women were not viewed to be as much of a problem as alcoholic men, as their numbers were smaller and as they were not believed to be particularly violent.[72] This second point is in stark contrast with men under the influence of absinthe.

There were, however, also voices who believed women in general to be more likely than men to fall for absinthe, as seen in Heilig's quote about women taking to absinthe "as ducks take to the water."[73] Amongst women, some were believed to be particularly liable to succumb to absinthe, depending on their morality, their age, what class of society they belonged to, and their profession. In 1900, the US newspaper *New York Sun* published an article on the topic of "Society Women's Drinking" in New York, for which the unnamed journalist had conducted a series of interviews. One of these was with a "successful [female] physician," who was not herself part of high society but whose patients were. According to the journalist, this unnamed doctor suggested that women destroyed their "nervous balance by excessive use of stimulants." For this reason, she recommended abstinence from all stimulants, as "the final result of their use is always disastrous. A man may be a steady moderate drinker for a life time, and be little the worse for it; but the same thing isn't true of a woman. She may never get drunk but she pays, in one way or another, for fooling with her nerves." The same understanding of a clear biological difference in male and female alcoholized bodies can also be found in a second interview by this unnamed journalist with a man belonging to New York's high society. This man apparently told the journalist that young women should not drink in "mixed company" and that they should skip all "mixed drinks": "Cocktails are deadly for any one; and a woman is too highly strung, nervously, to take the chances on tampering with nerves that a man will take. As for absinthe – that's a drink that's rapidly growing in favor over here; and it's a funny thing that the women seem to take to it more kindly than the men. Go to a certain tea room in one of our big hotels at 5 o'clock any afternoon and you'll see more absinthe drunk than you'll see drunk in all the saloons of the city in the same amount of time." To this, the unnamed man supposedly added: "The women ought to stop that. It's beastly bad stuff, even when one has the steadiest nerves."[74] Women were thus not only understood by some to have a particular taste for absinthe; additionally, it was believed that their bodies had stronger reactions to the substance. This made absinthe doubly dangerous for women.

Absinthe was not only depicted as dangerous for a woman's body, but also for her morals. Many of the French women drinking absinthe in cafés in the afternoons and early evenings were perceived and portrayed either as sex workers or as morally questionable.[75] Jad Adams explained that "women of uncertain virtue" would frequent cafés "in the hope of finding a bourgeois man to treat them,"[76] while sex work was understood as being part and parcel of the hour of absinthe. In his study of sexuality in Paris, *Love in Paris*, which was first published in 1894 and which already amounted to twenty-four editions four years later, Jules Davray described the hour of absinthe as the time when "girls" were on the hunt for free absinthe. Their clothes had, according to Davray, "a distinctive sign, a stigma which denounces the type of occupation to which the woman surrenders," and they could be seen "flocking from the heights of Montmartre, descending through the streets of the Martyrs, Notre-Dame-de-Lorette," "scattering on the boulevards … in search of dinner."[77] The historian Scott Haine described the behaviour of women who walked along the boulevards, "lur[ing] men into cafés for a couple of drinks and perhaps an evening together," as one of the two strategies of "café prostitution," and defined such women as the "femmes des boulevards." The other strategy was, according to Haine, that of the "filles de joie," who were looking for clients while already seated in the cafés.[78] Based on such assumptions, the mere fact that a woman strolled through the boulevards at the hour of absinthe or publicly drank a glass of absinthe could be interpreted as an invitation. The boundaries between a woman relaxing with a glass of absinthe in a café and a sex worker looking for work seem to have been strangely uncertain for nineteenth-century men. In a 2008 review on the secondary literature on absinthe, Haine pointed out that the selected images in Marie-Claude Delahaye's 2007 booklet on absinthe and women revealed "the difficulty the contemporary observer had in correctly distinguishing between the working woman, the prostitute and the bourgeoise."[79] For nineteenth- and early twentieth-century men, the mere fact that a woman drank absinthe, publicly, blurred the lines between respectability and sex work, which might explain some of the more outraged descriptions of what appears to be an innocent moment of women participating in France's hour of absinthe.

Women also turned to absinthe in France's colonial empire: "the abuse of drink is one of the great evils in Algeria, not only among men, but, unpleasant thing to say, among [settler] women, who are not free from all accusations of intemperance" is how Alphonse Marcailhou d'Aymeric addressed the alcohol consumption of European women in Algeria in his 1873 *Hygienic Manual of the Algerian Settler*. While Marcailhou d'Aymeric spoke generally about alcohol in this passage, the very next passage directly referred to absinthe.[80] As in France, absinthe drinking was believed to be a particular problem of working-class and marginalized European women in the colonies. In his 1889 book *Alcoholism*, the French doctor Ernest Monin referred to information gathered by a Dr Gautier in Algeria, who had explained that female absinthe drinkers, "who deny, by the way, with aplomb, all alcoholic antecedents … generally belong to the class of prostitutes and street girls."[81] Taking into account the difficulty that men seemed to have had in distinguishing "between the working woman, the prostitute and the bourgeoise" in France, to use Haine's formulation,[82] and that the mere consumption of absinthe might have been interpreted as a marker of sex work, such generalized statements should be taken with a grain of salt.

Marginalized women from amongst the colonized were also described as drinking large amounts of absinthe. According to Ernest Feydeau in an 1862 description of an evening of festivities in Algeria, which had been accompanied by female dancers, "one cannot get an idea of the quantity of liquor that a Moorish woman swallows without getting drunk. The glasses of rum and absinthe disappear down her throat with extraordinary ease, much to the great amazement of the Europeans, who do not have a strong head [for liquors]."[83] In addition to highlighting the often impossibly large amounts of absinthe allegedly consumed by North African women, accounts of the absinthe consumption of such marginalized Muslim women were often heavily Orientalized. This can be seen in an 1887 account by the French doctor Marius Bernard, who put absinthe-drinking women into a typically Orientalist tableau: "And when the muezzin sings at midnight, one will end the evening in the native cafés, where the Arabs are crammed together in a heavy and fragrant atmosphere, where golden women dance; in houses, whose courtyards have roofs of vine branches and where, covered in silk and gold, tattooed moukhères [i.e., a settler version of the Spanish "mujeres," women, prevalent in Algeria] drink absinthe and play the tambourine."[84] Both Feydeau and Bernard's accounts are clearly not reports of a traditional hour of absinthe, as celebrated publicly by settlers in all cities in Algeria. The absinthe consumption in these reports followed, apparently, none of the bourgeois rules of the hour of absinthe. In addition to the absinthe consumption occurring at the wrong time of day – into the night instead of before a meal – and to these women drinking several glasses, there are also no allusions to the established tools of absinthe. While it is not stated, this pointed lack of allusion to iced water, carafes, and sugar hints at these women – scandalously – drinking their absinthes neat.

As in France during the hour of absinthe, French observers often – deliberately or not – mistook these dancers, singers, and musicians for sex workers. It is therefore unsurprising that absinthe was also described as a drink connected to both European and local sex workers, not only in Algeria but throughout the Maghreb.[85] An early mention of this can be found in an 1853 book, *Prostitution in the City of Algiers since the Conquest*, by a French doctor with the name of E.-A. Duchesne. Duchesne explained that, immediately after the military conquest of the Algerian coast in 1830, "*lupanars* have been organized as in France" in the city of Algiers, with lupanar being the Latin name for a brothel. These brothels employed both European and North African sex workers: "Native prostitutes have learned and practised the refinements of debauchery from foreign prostitutes, with whom they have been in contact, either in brothels or clinics, or they had to submit to all the depraved tastes brought to them by our young soldiers, we must even say, by our young officers." Duchesne further added that these sex workers were, in their line of work in these French brothels, introduced to "wine, rum, and absinthe," which "did the rest" in their moral decline.[86]

While French women of all ages were described as falling for the lure of absinthe, absinthe was described as particularly detrimental amongst young women. In his 1897 article for the journal *L'Alcool*, Gustave Geffroy described "a barely adolescent girl" consuming absinthe, whom Geffroy intensely – inappropriately – sexualized. After providing a detailed description of her body, he added that, "like the others [i.e., the adults around her], she took an absinthe, and the blues in her eyes were reflected in the little green swamp [of the absinthe]."[87] The majority of sources depicted the absinthe consumption of young women as particularly dangerous. In his 1894 article, Heilig referred to Étienne Lancereaux's research, who had discussed the disorders of the "great nervous functions, the motor power, and the mental faculties," caused by repeated absinthe use, and who had suggested that it was possible to observe such "accidents" amongst "young women from 18 to 20 years of age."[88] The same passage of Lancereaux was also referred to by the French doctor Socrate Lalou in his 1903 study of wormwood. Lalou introduced the topic by quoting Lancereaux as having stated that "women have a particular taste for this drink [i.e., absinthe]; and, if she is rarely intoxicated with wine and alcohol, it must be recognized that in Paris, at least, she is frequently affected by aperitifs, and without fear of being taxed with exaggeration, adds this author, I would say that this kind of intoxication has for some years been as common in her as in the man. Mr Lancereaux affirms 'that it was possible for him to observe very clear accidents of chronic absinthism, after eight, ten months, a year, in young women or even young girls, from 18 to 20 years old.'"[89] While this passage did not depict absinthe drinking as being exceptionally high amongst young women, Lancereaux framed their consumption as particularly harmful. This highlighting of the dangers of absinthe amongst young women seems to be linked to contemporary fears of degeneration, as absinthic young women were not believed to be able to fulfil their duty of birthing healthy French children.

Finally, one of the biggest factors in how the absinthe consumption of women was judged seems to have been the class of the drinkers. In an 1899 article on the "fight against alcoholism," the biologist and physician Albert Dastre wrote the following about the alcohol consumption of female workers in France: "The women did not stay behind. The [female] workers in the mills take coffee and cognac in the morning, at random débits: at eleven o'clock, [they take] more coffee and cognac," accompanied by a little food, but Dastre informed his readers that these women "spend half as much money on solid food as on their drink." Yet it was not only women working outside the home who were viewed as susceptible to alcoholism. Women from all kinds of modest backgrounds were believed, by Dastre, to have turned to drink. "Women who do not work outside [the home, also] drink more than men. They do not go to a caterer, grocer, charcoal merchant, fruit seller, without having a little glass. The wives of sailors and day labourers have similar habits. Some carry flasks of brandy in their pockets, and they have recourse to it on every occasion. [Female] farmers are the same. The evil [of female alcohol consumption] is universal."[90] The absinthe consumption of working-class women was often explained, just like their general alcohol consumption, as stemming from them having to work like men.[91] While Heilig and others described a respectable absinthe consumption by middle- and upper-class women, on the terraces of the same cafés and in the same private salons as the men of the French bourgeoisie drank theirs, many nineteenth-century authors condemned the consumption of working-class and marginalized women.

Even though it was believed that the profession, morality, and class of women could have an influence on whether any of them fell under the thrall of the green fairy, the consumption of women of all classes and ages was viewed as fraught with risk because of their direct influence on the behaviour of children. Indeed, women and children often appear to fall into the same category in these reports about absinthe drinking from the Belle Époque. "From top to bottom of the social scale, the habit has become, as they say, second nature," stated a Doctor Ch. Ribouleau in 1901, "and, it seems, [that] neither the poor nor the rich can properly eat, without having moistened their digestive tube with absinthe. In Paris, in some neighbourhoods, women and children inhale the 'bleue' with a truly stupefying bravado."[92] Implicit in such a statement is the assumption that these women were, directly or indirectly, responsible for the absinthe consumption of children, by either encouraging it or failing to prevent it. Indeed, absinthe-drinking women were often blamed for having caused the absinthe consumption of their own children. An example can be found in Robert Hazemann's 1897 dissertation, in which he lamented that "the adult man has not retained the monopoly of this drink;

the women openly drink absinthe in the café, among the poor classes, with, around them, [their] little children who also taste it, if they have been good."[93] Similarly, Pierre Decroos exclaimed in 1910: "In certain milieus, women themselves begin to drink absinthe! How to qualify, finally, the strange aberration which sometimes pushes these senseless [women] to give a sample to their children 'to make them strong'?"[94]

The strong moral judgement behind these statements implies both that this was a regular occurrence and that something was very unwomanly in these women. Absinthe, it was feared, had made them forget their motherly duties. The well-known French author Maxime du Camp suggested in his 1885 book *Private Charity in Paris* – in the context of children being given to an orphanage despite still having families – that "absinthe drowned the paternal feeling and poisoned motherhood."[95] While du Camp mentioned the nefarious influence of absinthe on both fathers and mothers, these claims that absinthe made parents neglect their children were usually applied to women, and, amongst them, mostly to working-class women.[96]

Absinthe was also believed to cause more criminality and violence amongst working-class women.[97] In 1906, Camille Granier, a former judge, suggested that France was living through a clear increase in drunkenness amongst women. This, for him, was an "unfortunate indication, not for general morality, but for feminine tendencies." Granier believed that, "equal in crime, [women] would draw antisocial energy and impulse from alcohol more often than men."[98] While this belief was, as mentioned above, not mirrored in the admissions to psychiatric institutions, where alcoholism remained a mainly male disorder, nineteenth-century authors sometimes gave anecdotal evidence of how negatively absinthe affected especially working-class and marginalized women. Charles Mayet, for example, described in 1894 a scene in a café, in one of those quasi-anthropological reports, which showed, in his eyes, various stages of moral decay: "It is ten o'clock in the morning; already near us a laundress is drunk; she quibbles with the waiter about the quantity of absinthe that, for the third time, he has just served her. She wanted more. It is with great difficulty that she succeeds in enclosing her gray hair in a woolen scarf with holes in it. From time to time, she wipes her mouth with her damp canvas apron." This woman, like the female North African dancers, singers, and musicians described by Feydeau and Bernard,[99] broke several of the rules of absinthe drinking established by the French bourgeoisie, as she drank several glasses outside of the hour of absinthe. But this laundress was not the only woman drinking absinthe at this time of the day that Mayet observed:

"Next to her, in the company of a poor [male] wretch, sits a young woman of twenty; both also drink an absinthe at fifteen centimes; further on, other groups are swallowing small glasses worth five centimes. Brandies, absinthe, these are the poles around which gravitate the population of these hells which, with their gilding, their decorations … take on the air of paradise."[100]

While the women in Mayet's report were deemed to be questionable because of their open breaking of the rules of respectable bourgeois absinthe consumption, other women were described as disturbing the public order when under the influence of absinthe. A scene of mayhem, caused by absinthe drinking, was described by Henri Lierre in 1867, who wrote about the "adverse consequences, which its disorderly absorption brings with it." These consequences, he regretted, were "all too familiar": "It is sufficient, in order to note them, to roam, on a Sunday evening, the ancient boulevards on the outskirts of Paris, where, in certain populous neighbourhoods, you will find half-suffocated drunkards, lying on the ground; others half naked and covered in blood after a fight; and even women with hoarse voices, with dishevelled hair, with tattered clothes, prey to the madness of the Bacchantes!"[101] While they are not described as aggressive, Lierre nonetheless saw these women as part of the problem.

Fears about both the moral and racial degeneration of France led the discussion of the absinthe consumption of women. Female absinthe drinkers were reported to shun the rules of absinthe drinking established by men of the French bourgeoisie; were perceived and described as unruly, dishevelled, and morally questionable; and were, in the case of working-class mothers, feared to introduce their children to absinthe at an early age and so corrupt them. Once grown up, these corrupted, unhealthy children could not maintain the glory of France, so to speak, whether on the mainland or in the colonies.

Absinthe and the New Woman

One of the dangers of women's absinthe consumption, Sterling Heilig argued in 1894, was women drinking absinthe undiluted by water: "The great thing, what the specialists affirm and what the liquor sellers half admit, is that women very, very often take their absinthe neat, in little glasses, without water." This habit broke another of the rules of respectable absinthe drinking, the keeping of which, it might be argued, was believed to protect the majority of regular consumers from developing absinthism. Heilig set out to explain why women did not follow this rule: "They are women, after all, and, being so, have not been blessed with too much reasoning power. There may be, therefore, a simple reason why they drink their absinthe pure, a reason which the specialists have been too busy writing books to come across. The simple reason why women drink absinthe pure is that they are in corset. They come in their corsets, looking nice; and naturally they cannot take a large amount of water in, because they have to eat their dinner afterward. They want the absinthe taste and its effect. They also want their corsets. When a woman wants two things[,] she does not give up either. She takes both and makes them work tougher some way."[102]

It is questionable whether the belief in women in corsets not being able to consume food or drink was based on historical truth. What is clear is that the corset was demonized by some. In his 1979 article "Society, Physicians, and the Corset," Gerhart Schwarz explained that certain eighteenth-century physicians "blamed indiscriminately nearly every female disease on the corset."[103] How harmful a corset was when it came to eating and drinking seems to have been primarily a question of the amount consumed, and how tightly the corset was laced. The US historian Valerie Steele suggested in her 2005 book *The Corset: A Cultural History* that corsets led to a variety of both supposed and real medical issues, before adding that twenty-first-century "corset enthusiasts" informed her that it was "uncomfortable to eat too much at a time."[104]

In the course of my research, I have not come across another nineteenth- or early twentieth-century source that connected corsets to absinthe drinking, yet this notion can be found in some of the secondary literature on absinthe. Referring to Doris Lanier's 1995 book – who, however, quoted Heilig's passage above and did not confirm his dubious corset theory herself[105] – Bauer stated that "their tight corsets forced many women to drink absinthe neat."[106] It should also be considered that Heilig's 1894 linkage of the corset and absinthe took place in the midst of a wider debate. While Heilig presented women as vain and silly for drinking absinthe undiluted while corseted, feminists argued for the abandonment of the corset on medical grounds, as suggested by Ruth Iskin in a 2007 chapter on the depiction of French women in Belle Époque advertisements.[107]

Independent of the truth of Heilig's claim, the belief in French women often drinking absinthe without added water can be found in other publications. Indeed, for some this tendency was what defined the consumption of women.[108] Others believed that, while women did add some water to their absinthe, it was less than the men did. Gustave Geffroy remarked in 1897 that during the hour of absinthe, he had found himself in a café where absinthe was not served in "the usual big and tall glasses, but in small, stemmed glasses, Bordeaux glasses. Taken like this, absinthe seemed to lose its importance: we did not drink, we sample [it], in these little glasses, which were really children's glasses." These "children's glasses," he suggested, were particularly attractive to women, "who would perhaps recoil at first before the immense cup to be emptied." However, women drinking from small glasses aimed specifically at them did not consume less absinthe. "Simple illusion, by the way, created by the malice of the industrialist. The 'small absinthe' is worth [as much as] the big one, the quantity is the same: you have less water to add, that's all."[109] In Geffroy's explanation, drinking absinthe neat was not necessarily a preference of women, but due to cafés and débits trying to maximize their clientele by offering absinthe in glasses that they deemed more attractive to female customers.

One of the rare published case studies concerning a woman's absinthe consumption in the nineteenth century also described this gendered preference for neat absinthe, neither making it about corsets nor dainty glasses, but a question of taste, and, possibly, class. It was published in Albert-Joseph Devoisins's 1885 study *Women and Alcoholism*, but taken from an unspecified 1873 article in the journal *La Tempérance*. Devoisins recounted that a forty-one-year-old woman was found on a bench, "stiffened by the cold and giving no sign of life," and taken to the police station: "She had spent part of the night at wine shops, with several individuals; she had, according to her own statement, drunk forty-two glasses of absinthe, into which, she added, she had not put a drop of water, for fear of depriving the liquor of its aromatic flavour."[110] This collection of sources shows that a combination of factors might have propelled nineteenth- and early twentieth-century women – and men – to drink absinthe undiluted.

One striking critique of women's absinthe consumption occurs in Witold Lemanski's 1902 handbook for European settlers. In it, Lemanski blamed bicycles for women's growing addiction to absinthe. Bicycles had become popular in the 1880s,[111] but it was the decade between 1893 and 1903 that the French journalist and author Claude Pasteur described as the "universal triumph of the bicycle" in her 1986 book.[112] Lemanski based his assessment on a conversation he had had with Jules-Pie Braquehaye, chief surgeon at the Hôpital français in Tunis. Lemanski explained that, in "a recent conversation with my eminent colleague at the Hospital, Professor Braquehaye," Braquehaye had supported the "thesis of the contagion of alcoholism, for women, by the bicycle." Lemanski explained that "in the past, in many provincial towns, women were rarely seen keeping company with their husbands at the time of the 'parrot.'" Yet the bicycle gave these women the opportunity to take part in the "hour of absinthe," with or without their husbands. Due to bicycles, Lemanski regretted, "it is not uncommon to see pretty lips, [that] pleasant part of graceful faces, moist with adulterated liquors, detestable beverages, ignoble and horrible poisons."[113]

Lemanski believed that the theory of his colleague Braquehaye was correct. He was convinced that "the bicycle pushes the woman to alcoholism; and alcoholism in women is the worst [form of] social disorganization, the ferment that disintegrates the best unions [i.e., marriages] and compromises the future of the offspring." The danger in women having taken to the bicycle, which gave them more personal freedom, was thus, in Lemanski's eyes, degeneration. "Is it then necessary to enact severe laws of prohibition; restrict the bicycle, regulate the length of the skirts of these ladies and severely specify the duration of the stops at the terraces of the cafés?" Lemanski rejected these suggestions as infantilizing. He thought it more effective to let women "know that there are better things for them to do than to only imitate men!"[114] This idea of women's alcohol consumption – and their use of the bicycle! – being nothing but an imitation of male behaviour,[115] as discussed above, outlasted the prohibition of absinthe. An article published in the *New York Times* in 1925, for example, summarized a report given to the French Académie de médecine that same year: "With respect to women it is declared that their increased addiction to drink is merely part of the general tendency of the female to imitate the male, other aspects of this phenomenon being the boyish bob, the masculine cut in clothing and the readiness with which they take to cigarettes."[116] Aspects of women's expression and their striving for freedom were equated in both this 1925 article and Lemanski's 1902 book with women's consumption of alcohol and dismissed as nothing but an imitation of the behaviour of men.

Lemanski's bizarre diatribe against the bicycle is connected to the fact that the bicycle – and the changed costumes that came with it[117] – became associated with the New Woman in the late nineteenth century.[118] Women of the Belle Époque consciously used the bicycle to gain access to life outside of the house.[119] Indeed, in her 2007 chapter on women and transport in the Belle

Époque, Siân Reynolds described the bicycle as a means of transport for French women "within a small radius,"[120] as well as a "private means of escape," especially outside of the cities with their growing public transport.[121]

A humorous sketch in the newspaper *Don Juan* in July 1897, shown in Fig. 4.6, mirrored Lemanski in connecting the New Woman, bicycles, and absinthe. The artist Georges Conrad depicted five different scenes in this sketch, showing a young woman's relationship to her bicycle. The caption of the first image refers to the new freedom of the costumes presented to French women, focusing on the tight clothes these women wore when cycling. After an invasive sexualization of the woman bicyclist, Conrad continues, in the second sketch, in which he draws a direct connection between bicycling, freedom, and absinthe: "The bicycle for her is a pretext to flee to the suburbs. She gets tired quickly. She goes into cafés and taverns, and finds that one is better off in a large armchair than on the narrow saddle. But the bicycle and the suit give her the air of a cheeky little page, who happily empties her can, her absinthe." Conrad finishes by ironically saying: "Long live the bicycle that gives freedom!"[122]

While the image of the absinthe-drinking woman was used as a shortcut in the narratives of the Belle Époque for both women's irrationality and the figure of the New Woman, such notions were sometimes also turned on their head. The well-known French feminist Hubertine Auclert used the general prejudice against absinthe-drinking women in a moral tale in her 1900 book *Arab Women in Algeria*, attacking both the general cruelty of people and the easy association of certain forms of behaviour with the overconsumption of absinthe amongst women. Auclert recounts the story of Réïra,[123] a young Algerian woman, who has been picked up by the police in the streets with a young child: "She staggers when walking; an official that she comes close to, brutally pushes [her] away with his cane and, seeing her fall, exclaims: 'Dirty mouquière [i.e., woman]! She is drunk on absinthe!'" However, Réïra turns out to not be drunk, as Auclert explains in the following paragraph. After having been carried, "unconscious," to the prison, with local children following them, shouting "Hey! The drunk woman! ... the drunk woman! ... Réïra was locked up and left there: 'The next day, she still does not move. However, she should have digested her absinthe ... In the end, the jailer becomes alarmed. The doctor is called: he is told that the prisoner was arrested for drunkenness; he examines her carefully, then, his voice trembling from indignation: 'Thrice brutes! He explained, this woman died of hunger!'"[124] Auclert's message is clear: all those who treated Réïra callously could have

Figure 4.6
Drawing depicting a woman in trousers, sitting on a chair next
to her bicycle about to order a glass of absinthe.

helped the poor woman, if they had only listened to her and not immediately categorized her behaviour – caused by poverty and need – as a symptom of absinthe excesses amongst women.

In summary, it can be said that the absinthe consumption of women was interpreted in various ways by nineteenth- and early twentieth-century authors, reflecting the deep flexibility of how absinthe itself was seen and depicted. Absinthe drinking was practically always interpreted as women neglecting their dual duties of modesty and procreation. Absinthe-drinking women were viewed and depicted as enticing, but also – for male absinthe consumers in the same cafés – as being nigh impossible to differentiate from sex workers. If these women had children, they were accused of raising them unhealthily by introducing them at an early age to the green fairy. The question of why these women consumed absinthe was not generally asked, as, to nineteenth-century sources, it seemed obvious that they did so in order to imitate men, not only in their consumption of the green fairy, but also in their choice of fashion, their hairstyles, and even their discovery of the independence a bicycle offered to them. In addition, women who took their absinthe neat were described as doing this either due to their own vanities or wishes to attract men, or due to them falling for the insidious marketing campaigns of cafés aimed specifically at them. All of these reasons given by French, male, middle-class authors speak to the fact that Belle Époque women in general and absinthe-drinking women in particular were represented as to some degree irrational.

5

Undesirable Consumption

The previous chapters already touched on the clear influence of class on how a drinker's absinthe consumption was judged by nineteenth- and early twentieth-century sources. For example, while the absinthe consumption of all women was deemed suspicious, the drinking habits of working-class and marginalized women was overall depicted as more dangerous and morally reprehensible than that of upper- and middle-class women. This chapter specifically addresses the absinthe consumption of France's working classes and of the colonized populations in France's empire. The final part of this chapter is dedicated to the theory that working-class men from both France and the colonies became violent and deeply dangerous after having indulged in too much absinthe.

The Price of Absinthe

An author only given as L. M. wrote in January 1896 an article for the monthly temperance journal *L'Alcool*, describing a dinner where the conversation turned to alcoholism, a "usual conversation these days," as he remarked. The author, recognized by his dinner companions as being part of the French temperance movement, recounted the following conversation: "We came to talk about the campaign that is being waged almost everywhere and in the most diverse forms against the habits of unconscious intemperance, which are rapidly and surely leading our race towards decay and our country towards its ruin." In the course of this conversation, the temperance movement was "accused of clumsy fanaticism and cruelty: working towards depriving the worker of his little morning glass, of his evening drop … No doubt, one should not drink too much, but brandy gives strength, alcohol is a food; and then it is only in his glass that the worker finds joy and his share of dreams that one is no more entitled to deny to any man than his share of bread or sunshine!"[1]

As hinted in this reported conversation, the French temperance movement framed alcoholism mainly as a problem of the working classes. This notion was perhaps best summarized by the temperance advocate Louis Jacquet, who argued in 1912 that alcohol was less of a problem amongst the wealthy as "nearly 4/5 of alcohol is consumed in débits by the people; alcoholism is therefore, above all, a disease of the poor classes."[2] Prestwich contextualized Jacquet's suggestion by explaining that four-fifths of the *distilled* alcohol consumed in France was indeed "industrial alcohol," and not alcohol made from various fruit, from which cheap drinks were produced that were intended for sale in the débits de boissons. These drinks were, however, consumed "not only by workers, but by peasants, fishermen, office clerks, and small businessmen."[3] Prestwich's contextualization shows that non-distilled forms of alcohol – i.e., the "hygienic beverages" of wine, beer, and cider – seemed to have been excluded from Jacquet's calculation of alcoholism.

Before the 1870s, French workers, like the ones discussed in the course of this middle-class dinner conversation, had been mostly wine drinkers.[4] There were, of course, vast differences between wines, with many of them financially inaccessible to workers.[5] The workers discussed during M.'s dinner, however, were described as consuming distilled forms of alcohol. "Formerly, while the boulevardiers drank absinthe, the workers, upon leaving the workshops, drank wine … Today, it is no longer so," lamented Charles Mayet in his 1894 book. "Coming down from their scaffolding, carpenters, masons, roofers, painters, often act like consumers on the boulevards. They take one, two, three [glasses of] absinthe: each [pays for] his round."[6] While working-class women were also reported as absinthe drinkers, they were often excluded from such discussions of working-class drinking habits. When not otherwise marked, these sources used exclusively male descriptors in their texts.

Returning to the dinner party: M. felt that he had won the evening's moral argument on the topic of workers' alcoholism as soon as it turned to the true enemy of France's nineteenth-century temperance movement, absinthe. One of his dinner companions exclaimed that what "proves your thoughtless fanaticism is that you even attack absinthe. Tell the workers not to drink all those dreadful aperitifs, all those bitters, with which they spoil their stomachs; make them give up, if that is your pleasure, drinking potato spirit or gin for a sou [five centimes] a glass; but, for God's sake!, do not blame absinthe, good, restful, and refreshing absinthe!"[7] This argument was based on the widespread assumption that the consumption of alcohol in general, and absinthe in particular, provided strength and energy to the drinkers,[8] not dissimilar to explanations given by both French soldiers and settlers in French colonies for their own absinthe consumption. To M., who was caught up in the anti-absinthe frenzy of the 1890s, his opponent's defence of absinthe – as more nourishing and energy-giving for workers than other distilled forms of alcohol – proved his irrationality.

Described as an established fact in this 1896 description of a dinner conversation, workers had started to drink absinthe at some point in the late nineteenth century. Giant absinthe adverts were prominently placed in quarters of Paris where working-class consumers would see them on their way to and from work (Fig. 5.1). V.-S. Lucienne reported in an 1899 book that, after the habit of drinking absinthe had been imported from Algeria, it did not immediately spread to the working classes. In France, Lucienne explained, the consumption of absinthe remained "concentrated in the cafés, for some time; then it spread to the cabarets of the cities, and all the classes of society have today taken the disastrous habit of this drink. It is no longer only the rich who

51. LE BOURGET — Route de Flandre, le Pont du Chemin de Fer

Figure 5.1
Postcard of the Route de Flandre in Le Bourget, with an advert
for Absinthe Oxygénée Cusenier.

poison themselves with absinthe, but the whole working population that makes use of this beverage."[9] Similarly, Robert Hazemann believed that one could trace clear stages in the spread of absinthe consumption. According to him, absinthe had first been consumed only by "the rich or well-to-do," referring to descriptions in Auguste Motet's 1859 dissertation, before becoming the drink of the lower middle classes. Hazemann based his interpretation of this development on the aforementioned claims in Henri Legrand du Saulle's 1877 book.[10] By 1897, the time of the composition of his thesis, Hazemann believed that there had been a process of absinthe democratization,[11] adding that "in our time, it would be very difficult to determine which class of society drinks the most absinthe. Rich and poor, successful and failure, [all] drink absinthe."[12] As absinthe spread through the French class system, even "the most disadvantaged," as the French historian Henry-Melchior de Langle put it in 1990,[13] started to drink it. This absinthe consumption of "the destitute and alcoholics" can be explained, as Ian Hutton reminded his readers, through it being "the cheapest way of buying strong alcohol."[14]

Absinthe came to be understood as the "favourite drink of the working classes"[15] at some point between the 1870s and 1880s. From this point onwards, medical reports often focused on examples of excessive working-class consumption. In his 1899 book, for example, Raoul Brunon reported on the case of a blacksmith, who died at the age of thirty-seven from delirium tremens, and who had for the two years prior to his death "taken a litre of brandy with meals," as well as, between meals, "7 or 8 [glasses of] absinthe a day."[16] Nineteenth- and early twentieth-century sources framed the absinthe consumption of the working classes as being due to workers imitating the habits of the bourgeois,[17] something that workers could afford to do thanks to the lowering of the price of absinthe. Yet far from being an imitation based on admiration, so to speak, this new consumption of absinthe by workers might have been "encouraged in part by a sense of class transgression," as suggested by Marnin Young in 2008, as workers could now afford to consume a drink that that previously been reserved for the bourgeoisie's – and the bohème's – celebration of the "hour of absinthe."[18]

Once absinthe was produced with "industrial alcohol" – due to the shortages of grape wine after the phylloxera crisis in the 1870s and 1880s – absinthe became cheap enough to be consumed by the working classes both in France[19] and the French colonies.[20] For Pierre Decroos, in his 1910 dissertation, the "undeniable fashion of absinthe everywhere where she [absinthe] has made her apparition" could partly be explained through the "appeal of her essences and by her fine taste," but mostly by absinthe's "very affordable price compared to other alcoholic beverages. Absinthe has thus been put within the reach of all, and her ravages have multiplied in the working class in particular in at least equal proportion to the debasement of its price."[21] Absinthe, once limited to the wealthy due to its price, turned into an affordable everyday item for the masses. Absinthe prices also fell in the colonies. Lucien Raynaud reported that a glass of absinthe was sold for ten centimes in Algeria in 1896,[22] but, apparently there were even cheaper options, as ten glasses of absinthe could be bought by a legionnaire for fifty centimes in Algeria at the beginning of the twentieth century, according to Georges d'Esparbès in his 1901 book on the Foreign Legion.[23]

From the 1870s onward, absinthe could be obtained very cheaply in France, as can be seen in Sterling Heilig's 1894 article, who explained that "everywhere in the poorer quarters [in Paris] absinthe is three cents a glass (its price in the rich quarters is ten cents a glass)."[24] The prices varied according to the location of consumption. Like Heilig, Phil Baker informed his readers that there were differences in pricing, with absinthe being at its most affordable in bars surrounding markets, for example, where workers could get a glass of absinthe at the counter for ten centimes, while in the rest of Paris, a glass cost fifteen centimes.[25] While the difference between a glass of working-class absinthe and one of bourgeois absinthe was seven centimes, according to Heilig, and five according to Phil Baker, contemporaries of Heilig described respectable absinthe as being much more expensive. Émile Goudeau explained that absinthe, bitter, and Amer Picon were the most popular aperitifs in Paris at the time of the publication of his book in 1893. He clarified that this was due, in part, through there being "a decree issued from no one knows where, [that] these three aperitifs, pure or mixed, cost only fifty centimes, while for the others the price is higher." He further clarified that if you "take an absinthe or a bitter, put some gomme [i.e., sugar syrup], anisette, mint, curaçao in it; it's a drink of fifty centimes: if you ask for *only* gomme or anisette, or mint, or curaçao to be put in the same large glass, it's fifteen sous [seventy-five centimes], a franc, or even a franc twenty-five!"[26] In Goudeau's report on bourgeois Paris, fifty centimes was thus cheap for a glass of absinthe, either pure or mixed with one of these other substances, while at the same time, Heilig suggested it was possible to get one for three.

In his 1990 chapter on cafés and bars as "places of novelty," de Langle explained that in 1900 a litre of absinthe cost two to four francs in Paris, which meant, according to his calculations, that a glass of absinthe cost about fifteen centimes. As a means of comparison, de Langle added that a bowl of soup in a cheap restaurant cost ten and a kilogram of bread about fifty centimes. A daily glass of absinthe was thus a possibility for a worker with an average salary of about three francs a day.[27] In Switzerland, a glass of absinthe cost 0.10 francs in the 1900s, according to a 1907 brochure arguing for the prohibition of absinthe, which led the Swiss working classes, allegedly, to spend 10 per cent of their earnings on alcohol in general and absinthe in particular.[28] With such low prices, absinthe might even have been used as a replacement for meals amongst the low socio-economic classes.[29]

This spread of absinthe – and distilled alcohol in general – to the working classes was framed as having deplorable consequences on public health. In his 1865 monograph *Influence of the Moral State of Society on Public Health*, the French doctor Louis Cyprien Descieux sounded the alarm, based on his experience of forty years as a doctor in a hospital for the working classes in Montfort-l'Amaury, in a region "where the population is not known for being particularly immoral." Despite this reservation, his findings were dire, as Descieux claimed that "three-fifths of the sick are brought there [to the hospital] as a result of drunkenness and of disorders which are its ordinary consequence." The other two-fifths were mostly due to "debauchery" and the living situation.[30] Writing in 1865, at a time when absinthe was still at the beginning of its "meteoric career," to use the formulation by Michael Marrus,[31] Descieux did not blame absinthe specifically for the enormous number of alcohol-related cases. Indeed, Descieux did not mention absinthe at all in his book. When Dominique Thierrin, however, summarized these findings of Descieux in his 1896 book on the *Dangers of the Abuse of Alcoholic Drinks*, he implicitly connected these numbers with absinthe. According to Thierrin, Descieux's findings had shown that "*three-fifths* of the illnesses which strike the men of the people are due to the cabaret"[32] – and the working-class cabaret was, in the 1890s, inextricably linked with absinthe. Based on fears about working-class consumption, calls for bans of absinthe – or for the closure of débits de boissons – appeared. In 1888, Maxime du Camp mused that, "if we could close the débits de boissons, [and] throw absinthe down the drain," together with other drinks that were perceived to be of poor quality, then "the worker would complain less," which, in turn, would lead to less social unrest. While keeping them from absinthe was seen as a means of protecting the government from working-class discontent, du Camp himself saw the closure of these débits de boissons as a way of protecting Paris's working classes: "It is savings that have made the fortune of the Parisian bourgeoisie, it is the 'assommoir' [i.e., a working-class drinking establishment] that is ruining the Parisian proletariat."[33] Du Camp's assessment should be seen in the context of a backlash to the Paris Commune, during which there had been legends of "drunken women torching the city – *les pétroleuses* – in 1871."[34] The Commune was a "watershed in the bourgeois perception of drink," as the historian Ruth Harris suggested in 1991, with alcohol – especially absinthe – drinkers now being framed as dangerous.[35] Indeed, the Commune and France's defeat against Prussia were the very "beginnings of the first anti-alcoholism" in France,[36] as the defeat of the French army was blamed on the high alcohol consumption of the soldiers.[37]

Comparable to the notion of a loss of creative minds amongst the intelligentsia and artists, it was mainly the loss of sheer work force that was regretted when it came to working-class men's absinthe consumption. France's "working classes have been debauched and ruined physically by this subtle poison," lamented an article published in *The Times* in April 1915.[38] In his 1888 article, Georges Maillard explained that "thanks to the odious absinthe, the most able-bodied, the most vigorous men" ended up being removed "from industry, from agriculture, from useful production."[39] Men, at the prime of their strength, it was feared, were lost to France's industries, due to absinthe prematurely aging young working-class men, as André Pascal claimed in his 1864 book.[40]

This problem of an allegedly excessive, working-class absinthe consumption was believed to have spread from Paris to the rest of France as well as throughout the French Empire. The spread through France was possibly aided, as Roberta Lee and Michael J. Balick suggested in their 2005 article on absinthe, by the emergence of the train network. This development, which "allowed for more commerce," led to the spread of "a large French underclass of working poor." This, in turn, enabled the spread of the green fairy, as these exhausted workers liked to spend the "little money" they gained from their hard work on absinthe.[41]

Independent of the driving force behind absinthe's proliferation through France, it was soon possible to order the drink even in small villages. "The consumption of alcohol increases in the countryside as in the cities, under the influences of the same causes, and causes the same havoc there," stated the French doctor Jules Rochard in 1897. "Cabarets multiply in the villages with a frightful rapidity and they become a place of habitual rendezvous. They sell under the name of cognac, rum, eau-de-vie, drinks composed with alcohols [which are] cheap and consequently of inferior quality. Liquors with pretentious names, absinthe is also found there." Furthermore, Rochard informed his readers that in these villages, "women, children drink them as men do."[42] By 1897, the absinthe bottle had, apparently, achieved "the place of honour in the cabinet of the innkeeper of the most isolated hamlet of France," bewailed Robert Hazemann.[43] Some sources even suggested that absinthe had become a greater problem outside Paris. In his 1894 article, Heilig wrote "the religion of the apéritif lives in more vigor in the south of France than in the capital." Amongst the inhabitants of southern France, absinthe was, according to Heilig, a particular problem amongst certain working-class pockets, such as the "mining countries of the south."[44]

While the low price of absinthe was usually blamed for this development, some believed an assumed improvement of working-class lives to be responsible. Marrus explained that employers in nineteenth-century France often argued that an increase in the wages of workers – or them having more free time – would lead workers to spend their free time and their extra money in débits de boissons, in order to justify their opposition to both kinds of improvements in workers' lives.[45] According to Marrus, these working-class débits de boissons, much demonized by the bourgeoisie, came to play an important role for the working classes during the Belle Époque, as "the principal if not the sole place in which popular sociability could take place." Marrus argued that the uncomfortable living conditions of the working classes – overcrowded, poorly heated, and unhygienic – intensified the attraction of the "bright, warm and crowded world of cabarets and bistros."[46]

An article in the New York Times, published in 1925 with the title "Alcohol Drinking Doubles in France," proposed similar arguments against giving workers more time and pay. In his analysis of the situation in France after the 1915 absinthe ban, the unnamed author referred to a report by a French professor, Achard, of the Academy of Medicine in Paris.[47] While I could not identify this specific report, the author was presumably the French doctor Charles Achard, professor of pathology and therapeutics at the Faculty of Medicine in Paris.[48] According to the New York Times, this professor placed "emphasis in his report on the fact that the general increase in the consumption of alcoholic beverages may be attributed to the improvement of conditions of the working classes, particularly the increase of wages and the eight-hour working day. Both of these benefits, according to Professor Achard, have in many cases only tended to give the working man more time and money to waste in drink."[49] This patronizing depiction of working-class people continued, as, according to Achard, "the establishment of the eight-hour law should have been preceded by the education of the working classes into the employment of their leisure time. Drinking absinthe in disguised form is a practice which is becoming increasingly popular in France, and he urges rigid execution of the laws against cafés which keep open beyond the legal hours."[50] While this argument was from the post-ban period, it is impossible not to see an echo of the middle-class discourse on the evils of working-class absinthe consumption, especially with the reference to workers drinking "absinthe in disguised form."

Once work was done for the day, workers were described as rushing out of their workplaces and into the various débits de boissons. Raoul Brunon – director of the School of Medicine in Rouen[51] – explained in his 1899 monograph, *Alcoholism of City Workers*, that "at eleven o'clock, [there is a] hasty exit from the workshops. The débitant [i.e., the owner of the débit] has prepared a sufficient number of glasses of absinthe, more rarely of vermouth or bitters, in advance, and the consumer does not waste a minute; he swallows [it] quickly."[52] This description lacks the leisure, glamour, and ritual of the hour of absinthe of the boulevardier, focusing instead on an urgent need, and depicts workers as drinking at least their first absinthe neat.

From the point of view of the middle-class authors comprising most of my sources, absinthe began to dominate the lives of working-class men to the exclusion of most other drinks. A Doctor Daviller wrote in 1889 an article about "alcohol and alcoholism," in which he portrayed tea and coffee as healthy drinks, "but, unfortunately, these harmless drinks are not those that the public likes and seeks. Talk about tea or coffee to a worker or a peasant, they will not understand you." Daviller added that, while the prices for tea and coffee were excessively high for the daily budgets of French workers, "their preparation [is] too complicated for them to get used to." Just as Doctor Achard viewed working-class men – in the 1925 *New York Times* article quoted above – as incapable of knowing what was best for them without having first received detailed instruction from the state, Daviller similarly depicted the choice of "workers and peasants" of drinking absinthe as based on them being simple-minded or lacking knowledge. Additionally, Daviller supposed that tea and coffee did not provide these workers and peasants with "that well-being, that state of cerebral dizziness, that *bliss*, if I can put it that way, that those accustomed to alcohol seek above all else. The state of enjoyment in which absinthe drinkers find themselves is too well known for it to be necessary for me to dwell on it."[53] This idea of a diametrical opposition of tea and coffee on the one hand and absinthe on the other can also be found in other sources. In his 1885 article on absinthe, the Swiss journalist Franz August Stocker explained that drinkers should try to reduce their absinthe consumption, suggesting that "the replacement [of absinthe] becomes all the easier when a cup of coffee takes the place of absinthe."[54] In the specific context of the absinthe consumption of the working classes, such references to coffee were linked to notions of coffee as the alleged drink of reason and the industrial revolution, increasing both the intellectual and physical labour of consumers.

Such sources – condescending but also full of an authentic alarm about the rising numbers – should be seen in their broader political context. In her 1979 chapter "After the Commune," Susanna Barrows suggested that "after 1871 much of the bourgeoisie used alcoholism as a code word for working-class irrationality and as an overarching explanation of French defeat."[55] Confronted with sources that depicted this consumption as a steadily increasing working-class problem, it is difficult to estimate how much of this was moral panic, how much an expression of irritation about what was perceived to be "working-class irrationality," to use Barrows's formulation, and how much was based on an actual increase in consumption. While many of the sources exaggerated the issue, it is unquestionable that rates of alcoholism – and, once the price of absinthe fell, of absinthism – increased in the second half of the nineteenth century. In 1987, Patricia Prestwich commented on a paper by Catherine Kudlick, with the title "Fighting the Internal and External Enemies: Alcoholism in World War I France," suggesting that, while some of the evidence on the alcohol consumption of working-class men presented in nineteenth-century sources was deeply biased and "clearly flawed," alcoholism might indeed have posed a particular danger for working-class men in France.[56]

While alcoholism in general and absinthism in particular were undoubtedly problems amongst some working-class men in France and in France's colonies – just as they were amongst the bohème and the bourgeoisie – the normal, everyday joy of a shared glass of absinthe amongst workers was deeply pathologized by medical experts. As with women, the absinthe consumption of working-class men was explained both through them trying to imitate the habits of the bourgeoisie, and as them failing to participate correctly in the hour of absinthe, as they did not stick to the rules established by the French bourgeoisie. This was shown through reports of them drinking perhaps more than one glass of absinthe in one place, neat, sometimes alone, while standing at a counter. This, it was believed, could have serious consequences on their bodies, their ability to work, and on wider society. Indeed, as shown in Maxime du Camp's 1888 quote, discussed above, the absinthe consumption of workers was depicted by some as a source of social unrest.[57] This, in turn, explains why their consumption – unlike the refined hour of absinthe of the bourgeoisie – was understood as something that should be studied and controlled.

"Colonize by Absinthe"[58]

Absinthe was described as a cornerstone of daily life in France's colonies and it was sometimes suggested – humorously or not – that both the spread of French civilization and the presence of French citizens in a country could be measured by the amount of absinthe shipped there. In his 1914 account about his military experiences in Western Morocco, Captain F. Ceccaldi asked his readers, "is it not demonstrated that civilization will always start with the instilling of the vices of the conquerors in the conquered? Pernod and his imitators penetrate the country with our vanguards – that was all that the Moroccans needed!"[59] The somewhat sinister-sounding phrase of this being "all that the Moroccans needed" seems to imply that absinthe was important to the conquest. This could either be straightforward, in the sense of absinthe having helped to defeat the Moroccans, or it could have been meant ironically, in the sense of the addiction to absinthe being the last thing that the Moroccans needed.

Given the popularity of absinthe amongst French settlers, tourists, and soldiers in the colonies, it is not surprising that the colonized populations also turned to the drink. The secondary literature on the history of absinthe sometimes suggests that although absinthe spread to the French colonies, the colonized populations did not partake in its consumption. In her 1983 book *Absinthe: History of the Green Fairy*, for example, Marie-Claude Delahaye explained that "whatever the colonized country, absinthe was not drunk by the natives, but by the French soldiers and settlers."[60] Such statements are presumably based, amongst other things, on claims of absolute abstinence amongst Muslims in certain nineteenth-century sources.[61] However, they are inaccurate.

In the context of North Africa, where French alcohol drinkers were surrounded by what they believed to be strict adherents to the prohibition of alcohol in the Qur'an, the fact that some Muslims drank absinthe preoccupied French authors greatly. A curious footnote in the history of absinthe should be mentioned in this context. In 1896, the French doctor Philippe Grenier was voted into the French Chamber of Deputies for the Doubs region, i.e., the heart of France's absinthe production. Grenier came from a "strict Catholic family," according to Barnaby Conrad, but had converted to Islam after living in Algeria.[62] He was openly anti-absinthe, and his abstinence – based on his faith – was depicted as something very foreign and un-French. Upon his election in 1896, the French press described Grenier both as a "radical socialist Muslim"[63] and as "a kind of madman."[64] He lost his seat in 1898, whereupon an article published in *La Dépêche algérienne* openly mocked him, depicting a Mme Grenier offering him an aperitif, as consolation, while he was conducting his prayers and his reply to her offer: "Absinthe from Pontarlier … never."[65] While the press disagreed with Grenier's opinions, his stance towards absinthe was in line with the wider French understanding of how the prohibition of alcohol in Islam worked. However, the French did not understand that, despite the prohibition of alcohol in the Qur'an, some North Africans were able to reconcile a glass of absinthe with their Muslim faith.

Generally speaking, the French viewed their North African colonies as consisting of strictly divided societies – European alcohol consumers and abstinent Muslims. The French playwright Ernest Feydeau described Muslim society in Algeria in 1862 as symbolized by the traditional North African coffeehouse on the one side and European cafés on the other. During the day, the North African coffeehouses were busy places where information was exchanged: "News from France, with the arrival of each ship, is collected there and commented on by the passing Arabs who go at once to transmit it to their tribes." This North African space was open to Europeans, but only "French merchants of the city" and a few simple French soldiers entered them. "In contrast, there is no shortage of Arab leaders in the European cafés, and it is a pretty sad sight to see them publicly swallow glasses of absinthe and ape the manners of their conquerors, under pretence of civilization."[66]

Feydeau's offensive description of these "Arab leaders" shows that the absinthe consumption of colonized populations was believed to be merely an act of imitation of a "higher" group – just as women were believed to imitate men and workers to imitate the bourgeoisie. This echoes Paul-Maurice Legrain's 1897 theory of a hierarchical progress of absinthe – "from the bourgeois, the contagion spread to the worker, from man to woman, from woman to child"[67] – only here the "contagion" spread from the settler to the colonized.

In this understanding, the absinthe consumption of formerly abstinent Muslims was the fault of French settlers, who set a bad example to the colonized. In his 1892 study on the French in Tunisia, Eugène Poiré deplored how ineffective France's efforts of instilling civilization had been in Algeria. According to Poiré, most Algerians had chosen to flee South from the invading French, instead of assimilating: "Those who remain, sadly prone to contracting above all our vices, only fraternize with our settlers before [a glass of] absinthe."[68]

As the French believed that Muslims lost their religion when drinking, they framed the alcohol consumption of Muslims as following an all-or-nothing attitude: If they started to drink – risking their faith with every drop – they drank it immoderately. A French doctor with the name of Paul Remlinger gave a paper in November 1912 about the "Progress of Alcoholism in Morocco" that was published that same year in the *Bulletin de la Société de pathologie exotique*. Remlinger informed his audience that Muslim men gave "preference to absinthe, cognac, whiskey, and gin." Based on his observations, Remlinger believed that "if the European drinks in general for the pleasure of drinking, despite the intoxication which may result from it, the Arab never or almost never drinks by taste. It is the drunkenness that he looks for. The more easily it is obtained, the more satisfied he is." The joy of the taste, sweetness, and fragrance of a glass of absinthe, prominent in many accounts of the hour of absinthe amongst the French, was, according to Remlinger, irrelevant to "Arabs." Instead, it was this desire for drunkenness that explained, in the eyes of many, the preference of many North Africans for absinthe, one of the strongest alcoholic drinks available to them. "It follows from this that the Arab does not know in the consumption of alcoholic beverages any moderation. While it is very embarrassing [i.e., socially difficult] to rank a European among the drinkers or the non-drinkers, this is not the same with the Arabs. He drinks or he does not, and if he drinks, he is drunk."[69] North Africans were not only believed to drink too much absinthe but, like corseted French women and exhausted workers at the counter – and female North African dancers, singers, and musicians[70] – they were also sometimes described as drinking it neat.[71]

This suspicion about North Africans not being able to consume absinthe moderately made their absinthe consumption appear particularly dangerous, even potentially fatal. Some settlers were reported as believing that this could be used to France's advantage, suggesting that, with the help of absinthe, the colonized could be basically eradicated from France's North African colonies. One such example can be found in Henri Richardot's 1905 travel account about his journey through Tunisia and Algeria. In Tunisia, he came across

Black and Arab mine workers who drank absinthe. Observing this, Richardot stated: "And I remember the words of one of these fierce settlers who dream of the destruction of the native race: 'It would need a few thousand litres of absinthe.'"[72] While Richardot condemned the genocidal fantasies of this un-named settler, it is still telling that the mere sight of absinthe-drinking Tuni-sians reminded him of this.

After the prohibition of absinthe in France and French colonies in 1915, similar descriptions of an inherent North African immoderation can be found about one of absinthe's heirs, anisette. According to Pierre Pinaud – in his 1933 medical dissertation "Alcoholism amongst the Arabs of Algeria" – the "scourge" of the various anisettes was disastrous in Algeria. "In recent years, [anisette] has exerted its toll as much among the European population as among the Arabs. But the natives seem more particularly affected." Pinaud warned his readers that this had consequences for the lives of French settlers, as "cases of acute intoxication assume among the Arabs particularly grave forms … Under the influence of anisette, they become violent and quarrel-some. Cases of delirium due to the absorption of this drink often end tragi-cally, and it is enough to consult any newspaper in order to observe the considerable number of criminal acts, attacks, and murders committed by natives in a state of [anisette] drunkenness."[73] It was, however, not only ab-sinthe – and anisettes! – that was dreaded as unmasking an innate savagery amongst the colonized, as very similar fears were also voiced in French pub-lications dissecting the role of hashish in North Africa.[74]

French sources often viewed Muslims willingly breaking with the laws of their religion after contact with France in the context of the question of as-similation. In his 1905 dissertation, Henri Duchêne-Marullaz explained that "if the Qur'an defends a single drop of wine, the Arab takes this less and less into account. By civilizing, or rather, by wanting to imitate us, he mainly took our faults. At present it is no longer uncommon to find natives drinking wine, and, as in everything, they do not use it, they abuse. They mostly drink ab-sinthe and anisette."[75] In Duchêne-Marullaz's simplistic framing, Muslims had started to drink absinthe in order to acquire civilization, since it was a drink that – for better or for worse – embodied Frenchness.

Some French sources accused both absinthe-drinking North Africans and other French people of having genuinely believed that Muslim colonized men (and women, to a lesser degree) could potentially become more French and "civilized" through the consumption of alcohol in general and of absinthe in particular. During the colonial period phrases such as "people who colonize by absinthe"[76] were most often used disparagingly – mocking those who believed it was possible. In his 1893 study *France in Algeria*, Louis Vignon, professor at the Colonial School in Paris, explained that, in the major cities of Algeria, a French traveller "will meet [Algerian] people, in traditional clothes," willing to work as porters, "who boast that they never enter a mosque, that they never pray, that they drink absinthe. Perhaps some convinced 'assimilationists,' still attached to their ideas, rejoice; they judge that an Arab who drinks absinthe is an 'assimilated man.' This opinion is not ours."[77] The majority of French nineteenth- and early twentieth-century sources agreed with Vignon and rejected this narrative of absinthe-drinking representing a sign of assimilation amongst the colonized. Similar negative comments about the absinthe consumption of colonized populations can also be found for other French colonies. In an article written for *Le Temps* in September 1896, for example, Jean Carde described Madagascar as "flooded with absinthe at twelve sous a litre." This development displeased Carde and made him ask: "Is it necessary to brutalize before civilizing?"[78] France's *mission civilisatrice* theoretically had the end goal of civilizing the local populations. By brutalizing, Carde meant the introduction of absinthe drinking and its consequences, making it apparent that absinthe must have been consumed by the local population in Madagascar.

It was generally believed that, amongst the colonized, those in direct contact with France – mainly those living in the coastal cities, soldiers in France's army, servants, and sex workers – were most likely to drink absinthe, again hinting at the idea of absinthe-drinking being somehow contagious and transmittable – or, more accurately, learnable. In the French army, drinking absinthe had been part of the French way of life that these North African soldiers adapted to, despite the prohibitions and bans of the 1840s and 1850s. In his 1896 article "Alcoholism in Algeria" the French doctor Lucien Raynaud discussed this, stating that "the Arab of the cities, the one who becomes civilized (!) through our contact, naturally finds what is best amongst our morals and begins to drink absinthe. It begins in the regiment, which may be called the primary school of alcoholism."[79]

As seen in the quote by Duchêne-Marullaz, descriptions of absinthe-drinking Muslims were often framed by European observers as *assimilation gone wrong*. In his 1862 book *Notes in North Africa*, W.G. Windham described how, in general, "the moors and Arabs … will never, I believe, adopt European civilisation; they seem to recoil from before it, like the wild beasts of their native deserts." To this, Windham added: "The French people certainly pointed out to me in the towns one or two *Europeanised* Arabs, and laughed at the idea of their even becoming *'Français.'* From what I saw, the natives merely adopted the vices without the good qualities of the dominant race. If to be civilised consists in sitting in the cafés, drinking absinthe, playing cards, and speaking bad French, I certainly saw one or two most unquestionable specimens of the Arab adaptability to Gallic impressions."[80] A similar dismayed quote about France's superficial influence on North Africa can be found in the report on the travels through 1860s precolonial Morocco by the German geographer Gerhard Rohlfs: "Those in the cities have adopted all the bad manners of the French and assist the French rabble in drinking absinthe, but that they would have accepted Christian religious principles even in the slightest in return is unthinkable."[81]

Like these English and German travel reports, French sources suggested that assimilation had failed in North Africa because the colonized had only acquired France's "bad manners" and vices – chief among them absinthe – instead of France's broader civilization.[82] As early as 1863, an anonymous book with the title *Algeria and the Letter of the Emperor* declared the discussion about the possibilities of assimilation amongst North Africans as being over. The position of the anonymous author – that assimilation was impossible, and that association was the only possible solution to the societal challenges France faced in Algeria – was explicitly linked to absinthe drinking: "There is a word that has cast a regrettable confusion onto the problem, an unfortunate word in that it renders very inaccurately a fair idea: it is that of *assimilation*. What interest have we to assimilate the natives, that is to say, to make them absolutely similar to us? What do we care if they wear varnished boots and round hats? Is it important that they frequent the cafés in our main towns? Certainly, it is not the absinthe professors that are lacking in Algeria; but God forbid that they produce a lot of students!"[83]

To tackle the problem of a potentially growing, unrestrained absinthe consumption amongst the colonized, absinthe bans applying exclusively to the colonized were discussed in some French colonies. Gaston Doumergue, minister of the colonies between 1914 and 1917, raised the issue of alcoholism amongst the colonized in French West Africa in November 1914. As part of measures suggested by the colonial government in 1912 and 1913, Doumergue mentioned "the prohibition of the sale to the Natives of spirits of the type of 'absinthe,' particularly sought after by the blacks." Such prohibitions were regionally put into effect, but "partial prohibitions applying only to the natives would remain illusory if the Europeans established in these regions can freely import and consume 'absinthe.'" Doumergue asserted that absinthe was as dangerous to Europeans living in French West Africa as it was to the colonized. Because of this, Doumergue proposed a decree with the goal of the "absolute and general prohibition of the introduction, manufacture, circulation, and sale of spirits of the type 'absinthe' throughout French West Africa." This step, Doumergue suggested, "marks a new stage in the fight against alcoholism in our overseas possessions, responds to the duty imposed on metropolitan France by the concern for the protection of the black races, for the future of colonization, and the good name of our civilizing work in these regions."[84]

Similar to the absinthe consumption of both women and the working classes, the consumption of absinthe amongst the colonized was interpreted, by the male, French, middle-class authors used for the composition of this book, as a form of imitation of the consumption of others, in this case the allegedly heavily absinthiated French settlers. This imitation was often framed negatively, as a form of "aping,"[85] i.e., as a form of *assimilation gone wrong*. Technically, the adoption of the habits and behaviours of the French was one of the goals of French colonialism, yet the medical and psychiatric sources did not subscribe to the belief that the consumption of absinthe fell into this category. Instead, they can be found reacting negatively to unnamed others, often settlers, who allegedly believed the consumption of absinthe amongst the colonized to be a step in the direction of French civilization. The consumption of absinthe by the colonized was, overall, seen as a regrettable development, due in large parts to a violence that was believed to come with excessive absinthe consumption, as will be discussed below. The malleability of how absinthe could be interpreted is again demonstrated in these descriptions of consumption amongst colonized populations: absinthe could be seen as a tool in France's civilizing mission, as well as something that needed to be stopped for the safety of the colony, while others framed it as a weapon that the colonial state could aim at the colonized.[86]

Under the Influence of Absinthe

The absinthe consumption of bourgeois men – be it in France or in France's colonies – was generally not viewed as particularly perilous, due to what was believed to be their innate "restraint." The most worrisome aspect of their consumption was that their bourgeois habits were – allegedly – badly copied by others with less constraint: women, the working classes, children, and the colonized. When the bohème and the intelligentsia of France turned to absinthe, their drinking habits were mainly understood as dangerous to themselves, with drinkers ruining their creativity and health before their time. While absinthe-drinking women were also understood to pose a danger to themselves, it was mostly their offspring that nineteenth- and early twentieth-century sources worried about, due to contemporary fears about depopulation and racial degeneration. With (male) workers, farmers, and the colonized starting to drink, these various perceptions of the danger of absinthe accumulated: these men were a danger to themselves, to their offspring, and, above all, to those around them. This was also connected to fears that the change from wine to absinthe could lead to "working class agitation."[87] Indeed, once absinthe reached the working classes, "it started to be regarded as a threat to society."[88] In the context of working-class unruliness, absinthe drinking was often connected to the Communards, the revolutionaries in power after the siege of Paris between March and May 1871, with absinthe blamed for the uprising itself. Maxime du Camp described these Communards in 1877 as "murderers, gorged with absinthe,"[89] adding in 1881 that they believed themselves to be "knights and apostles of an unappreciated cause," while, "in truth, they were the knights of debauchery and the apostles of absinthe."[90] For many, absinthe turned – in the hands of workers and the colonized – into the "green poison,"[91] a "national peril,"[92] the "French poison,"[93] and more. In his 1897 dissertation, Robert Hazemann gloomily stated that "nowadays alcoholics, and absinthics in particular, we believe, are no longer content to shorten their [own] lives, they begin ending those of others."[94]

The journalist Henri Lierre suggested in his 1867 study of absinthe that its consumption could be divided into phases. To come to this conclusion, Lierre had both consumed absinthe himself and interviewed absinthe drinkers, stating that "the drinker always goes through three periods: that of exhilaration; that of violent overexcitement; that of torpor. Well! These three periods exist in all drunkenness, and they were admirably characterized in the Qur'an, by Mahomet, who said that Noah successively watered the vines with the blood of a monkey, a lion, and a pig."[95] Despite Lierre's claims, this story is not part of the Qur'an and seems to be, instead, part of Christian and Jewish folklore.[96] Absinthe's middle – lion – phase of "violent overexcitement" was believed to be particularly dangerous.

Violent crimes were attributed to the overconsumption of absinthe. "Absinthism predisposes in a quite special way to violent reactions and therefore to crimes of the blood," explained the French doctor Paul-Lucien Wahl in 1910.[97] In this, absinthe was, again, singled out amongst all forms of alcohol by French doctors and psychiatrists as well as the temperance movement and the press. Indeed, the absinthe bans of the early twentieth century are often credited by the secondary literature to stem from outraged reactions towards the so-called "absinthe murders" in Switzerland in 1905.[98] The connection between crime in general – and murder in particular – and absinthe seemed obvious to many nineteenth- and early twentieth-century sources.

The doctor and temperance advocate Paul-Maurice Legrain discussed the influence of absinthe on crime in an 1899 article published in *L'Alcool*, in which he first explained that humanity found only "misfortune, ruin, decrepitude, and disease" in alcohol. Under the influence of alcohol, Legrain assured his readers, man was willing "to debase himself, to lower himself to the level of the brute, to kill himself in small doses, to destroy his domestic happiness, to breed idiots, [and] to ruin his fatherland like a bad citizen." This would have been bad enough, but man's "gluttony and his base instincts needed more. He needed the sovereign liquor which not only produces all these ravages, but makes one see red, drives [one] to crime, and deprives man of the conscience of his actions as a result of healthy remorse. He invented *absinthe!*"[99] While Legrain understood alcohol as causing physical and mental issues as well as degeneration, he credited absinthe specifically with inciting unprecedented levels of violence and criminality. This action of absinthe was not only feared in France but also – perhaps even more so – in the colonies, where a minority of French settlers was believed to be surrounded by hostile masses of the colonized, who had a predilection towards absinthe and anisettes.[100] In a book entitled *Sketches of Algeria during the Kabyle War*, the army officer and author Hugh Mulleneux Walmsley described in 1858 a stroll through Algiers, in which he observed "an Arab" drinking a glass of absinthe in a café, having "previously drugged himself with opium." Walmsley explained that "the moment the fumes of the burning liquor he had superadded [to the opium] began to work, he was seized with a fit of sudden madness" and randomly attacked the people around him.[101] Walmsley clearly supposed that the unexpected violence of this "Arab" was caused by this mix of both the French opium of the West and opium itself.

An April 1915 article with the title "French National Curse Suppressed," published in *The Times*, claimed that drunkenness from absinthe was sometimes accompanied by convulsive phenomena, and could cause "nervous agitation, insomnia, and nightmares," as well as "hallucinations and profound mental troubles, which may lead to the Assize Court or to the asylum, or to both." Due to these specific symptoms of absinthe intoxication, "absinthe is a poison more powerful in murderous impulses than any other. Its victims sometimes run amok in provincial France. In a case under my notice a labourer, maddened by absinthe and armed with a long knife, rushed down a village street not far from Paris. The affrighted inhabitants sheltered in their houses." This, the unnamed journalist assured the readers of *The Times*, was not a unique occurrence: "Instances of the sort might be multiplied to show the effects of absinthe."[102] In this, *The Times* echoed opinions propagated by the French temperance movement. Legrain – and the French temperance movement he co-led – believed absinthe to have far-reaching consequences for society. For Legrain, the "hour of the aperitif is, among all [hours], the dark hour. Who will be able to count the offences, the crimes, the acts of savagery, the outbursts of fury engendered by the green fairy, this modern purveyor of prisons and the madhouse."[103] For many it seemed as if violence was intrinsically linked to the consumption of absinthe. Similar accounts of violent crimes committed by absinthe drinkers can also be found in Swiss sources. The aforementioned 1907 pamphlet arguing for the prohibition of absinthe in Switzerland, for example, quoted the unnamed director of the prison of Lausanne, in the canton of Vaud, as having stated that "*in the canton of Vaud all serious crimes (murders) in recent years have been committed by schnapps drinkers and especially by absinthe drinkers.*"[104] While not further clarified in the pamphlet, it is likely that this statement was made after the 1905 "absinthe murders" in Commugny in the canton of Vaud, and seems to have been coloured by the absinthe panic that swept Switzerland in its wake.

The most detailed nineteenth-century study of crimes committed under the influence of absinthe was Robert Henri Hazemann's medical dissertation on the topic of "Homicides amongst Absinthists," which he wrote at the University of Paris in 1897. Hazemann was active in the temperance movement and saw himself as part of a larger group who had taken on the task to "show the public authorities that the manufacture and sale of absinthe and similar liqueurs must be prohibited in France for public health and safety."[105] He was of the belief, based on his research of "authors who have dealt with the alcoholic in forensic pathology," that "most alcoholics who have committed homicides are absinthe drinkers," adding, however, that "absinthe does not lead all its enthusiasts to crime." Indeed, Hazemann believed that absinthe exacerbated existing "hereditary or accidental" issues.[106]

In his dissertation, Hazemann examined seventeen cases of homicide, "committed under the sole influence of absinthe,"[107] deducing from them that "homicide is frequent during acute or chronic absinthism."[108] For his 1897 report on Hazemann's dissertation for *L'Alcool*, Doctor L. – presumably Paul-Maurice Legrain – chose to focus on one of these cases, which concerned a thirty-four-year-old man who, after having been offered absinthe, "suddenly finds himself completely dazed." Once home, he murdered his wife, but it was only during the inquest that "he learned all these details which were unknown to him." From the perspective of Doctor L., Hazemann's case study showed how unpredictable absinthe drinkers were. He added, however, that absinthe drinkers did not necessarily "have to be imbued with absinthe [i.e., at a specific moment] to be driven to crime." This statement suggests that, according to Doctor L. at least, regular absinthe drinkers were so saturated with absinthe that crimes committed by them when they had not consumed any were still attributable to the green fairy. This turned every regular absinthe drinker into a potential threat, at any point of their lives, but especially during the hour of absinthe: "The absinthic is an easily triggered firearm. Let us beware of ever teasing a drinker, at the supreme hour of the green."[109] Abstinence advocates like Doctor L. were thus convinced that an absinthic person could pose a threat, even if the drinker had only consumed a small amount of absinthe and perhaps even – in the case of chronic absinthists – if they had not consumed any absinthe at all that day.

Hazemann explained that in all his case studies he had "noticed very special characteristics in the performance of the act itself." He mentioned the "horrible coolness" and lack of motivation behind the crime, and that these murders were "distinguished by violence, strange brutality, speed of the execution," as well as by a loss of memory after the fact. He further defined three categories of absinthic murders in his conclusions, stating that these murders were committed by somebody "1) obeying a sudden, irresistible, unconscious, automatic impulse, similar to the impulse of epileptic vertigo; 2) Under the influence of terrifying hallucinations … 3) Because the absinthic, like the epileptic, is often morally unbalanced."[110] These bizarre comparisons with epilepsy were based on the idea that absinthe caused epileptiform attacks in consumers. Like absinthe, epilepsy was believed to cause sufferers to commit "crimes and acts of violence," as can be seen, for example, in the 1907 pamphlet by Swiss absinthe opponents.[111] While the first two of Hazemann's factors were, presumably, created by the overconsumption of absinthe, the third was, clearly, a preexisting failing of the drinker. In all these cases,

Émile Laurent explained in his 1898 review of Hazemann, "affective sensitivity has disappeared in him. The suppression of a human being seems to him a trifle, a fact of little importance."[112]

In his 1897 article for *L'Alcool*, Doctor L. clarified that the characteristic loss of memory was caused by the phenomenon of "absinthic vertigo," which he compared – like Hazemann – to that caused by epilepsy. Speaking about the experiences of a friend of his, Doctor L. stated that "during his dizziness, he had kept all the appearance of a normal man, except for brutality; he had behaved like an automaton, a dangerous automaton." This, Doctor L. believed, was common to all absinthe drinkers, who would afterwards "sincerely deny [his crimes], because he will have accomplished it in a forgotten nightmare."[113] This same loss of memory can be found in one of the few case studies of a crime committed by a woman under the influence of absinthe. Ernest Monin referred in his 1889 book to a case study by Auguste Motet, which concerned a "woman injured in the face," who was arrested on the street and brought to the Hôtel-Dieu Hospital in Paris. In her home, they found her brutally murdered lover. The woman had "lost the memory of the murder she committed; she has terrible hallucinations and all the symptoms of acute alcoholism. This woman is, indeed, an alcoholic. For a long time, she had been drinking eight to ten glasses of absinthe a day: and under the influence of this intoxication, she had become wicked, jealous, violent." During the psychiatric investigation, this woman was declared not responsible for her crime.[114] Absinthe, it was believed, could lead to such moments of madness – and France was full of absinthe drinkers. The April 1915 article in *The Times* simply stated that many people in France's psychiatric institutions were absinthe drinkers, adding, however, that statistics "scarcely help us in estimating the number of the half-insane, for the majority go unrecorded until they call attention to themselves by the commission of some crime or become inmates of an asylum."[115]

These specific characteristics of crimes committed by people under the influence of absinthe led experts to question their responsibility, for instance Augustin Hamon in 1898, professor at the New University of Brussels: "Chronic hashishists, [and] alcoholics are considered irresponsible by most alienists. The same is true for chronic absinthists. But acute alcoholics, absinthists, and hashishists are still seen as enjoying their responsibility." Hamon added that Hazemann had pushed for both acute and chronic absinthists to be recognized as not responsible for their crimes, referring to Hazemann's first two reasons for absinthe murders detailed above, "for they acted under the influence of irresistible impulses, of terrifying hallucinations." Yet despite the opinions of people like Hazemann, the courts were "reluctant to see in [acute] alcoholism, [or] absinthism, a cause of irresponsibility."[116] This idea of absinthists not being responsible for their crimes seems to have been commonly accepted before Hazemann's thesis, however, as it was taken up in 1888 by Pierre Marie Lucas, who was accused of the attempted murder of a Louise Michel in Le Havre. In her 2006 article on this attempted murder, Marina Daniel explained that the accused "excused his attempted murder, saying it was [due to] *'drinking madness.' 'It was absinthe that drives me crazy,'* he said." The court looked into this but realized that his claim of having consumed absinthe that day could not be corroborated, as he had only been observed drinking rum.[117] This idea of diminished responsibility was not unique to absinthe, with Haine suggesting in 1996 that alcohol in general was often used as a defence in court between 1870 and 1900, but that this explanation was no longer referred to after 1900.[118]

In her book *Murders and Madness*, the historian Ruth Harris showed that about 25 per cent of cases of actual or attempted murders in Paris between 1880 and 1910 were committed by men who "cited alcohol as an excuse, had a drinking habit, or had been drinking before the crime."[119] While this number is high, it perhaps shows not so much how frequent murders were under the influence of absinthe, i.e., the basis of Hazemann's research, but rather that absinthe – and alcohol in general – was used as both an excuse and explanation. Harris further added that despite the consensus about absinthe's murderous impulses amongst people like Hazemann, who studied absinthe specifically, "physicians, judges, and juries generally saw absinthe-drinking as an aggravating rather than extenuating circumstance," stating that those who tried to use it in their defence were often treated harshly in court.[120]

French society came to fear crimes committed by men – and occasionally women – under the influence of absinthe, especially in the 1880s and 1890s. Newspapers of the time published sensationalized accounts of violent crimes, often focusing on the fact that, during their drunkenness, the culprits had acted in a way that did not adhere to their sober intentions[121] or that they became completely different people once they started to drink absinthe.[122] An article published in *La Presse illustrée* in October 1883 with the title "The Crimes of Absinthe," presented a series of murders and attempted murders attributed to absinthe. The first of these cases was the attempted murder of a Doctor Rochard. The culprit, who had been unknown to Rochard, had confessed, explaining that he had heard voices inciting him to kill, "to ward off bad luck." He had shot, at random, at a man in the street, who turned out to be Rochard. The psychiatrist Legrand du Saulle analyzed him and recognized him "as an alcoholic by absinthe." The next of the cases described took place in Levallois. The culprit was a Belgian brickmaker who was arrested as he attacked customers at a *marchand de vin*, as well as the owner as she intervened. The husband of the attacked woman fired his revolver in the air. "Cause of this criminal act: absinthe," concluded *La Presse illustrée*. The third case concerned the murder of young woman by her husband, "the wretch [who] was then under the alcoholic influence of absinthe." The final case took place in Belgium, where the accused, Pinktens, attacked a woman who wanted to intervene after he had publicly exclaimed that he wanted to kill his wife: "Pinktens' outbursts were caused again by the abuse of the fatal potion."[123] All these cases had happened, according to *La Presse illustrée*, within one week.

While it is possible that there were four cases of absinthe murders or attempted murders within the span of one week, *La Presse illustrée* was biased against absinthe. This bias can be clearly observed on the front page of this same issue, which showed an illustration of a skeleton next to a visibly drunk working-class man. The skeleton can be observed as pouring a glass of absinthe with its right hand, while placing a spider on the man's head with its left. This is a representation of the French saying "avoir une araignée dans le plafond" – "having a spider in the ceiling" of the head, i.e., the skull – which is a metaphor for having gone slightly insane. In this context, the spider might either represent the skeleton putting fears into the drinker's brain or be interpreted as a metaphor for the hallucinations allegedly caused by absinthe. Above the man is a row of graves. Below him are three other illustrations, marked as "madness," "infanticide," and "suicide," i.e., three of the alleged consequences of the overconsumption of absinthe. "Suicide" is represented by a man who hanged himself from a rope held by a devil sitting astride a bottle of absinthe.[124]

The conviction that absinthe caused violent reactions in people led some to view all absinthe drinkers – even occasional ones – as potentially dangerous. In his 1897 article for *L'Alcool*, Doctor L. stated that, in the presence of people suffering from absinthism, "one experiences the impression that one is in the presence of a battery charged to burst; one is instinctively on one's guard, for one senses that the slightest incident can provoke a terrible reaction. It is, alas!, what we see too often in the streets."[125] Similarly, in his 1906 book about legal aspects of mental medicine, Paul-Maurice Legrain – presumably the same Doctor L. – warned that when consuming absinthe, one should "beware of sudden, brutal, hallucinatory reactions," as drinking absinthe was a lottery:

"Never will a consumer, sitting down in full lucidity in front of his glass of absinthe, be able to affirm whether in a few moments he will not be committing a crime. The green hour is the red hour."[126]

Hazemann believed that something needed to be done to protect society from these absinthic murderers, explaining that "preventing unfortunate feeble-minded [people] from arriving [at the point of] homicide [through absinthe]" was the only way of achieving this goal: "Now, to prevent the effect, the cause must be removed. Absinthe is frequently the direct agent of homicide."[127] This led Hazemann to the conclusion that a ban on the "the manufacture and sale in France of absinthe and similar liqueurs"[128] was necessary to protect France's population from the dangers of crimes committed under the influence of absinthe.

In summary, it can be said that the idea of absinthe being a unique drink also found its way into these accounts of crimes allegedly committed by occasional absinthe drinkers as well as by chronic and acute absinthics. In addition to the conviction that absinthe caused hallucinations, the medico-psychiatric experts discussed a loss of both conscience and memory in drinkers, which was for them not characteristic of drunkenness in general, but specifically of the consumption of absinthe. The theories of chronic and acute absinthism allowed medico-psychiatric experts to both diagnose a chronic drinker, who was not currently drunk from absinthe, as acting out an absinthic madness, and to explain how somebody could commit absinthe crimes after even their very first celebration of the hour of absinthe.

Fears of absinthe crimes fuelled the absinthe panics of the 1890s and the early twentieth century. Crimes under the influence of absinthe, according to the understanding of these nineteenth- and early twentieth-century authors, were mostly committed by working-class men, as well as the occasional woman, in France, and by colonized men in France's empire. It should be added that not many case studies of crimes committed by colonized absinthe drinkers can be found in the source material, which, however, did not seem to lessen general fears about their absinthe- (or, later, anisette-)soaked criminality, as described by Pinaud,[129] in the minds of French settlers.

6

Weapon of Mass Destruction

While the diagnosis of absinthism has been discussed in passing in the previous chapters – especially in the context of the criminality caused by absinthics – nineteenth-century medico-psychiatric theories about the bodily and psychological consequences of both absinthe drinking and its overconsumption will be examined in detail in this chapter. In addition to the diagnosis of absinthism, this chapter also focuses on ideas about absinthe's addictiveness, in the context of its effects being comparable to those of opium, and explores the notion that absinthe was the biggest danger to French people in the colonies.

"Epilepsy in Bottles"[1]

The 1860s saw the emergence of the diagnosis of absinthism, based on the diagnosis of alcoholism, which had only been developed in the 1850s. According to Scott Haine, the diagnosis of alcoholism – first proposed by the Swedish doctor Magnus Huss in 1853 – was initially ignored by French doctors, who supposed it to be a problem of Northern Europe.[2] From the 1860s onward, however, French medical and psychiatric experts believed they were observing an overall increase in cases of alcoholism. Valentin Magnan, at the time a psychiatrist at the Sainte-Anne asylum in Paris,[3] gave a presentation on the topic of "alcoholism and degeneracy" with a doctor, Alfred Fillassier, at the First International Eugenics Conference, held in London in 1912. In their paper, they asked "among the unfortunates brought by insanity to the asylum, how many are driven by alcohol? The part here played by alcohol is considerable, and since 1867, has been constantly on the increase. Nay, more: since its appearance, alcohol has modified the very appearance of our asylums." This change of "appearance" of French psychiatric institutions after 1867 was mostly due to gender. Magnan and Fillassier explained that before the early 1860s, most cases admitted to the asylums of the Seine had been women, which "was attributed to her [i.e., the woman's] more nervous temperament, to her higher sensitiveness and emotionalism." Yet from the early 1860s onwards, there had been an increase in male patients, which Magnan and Fillassier put down to a "new factor, alcohol, [that] has entered the scene, more perilous for man than for woman; it poisons him, makes him mad, and brings him to the insane asylum."[4]

Prestwich explained that from the 1860s onwards – parallel to this discovery of alcoholism – French medical and psychiatric sources started to depict absinthe as having "supposedly unique characteristics that made it more dangerous than any other type of alcohol."[5] This singling out of absinthe as a uniquely hazardous drink was not limited to France. "We are not aware of any liqueur that causes such devastation in Switzerland as absinthe. Absinthe tempts abuse like no other liqueur," stated three professors, only identified as Gaule, Jaquet [*sic*, but possibly Louis Jacquet], and Weber, in a pamphlet written by Swiss absinthe opponents in 1907.[6] In his book *Taming Cannabis*, David Guba identified the 1860s and 1870s as the moment when French doctors and psychiatrists based in Algeria started to write about "hashish poisoning" and "hashish-induced insanity," which, he explained, further added "to the negative swing" in the perception of cannabis that had, up to that point, been used medicinally in France.[7] While opium was presented as a Chinese drug, hashish was perceived as clearly Muslim – and thus closely connected to France's North African colonies. Both of these intoxicating substances – absinthe and hashish – that were, in the French consciousness, intrinsically linked with Algeria, thus underwent a process of broad medical condemnation at the same time.

The first medical publication that defined the addiction to absinthe as a separate diagnosis from alcoholism seems to have been Auguste Motet's 1859 medical dissertation, with the title "General Considerations on Alcoholism, and More Particularly on the Toxic Effects Produced in Man by Absinthe." Motet did not yet define this diagnosis as absinthism. Who came up with the term is difficult to determine, but comparable vocabulary seems to have been around before the 1860s. In his 1854 article about the colonization of Algeria, for example, the aforementioned Jean-Gabriel Cappot – under the pseudonym of Capo de Feuillide – described those addicted to the drink as "absinthists." It can therefore be said that Cappot conceived the addiction to absinthe as being a separate diagnosis to alcoholism.[8]

Following contemporary definitions of acute and chronic alcoholism,[9] Motet divided absinthe drinkers into acute and chronic consumers. Acute absinthism occurred in people who did not drink absinthe regularly, but who "managed in a very short time to drink rather considerable quantities of absinthe." Chronic absinthism, on the other hand, arose in people whom Motet called "professional drinkers," who consumed absinthe regularly over a long period.[10] Yet Motet admitted that he was not "writing the story of a new disease here. What we say about absinthe relates to the great chapter of alcoholic intoxication."[11] It was chronic absinthism that particularly worried medico-psychiatric experts. The 1907 pamphlet by absinthe opponents in Switzerland highlighted this fear by referring to a definition of chronic absinthism proposed by Swiss doctors. These doctors had warned that, amongst normal consumers, "it is of little importance that each dose is too weak to cause perceptible poisoning on its own: long-lasting repetition can lead to chronic intoxication even with these small amounts."[12] Similarly, Ernest Monin explained in 1889, "relatively minor doses of this liquor suffice" to cause very serious effects.[13] The diagnosis of absinthism could, therefore, be applied to people who were not necessarily heavy absinthe drinkers, just as crimes attributed to absinthics were not necessarily committed when drunk from absinthe. This conception of chronic absinthism made every absinthe consumption – however moderate – suspicious and potentially dangerous.

Despite Motet's admission of family resemblances between absinthism and alcoholism, so to speak, absinthism was generally understood as a separate diagnosis from the 1860s onward, with distinct physical and mental symptoms, not only in France and its colonies, but also in neighbouring Switzerland, where the "anti-absinthic movement" had been well-established by the late 1890s, as explained the Swiss journalist Paul Pictet in 1908.[14] Even publications that did not use the vocabulary of absinthism as a separate diagnosis, accepted this idea of absinthe being distinct from other forms of alcohol. A 1908 pamphlet composed by Swiss absinthe opponents, for example, explained that, within the field of alcoholism, absinthe took on a "special role," due to its "particular dangers."[15]

Yet this distinction might not have been as clear in practice as it was depicted in the theoretical texts of these nineteenth-century doctors and psychiatrists. Lachenmeier et al. suggested, for example, that the "word 'absinthism' soon came to lose its specific meaning. Absinthism and alcoholism were confused, and alcohol dependent people were simply deemed 'absinthe drinkers.'"[16] As the diagnosis of absinthism became somewhat fashionable amongst the medico-psychiatric experts of the Belle Époque, diagnosing an alcoholic who occasionally also drank a glass of absinthe as an absinthic became easier. In an 1897 article published in *L'Alcool*, Doctor L. – presumably Paul-Maurice Legrain – explained that visible symptoms of absinthism, such as the "altered faces" with "brutal expressions" in their "bright, mobile, worried gaze," made it easy to recognize "brains under the influence of absinthe." L. suggested that "in our asylums, we do not need to question drinkers at length to find out their habits."[17] Under such circumstances, misdiagnosing patients with absinthism would have been easy.

Generally speaking, a person who consumed both absinthe and other distilled forms of alcohol was usually defined as absinthic and not as absinthic and alcoholic.[18] Absinthe was singled out as a unique drink, whose consumption outweighed the consumption of other alcoholic drinks. The symptoms of absinthism were believed to be severe. The article in the *Indiana State Sentinel*, published in April 1861, summarized Motet's findings of absinthism as "a general poisoning of the system, which terminates in insanity and death." Physical symptoms included "trembling of the forearm, of the hand and inferior members," a "tingling and pricking of the skin, heaviness of the limbs, and numbness," as well as a "sad and sorrowful" look to the eye. Lack of sleep, nightmares, "hallucinations, illusions, blinding of the eyes, vertigos," and more were understood to be absinthism's mental symptoms.[19] In their 1912 paper on "Alcoholism and Degeneration," Valentin Magnan and Alfred Fillassier also highlighted the occurrence of "terrifying" hallucinations as a core symptom of absinthism, which they believed as "sometimes provoking most dangerous reactions of extreme violence."[20] Due to the mental consequences associated with absinthism, absinthe became popularly known as "la correspondence," short for "la correspondance à Charenton," the quick coach to the psychiatric asylum in Charenton.[21] A short note on absinthism in the *Journal de Genève*, published in 1893, explained that there were, indeed, several "current expressions which designate this poison," each connected to one of the specific dangers commonly associated with absinthe – i.e., insanity, death, and addiction: "it is the green-eyed fairy; it's the high speed [i.e., the quick coach] to Charenton; it is the aperitif of the grave; the opium of the West."[22]

The symptoms that differentiated alcoholism and absinthism the most, in the eyes of nineteenth-century experts, were epileptiform crises. In the early 1860s, Valentin Magnan started to experiment with both alcohol and absinthe on various animals, which led him to the conclusion that the essence of wormwood caused epileptiform crises in these poor creatures.[23] In an article on "Accidents Determined by the Abuse of Absinthe," published in 1864, as well as his 1871 book on alcoholism, Magnan discussed a case study regarding a "professional drinker," a thirty-two-year-old man, who had been his patient at the Bicêtre Hospital in Paris.[24] In his 1871 book, he suggested that this case served "as a good demonstration of the special action of absinthe." This patient had been healthy before he became a wine seller in 1861, after which he started to drink various types of alcohol. In 1863, due to his consumption of absinthe, he underwent "two attacks with sudden loss of consciousness, a fall, grimacing face, convulsions of the arms and legs, bloody frothing at the lips and biting of the tongue," followed by "frightening hallucinations." The patient was institutionalized at the Bicêtre Hospital, showing signs of "acute alcoholism." He recovered quickly, however, and was released after a month. At home, he started to drink again, and "following further abuse of absinthe, an epileptic attack similar to the previous ones occurs." When only drinking wine and eau-de-vie, he slept badly, lost his appetite, and had hallucinations, but the epileptic attacks only occurred in connection with the overconsumption of absinthe, Magnan explained.[25] In an 1874 article published in *The Lancet*, Magnan further suggested that these epileptiform crises were a defining characteristic of absinthism and that "never, in the experiments with alcohol, is an epileptic attack produced, whilst this, as we are about to make evident, is the principal manifestation of poisoning by absinthe." His experiences and his research proved to Magnan that the epileptiform consequences of absinthe drinking were due to the essences in the drink.[26]

While it is possible that such seizures might occasionally have been caused by substances that were fraudulently added to absinthe, these descriptions are reminiscent of classical crises of hysteria, which were, according to Jan Goldstein's 1982 article, defined by "convulsions and spasmodic seizures," fainting, paralyses of the limbs, "losses of sensation in the skin," coughing, trance-like states, delusions, and more.[27] Jean-Martin Charcot started his research into hysteria in the 1870s, while he was chief physician at the Salpêtrière in Paris, i.e., after Magnan's initial 1864 study on these attacks in absinthics. Goldstein further suggested that Charcot's four stages of a hysterical crisis had been publicized so widely through the use of photographs that it became, towards the end of the nineteenth century, almost a guide to how "insane" people ought to express themselves.[28] The same might be true, to perhaps a lesser degree, with Magnan's discovery of epileptiform crises amongst absinthics. Sara Black discussed in her 2022 book *Drugging France* that by the 1880s, French doctors discussed morphine addiction and hysteria as "associated pathologies," with both believed to be able to cause the other.[29] While to my knowledge there has not yet been any research conducted on potential overlaps between hysteria and absinthism, it is possible that a similar correlation might be discovered.

Magnan's understanding of absinthism as defined by these epileptiform attacks was taken up by the temperance movement. The aforementioned L.M. described absinthe in his January 1896 article for *L'Alcool* as "epilepsy in bottles; it's epilepsy on the cheap, epilepsy within the reach of all budgets."[30] These attacks were described as at once very serious and rather common. The severity shows itself in the 1910 book *Crime according to Science* by the French doctor Paul-Lucien Wahl, who described these crises as "pseudo-rabies attacks and [attacks] of classical epilepsy."[31] The commonness of these attacks, on the other hand, is apparent in accounts that alleged that one could observe severe epileptiform absinthe crises in the streets. Ch. Ribouleau described in 1901 such a scene, whose sequence and vocabulary were clearly inspired by Magnan's reports: "Sometimes in the street you see a crowd; you approach them. In the middle of the circle, on the ground, a man twitches convulsively; the face is grimacing, the eyelids blink, the jaws clash, saliva tinged with blood from the biting of the tongue soils the lips, the legs are shaken by incessant movements, the breathing is anxious: he is a drinker of absinthe."[32] Ribouleau's nonchalant claim – who was himself a doctor – that such a shocking scene was just one of these things you encountered from time to time when out and about in Belle Époque France, has to be seen against the absinthe panic of the 1890s.

Once somebody started to drink absinthe, it was widely believed that there might be no escape from eventually falling victim to the dire consequences of absinthism. In his 1862 article on the "Pernicious Effects of Absinthe," Louis Figuier referred to an unspecified article in the *Feuille commerciale de Cette*, i.e., from the French city of Sète, which stated, "you can be cured of everything, except from the disease of absinthe."[33] Once a person was infected with absinthe, many proponents of the medical profession warned, it could only end in their death. Motet explained in his 1859 dissertation that "in recent years," enormous quantities of absinthe had been consumed by in France, adding that "all classes of society have accepted it, and in all classes circulate these funeral words: 'X … is dead; it was absinthe that killed him.'" Yet even this threat of certain death did not stop consumers from enjoying their glass of absinthe. "Every drinker knows what danger threatens him and, fascinated by its greenish liquor, he always comes back to it."[34] Nothing, Motet believed, could stop the progress of absinthism.

In addition to these severe consequences for the drinkers themselves, it was mostly the idea that defects caused by absinthe could be passed on to future generations that preoccupied French medical and psychiatric experts. In his 1862 book *Poisoning by Absinthe*, Victor Anselmier suggested that "from the point of view of the individual and the species, absinthe is equally redoubtable," as "the most varied troubles of functions, an irregular development of the body, epilepsy, and idiocy, this is the only legacy that the absinthe drinker bequeaths to his children."[35] Similarly, in their 1912 presentation at the First International Eugenics Conference, Magnan and Fillassier suggested that the high rates of alcoholism amongst men and women often "bring to bear on the children an hereditary taint from both sides,"[36] before lamenting that absinthism did not cause infertility,[37] as that would have been better for the French than a nation of such "tainted" children.

This degeneration of the children of absinthe drinkers was believed to be dangerous for the future of France itself, as France needed healthy citizens for both the upkeep of its position within Europe and for the maintenance of its colonial empire. The journalist Georges Maillard summarized this train of thought in his 1888 article, stating that "absinthe is a poison that wreaks incalculable havoc on the French people; it affects not only the physical health, but also the intellectual and moral health of our country." He further added that "the fatal habit of absinthe worsens every day in a hopeless way for future generations, who are affected before [even] existing. Let's continue, and soon we will not have to envy opium smokers, we will be as foolish as they [are]."[38] The fear of France falling behind, in comparison with other European nations, often led to these comparisons of the absinthe consumption amongst the French with opium, as will be discussed below. Its absinthe habit, it was feared, might turn the whole of France into something *different*. In his 1906 article, Sterling Heilig proposed that it was only the allegedly characteristic restraint of French people that had stopped France's full degeneration through absinthe: "Only the instinctive parsimony, the habitual self-watching of the

French has permitted them to play with this green fire. Its slow work is unseen – it is hidden by the pride of families, given other names by doctors, but the long effect is race degeneracy."[39]

While fears about absinthe grew, especially in the last decade of the nineteenth century, there were people who refuted the idea that the consumption of absinthe should be viewed and treated differently to other drinks. Criticism came from both absinthe enthusiasts and members of the temperance movement. Critics of the diagnosis of absinthism often highlighted the effects of alcohol in general in their publications. Henri Lierre blamed the alcohol in absinthe in his 1867 book, *The Question of Absinthe*, for the medical and social consequences of its consumption, stating that "alcohol is the big culprit!" He further added that absinthe "does not have exceptional circumstances; it is in the ordinary conditions of alcoholic beverages."[40] By contrast, others, like the psychiatrist Henri Legrand du Saulle, believed that the discovery of the damage done by the essences in absinthe somewhat contradicted Magnus Huss's diagnosis of alcoholism itself. Focusing on a report by Louis-Victor Marcé in 1864 about the epileptiform effects of these essences,[41] Legrand du Saulle wrote in 1877 that "with a stroke of the pen, he [Marcé] crossed out all the admirable research of Magnus Huss."[42] Legrand du Saulle thus argued that, with essences singled out as the ingredient that made certain substances especially dangerous, alcohol should, again, be viewed as more or less harmless.

The French politician Yves Guyot, on the other hand, critiqued the allegations against absinthe in his 1917 book *The Question of Alcohol*. He referred to a case study by Lucien Raynaud, from Algiers, who had given examples of people affected by alcohol in general, and absinthe in particular, in his 1896 article. This specific case study concerned a mason who had lived in Algeria for sixteen years, drinking four to five glasses of absinthe on weekdays and fourteen to twenty on Sunday, as well as several glasses of eau-de-vie, anisette and wine each day.[43] "I admire the innocuousness of these [glasses of] absinthe, these glasses of brandy, and these litres of wine consumed for sixteen years, which, in a hot climate, have not killed this consumer," Guyot wrote with irony. "This man has certainly abused [absinthe]. Does this prove that it is necessary to prevent others from using it?"[44] In this passage, Guyot criticized the widespread view of absinthe as a unique beverage, whose consumption was more grievous than that of other comparable drinks.

In a subchapter of his book, entitled "The Crimes of Absinthe and the Reality," Guyot further expanded on this issue. In Guyot's eyes, it had been scientifically proven that absinthe was no more harmful than other forms of alcohol. Looking at statistical evidence provided by psychiatric institutions, he concluded that fewer patients had been admitted to these institutions for their absinthe consumption than for the consumption of the hygienic drinks of wine, cider, and beer: "If absinthe is a poison, wine, cider, beer, spirits, all other aperitifs, all liqueurs, [and] all fermented and distilled drinks must also be prohibited; because the victims of these drinks account for 85 per cent [of the alcoholic patient population of these asylums], while absinthe only [accounts] for 15 per cent."[45] From Guyot's perspective, these numbers alone were a complete refutation of the 1915 absinthe ban. Indeed, for Guyot, absinthe was a scapegoat that he ominously compared to the historical role of Jewish populations in France. According to Guyot, Jules Michelet, a French historian, explained that when "the ancient Orthodox" wanted to "engage in a good persecution against heretics, which would bring them glory and profit, they began by attacking the Jews, weak, few in number, more accessible than all others to popular suspicion and prejudice. For the leaders of anti-alcoholism, absinthe played the role of the Jews." While the comparison with the Jewish population in France is uncomfortable, Guyot rightly pointed out that the French temperance movement had the ultimate goal of weakening the influence of alcohol in general, yet singled out absinthe first because it was a smaller opponent – compared with France's wider alcohol industry – and more open to attacks.[46] In Guyot's eyes, this decision was both biased and ineffective as, based on the statistical evidence provided by him, this ban would make no difference to 85 per cent of alcoholics.

The medico-psychiatric diagnosis of absinthism singled out absinthe as a uniquely harmful drink, an idea that might have been accepted widely during the Belle Époque because absinthe's uniqueness had always been part of its attraction, so to speak: it was, for many, the only drink that caused pleasant hallucinations, that represented France's presence in Algeria, and that stimulated the brains of artists and the intelligentsia. The opponents of absinthe, such as the French temperance movement, similarly highlighted absinthe's uniqueness in their texts, often focusing on its transformative powers that turned drinkers into something unrecognizable. For people used to the established discourse of the green fairy's uniqueness, it might not have been such a big step to accept that absinthe was also the only drink that instigated widespread criminality and madness amongst drinkers, that debased future generations, killed its consumers, and threatened the future of the nation itself.

Opium's French Counterpart

The entry on absinthe in the 1875 *Universal Dictionary of Ideas* by Serge Ernst defined the drink as "the opium of the West, a *slow but terrible* poison, because it threatens *at the same time the intelligence, the constitution, and the life!*"[47] To nineteenth-century critics of absinthe, the dangers of the drink mirrored the dangers of opium. Such comparisons were used to communicate absinthe's threat to potential consumers. "For the past ten years, in the large centres of populations, but primarily in Paris and Algeria, a disturbing consumption of absinthe happened! All classes of society have accepted with an inexplicable eagerness the use of this strange drink: undoubtedly, there is something in this as disastrous as what happens in China with regards to opium," wrote the psychiatrist Henri Legrand du Saulle in 1864.[48] Like Legrand du Saulle, many contemporary French – and Swiss[49] – observers believed that the sought-after hallucinatory effects of both absinthe and opium, their addictive natures, and the medical consequences of these substances were all comparable. A further connection between these two substances was that many of the famous absinthe drinkers – such as Charles Baudelaire and Arthur Rimbaud – were also avowed opium smokers.[50] Indeed, both absinthe and opium were believed to deeply incapacitate consumers. "Absinthe is the opium of the West," explained the French doctor André Pascal in 1864, and "like opium among the Orientals, absinthe today exerts a disastrous attraction amongst city workers; it is to absinthe that the unfortunate father of a family turns to forget his miseries; it is still in absinthe that he seeks a remedy for the diseases which devour his children, and who, more often than not, would only need bread and more substantial food to repair their weakened forces, and not this disastrous poison, which wears them out more and more, [and] finally leads them to death."[51] This passage, framing absinthe as a working-class problem even before its prices fell during the phylloxera crisis, depicted the addition to absinthe – similar to that of opium – as having disastrous consequences not only for the individual, but their children and, implicitly, the French nation, thus depriving it of healthy citizens.

These comparisons between absinthe and opium highlight the frightening, mysterious and scandalous role that absinthe played in the imagination of many French people in the last decades of the nineteenth century. Absinthism was an addiction, just like the addiction to opium. Absinthe was also occasionally compared to other drugs. The French doctor Georges Saint-Paul – under the pseudonym of Dr Laupts – described absinthe in 1896 as the most dangerous form of alcohol, "this morphine of the vulgar."[52] Yet from the early 1860s onward, some French authors, critical of absinthe, started to openly liken it to opium, framing opium as an "Oriental" drug and absinthe as its French counterpart. This interlinking of absinthe and opium must be seen in the context of the Second Opium War, in which France and Britain fought against the Qing dynasty in China. The Second Opium War started in 1856 and lasted until 1860, the very year of Paul de Saint-Victor's article – with the first mention of absinthe as the opium of the West – published in *La Presse*.[53] During this period, both China and opium were on the minds of the French, reflected by the fact that 1862 was the year of the publication of the advert for Absinthe chinoise (see Fig. 3.3).

Additionally, since 1858 the French had been militarily – and economically – involved in parts of the world that later became the French colony of Indochina, with Cochinchina – southern Vietnam – officially becoming a French colony in 1862.[54] While some of the opium consumed in France came from Indochina, those in France who warned of opium as an evil often believed it to come from the "Far East," according to the historian Hans Derks's 2012 book *History of the Opium Problem*, a mechanism which hid the actual producers of opium – French settlers – and instead blamed the "Chinese."[55] Indeed, as Sara Black pointed out, much of the opium sold and used medicinally in France in the second half of the nineteenth century actually came from Smyrna, i.e., İzmir in modern-day Turkey,[56] or was even grown in France itself,[57] yet the comparisons of absinthe with opium depicted the latter as plainly anchored in "China." The French instituted a state monopoly on opium – a so-called *régie* – in 1882 in Indochina, which they believed would help them in making the colony profitable.[58] Derks further explained that, unlike other Western countries, the French viewed opium as a sort of "oriental luxury," fitting in with the fashion for *chinoiserie*.[59]

Outside of France, opium was understood as being far more dangerous than alcohol. In a 1910 article for the *American Journal of Sociology*, for example, Johann Friedrich Scheltema, who had himself lived in Java, described opium as an "unmitigated curse, corroborated on high medical authority. The moderate and even the minimum opium-eater is a slave to his stimulant as the moderate alcohol-drinker is not."[60] This belief in even small amounts of opium being dangerous was openly contradicted by some French authors, who instead reminded their readers that moderation and self-control were the important factors in deciding whether these substances were dangerous or not. "But it is with opium in China as with absinthe in Algeria; not all those who use it, abuse it," advised the French military doctor Louis de Santi to readers of his book about medicine in Cochinchina.[61] Lack of restraint was often depicted, by nineteenth- and early twentieth-century sources, as a characteristic of non-French populations, which made the consumption of the same substance more dangerous in the hands of the non-French.

As Frank Proschan explained in a 2002 article, those in France who agreed with Scheltema's dire assessment only worried about the opium consumption amongst the European population of their colony of Indochina, not about that of the colonized,[62] the latter's consumption often only discussed in terms of spreading the habit to the French. In 1912, for example, the eminent French psychiatrist Emmanuel Régis explained that the habit of smoking opium had been imported to France by returning "civil servants, civilians, sailors and military," who had contracted the habit from the colonized populations in Indochina. In Régis's eyes, the spread of opium in France was the revenge of the colonized: "And this is how the vanquished avenged himself on his conqueror by inoculating him [i.e., the conqueror] with his dangerous atavistic passion."[63] When directly discussing the opium consumption by local populations in China or Indochina, their habits were also sometimes used to attack the absinthe consumption in Europe. An 1865 article published in the Swiss journal *Le conteur vaudois*, for example, by an author only given as E.G., exclaimed: "O Chinese [man]! Do we really have the right to throw stones at you? You savour opium, because it gives you ecstatic pleasures; because you do not realize the havoc it wreaks on your morale; because in the end you are there [in the addiction to opium], without knowing it, pushed by the Englishman who provides you with contraband?" This hypothetical Chinese opium consumer was, in the eyes of this journalist, not fully responsible for his consumption – unlike the absinthe consumer in Europe: "We drink absinthe [which is] just as pernicious as opium, but which does not give ecstasy; we drink it, knowing very well that it is harmful; finally, we drink it spontaneously and without being pushed by any smuggler."[64]

This conception of absinthe being on a par with opium hints at fears about wider societal decay, as well as deep worries about individual French people losing their Frenchness by becoming addicted to it. In his 1863 book on absinthe, the French doctor Ferdinand Moreau explained that, in addition to the purely medical consequences of absinthe consumption in France, there was also a serious social component, as "absinthe has been seen as a social plague threatening to invade all classes of society, and as being for us what opium and hashish are for the Oriental civilizations."[65] In these comparisons with opium, opium consumers were often depicted as living in misery, disorder, and – not dissimilar to those partaking in the hour of absinthe – in languor and lethargy.[66] Such comparisons should be viewed as a warning about a state of misery that French absinthe consumers might slip into under the thrall of the green fairy. This idea of absinthe being both a danger to the individual consuming it and a social plague for the whole nation justified calls to oust absinthe from France.[67]

The French medical profession consciously used these direct comparisons with opium to attack absinthe. The earliest of these comparisons found during my research was in Auguste Motet's 1859 medical dissertation, in which he stated that, in France, "there is something as fatal and as stupid, as what is happening in China with regard to opium" – namely absinthe. Additionally, according to Motet, the "general disturbances" of opium and absinthe were "almost constantly the same."[68] This conviction of a deep connection between opium and absinthe also shaped the view of absinthe drinkers, as "the identity of the drink eventually rubs off on the drinker."[69] Three years after Motet and two years after Paul Saint-Victor's article, the French doctor Louis Figuier's description of absinthe mixed the vocabulary of both Motet and Saint-Victor: "The strange and universal fascination exercised by this liquor has something inexplicable and fatal; it reminds [us] of what happens in China with regard to opium, and one could say that absinthe has become the opium of the West."[70] This passage of Figuier's was, in turn, referenced by other nineteenth-century sources. It was quoted, among others, by Apollinaire Bouchardat and Henri Junod in 1863,[71] by Louis François Étienne Bergeret in 1870,[72] and by Daviller in 1889.[73]

This development of comparing a substance prevalent in France to opium was not unique to absinthe. In an 1844 book, the Belgian photographer Jean-Baptiste-Ambroise-Marcellin Jobard referred to beer as "Occidental opium"[74] – the very same year that saw Karl Marx's formulation of religion being the "*opium* of the people."[75] From the mid-1850s onward, some French authors started to decry tobacco as the opium of the West. In 1855, the writer Édouard Gorges described tobacco in a way that is reminiscent of comments about absinthe, suggesting that, through its consumption, "the races of Europe" would fall into depravity and degradation, plunging them "into the stupid stupefaction of the peoples of the East. Tobacco is the opium of the West."[76] Gorges's offensive comment about the "peoples of the East" shows that such comparisons with opium – while being disrespectful about non-French populations

– were meant to ridicule those French individuals who behaved like people who were understood to be inferior to them.

While the idea of absinthe having earned the title of opium of the West became prominent after Paul de Saint-Victor's 1860 article, comparisons between tobacco and opium continued.[77] The phrase opium of the West also came to be applied to substances other than beer, tobacco, and absinthe. Articles published in *Le Soleil* in October 1882,[78] *Le Figaro* in June 1883,[79] and *Rapports et Délibérations* in August 1900[80] applied the phrase to alcohol in general, while an 1891 article in *La Petite Presse*[81] and Laurent Tailhade in a study on morphine addiction in 1907 described morphine as the "opium of the West."[82] After the prohibition of absinthe, other drinks were also sometimes compared with opium by French authors. The weekly journal *L'Eveil de l'Indochine* published an article entitled "The Abuse of Tea Is Worse than the Abuse of Opium" in May 1933, written by R. de la Porte.[83] This article was based on fears about an addiction to tea ravaging Tunisia at this time.[84] De la Porte suggested that the motivations behind – and potentially the effect of! – the consumption of tea and opium were, essentially, the same: "What does the opium addict search for, the alcoholic, the tea drinker? He tries to get out of himself, to forget his worries, the miseries of his existence for a moment."[85]

Independent of who first applied the phrase *opium of the West* to an addictive substance that was perceived as problematic – and deeply harmful to the nation – its application to absinthe was rapidly accepted, both in France and abroad. Four months after Paul de Saint-Victor's article in *La Presse*, the phrase – and the associated fears of the medical and social consequences of masses of absinthe drinkers – had crossed the Atlantic. On 10 April 1861, the article in the *Indiana State Sentinel* warned its US readers about absinthe, stating that due to "the actual irresistible power which it wields over its victims as well as ... the similarity of its effects and the general and increasing popularity it has acquired, [it] may not improperly be called the 'opium of the West.'"[86] This direct comparison with opium acted as a shortcut, allowing those readers of the *Indiana State Sentinel* who did not know what absinthe was to understand that it was dangerous and highly addictive. Even a single glass of absinthe, it was believed, could start consumers on their road to addiction. In a 1908 article on absinthe, published in the *Journal de Genève*, the unnamed author explained that if somebody who had just consumed his first glass of absinthe was told that "he poisoned himself, he will shrug his shoulders. He will not believe you any more than the morphine beginner or the one who smoked his first pipe of opium."[87] If one started to consume absinthe – or opium – there was a steep price to pay, is the clear moral of such accounts. "The *opium* of the Orientals and the *absinthe* of the Occidentals are, in the twentieth century, the two great knock-out blows to human reason: *black poison* and *green poison* make people pay dearly for the moment of voluptuousness that one asks of them," wrote Éphrem Aubert in 1904,[88] quoting a French doctor with the name of Solmon.[89] What I have translated here as "knock-out blows" was given in the text as "assommoirs." While this was commonly used as a name for a drinking establishment, the author referred to the original meaning of the verb "assommer," which means to knock out.

Absinthe was depicted as a real threat to both France's national interests and to France's colonial empire. In his 1863 monograph, Casimir Frégier stated that the dangers of habitual absinthe consumption "remind [us] of what happens in China with regards to opium … and one could say that absinthe has become the opium (and the hatchich [hashish]) of Western Europe and North Africa."[90] From the 1830s onward, i.e., at the very moment of absinthe's initial spread throughout the French army in Algeria, hashish came to be seen, in certain circles, as a "dangerous, violence-inducing intoxicant" in France, as Guba showed.[91] Comparing absinthe with opium and hashish – both viewed as dangerous and destructive not only to individuals but also to nations – must have stirred up deep fears in a metropolitan, or, in the case of Frégier's book, settler readership, which probably included occasional participants in the hour of absinthe. As the phrase opium of the West was used as a shortcut by authors trying to conjure up alarm and fear in their readers, it was also connected to debates about the particular violence of absinthe drinkers. In an article in the daily newspaper *Le Vélo*, published in January 1897, the French journalist Pierre Robbe asked whether Paris was on its way to "become another Java?"[92] This question alluded to the European fascination with "running amok," i.e., the conviction that Malay people – under the influence of spirits – suddenly attacked people in a blind rage. Jenny Wade explained in a 2022 article that amok was "misrepresented, degraded, and pathologized" by European observers as a blind rage and that it was instead originally a "combat tactic."[93]

In reference to this phenomenon of random violence, according to Robbe, French people "are led to believe it," when reading "the details of this savage crime committed the day before yesterday near the Place des Victoires, in broad daylight, in the middle of the teeming crowd of a business district."[94]

The attempted murder of a man by the name of Guy de Malmignati by Octave Blin was reported by many newspapers.[95] Robbe suggested that this crime had been committed under the influence of absinthe: "It was the Western opium, the horrible adulterated absinthe of the assommoirs [i.e., working-class drinking establishments], that infuriated this malevolent brute to insane rage, of which an unknown, the first [person] he met, became the victim. Octave Blin, gorged with the 'green,' ran his 'amok' and it's lucky that he did not disembowel twenty people before being arrested."[96] Robbe was not alone in likening absinthe's effect to both opium and "running amok." The French doctor Gabriel Pouchet similarly wrote in a 1901 book that Black people in general – using the worst possible slur – and "the Javanese, but especially the Malay, display under the influence of opium a more or less violent excitement that I cannot compare better than to the excitement caused by absinthe: disorders, violence, murder, such are, in fact, the results that are most often observed and that have been noticed a very long time ago."[97]

The danger of the green fairy was often directly connected to fears of racial degeneration, reminding readers that their innocent participation in the hour of absinthe had severe consequences on future generations. One example of this can be found in Dominique Thierrin's 1896 monograph, in which he described absinthe as having been "nicknamed the opium of the West."[98] According to Thierrin, opium was in fact less dangerous than alcohol, asserting that "nothing is more lamentable than this bastardization of the race. As we have said, opium does not wreak such great havoc among the Chinese [as alcohol amongst the French]. The drunkard's child is almost inevitably a drunkard, an idiot, or a danger to society. The drinker therefore not only ruins his health, but he compromises in advance that of his descendants … He wastes his energy, his virility at the cabaret, he *drinks* the health and reason of his children."[99] In addition to striking fear into the hearts of absinthe drinkers, these comparisons with Chinese opium smokers, as mentioned in the context of Gorges's quote about tobacco,[100] were meant to shame French absinthe drinkers. In his 1889 article, the French doctor Daviller compared French absinthe drinkers with "the opium smoker or the hatschis [hashish] eater, with this difference that it [the scene of absinthe consumption] is in the West and not in the East, in France and not in China or the Indies, in the most civilized city in the world, the most educated and most enlightened [city]. The Oriental can draw an excuse from his ignorance and his misery, the intelligent Frenchman has none; it is willed degradation, it is a knowingly acquired vice, it is the fatal crowning of a pernicious habit," which left the drinkers with an existence that was "useless and often harmful to society."[101] While the consumption of opium by populations in the "Orient" was understood as them not knowing any better, the consumption of absinthe was depicted as degrading and unworthy of Frenchmen. Such statements should be seen in the context of contemporary theories, which claimed that there were not only differences between the races, but a clear racial hierarchy, cemented by France's colonial experiences.

In the context of absinthe being presented as having the power of *un-Frenching* consumers, it should be mentioned that that there were also antisemitic attacks on the drink. These started after Arthur and Edmond Weil-Picard had acquired a large share of Pernod Fils in 1894, prompted by the fact that they were of Jewish descent. Jad Adams further explained that, from this point on, antisemitic voices in France, led by Edouard Drumont – himself a French settler in Algeria and founder of the Ligue nationale anti-sémitique de France in 1889 – started to depict absinthe as non-French and "a tool of the Jews."[102] There were even two absinthes produced with the stated intentions of making this now foreign absinthe French again, under the highly offensive name of "anti-Jewish absinthe" ("absinthe antijuive"). One of these was produced in Montbéliard, in the Doubs region of France, and one in Algiers,[103] showing once again this duality of absinthe as both French and as intrinsically linked to French settlers in Algeria.

Unsurprisingly, these comparisons of absinthe and opium were used to demand governmental action against the former. In 1867, Henri Lierre referred to absinthe as not "less compelling than the opium in the Orient," and, referring to a petition asking the French senate to ban absinthe, asked whether it was "true, as stated in the report of 20 March 1867 [on that petition], that absinthe is comparable to opium? Is it true that it is *the dangerous liquor, the fatal liquor, the pernicious liquor* par excellence? Should it be banned in the name of morality, in the name of public health?"[104] This idea of absinthe deserving to be restricted, based on its similarities with opium and other drugs, can also be found in publications linked to other countries and French colonies. In 1907, for example, Swiss opponents of the drink suggested that absinthe, "recognized as particularly dangerous," should be banned by the Swiss national government, just like morphine, "which is only available on medical prescription."[105] This likening of a potential absinthe ban with existing limitations of drugs can be found very regularly in medical publications. "An intelligent government should outlaw [absinthe] on a par with opium, arsenic, and digitalis," wrote Émile Delauney in 1877, quoting a French doctor, whom he called "Doctor xxx," who had been working in the Algerian city of Misserghin.[106] Similarly, the French doctor Paul Remlinger suggested in his 1912 article about alcoholism in Morocco that "France must preserve the soldiers and settlers that she sends to Morocco as much as possible from the alcoholic peril." In addition, as the "protective state" in the protectorate contract, France also had duties towards the Moroccans themselves, Remlinger believed: "The importation of opium, that of hashish, even that of snuff is banned in Morocco. Could it not be the same for absinthe?"[107]

Once bans on absinthe were introduced outside of France, this development was compared with opium too. In May 1907, an author only given as St de H. wrote an article on the Ligue nationale contre l'alcoolisme, which had been initially founded in 1895, for the daily Catholic newspaper *La Croix*. This article claimed that it was "necessary to succeed in eliminating absinthe, and [that] in this respect, Switzerland is a lesson for us. In the canton of Geneva, the retail sale of absinthe has been prohibited. China itself has resolved to get rid of opium. We can do no less than emulate the example set by these countries."[108] Here, for the first time, China and the Chinese were not portrayed in a bad light per se; instead, France was somewhat humiliated by being behind China – and its neighbour Switzerland – in its progress.

These direct comparisons between absinthe and opium were mocked by some. The French doctor Adolphe Armand wrote in 1873 a *Treatise on the General Climatology of the Globe*, in which he discussed the issue of opium smoking in China. Having travelled through China, he suggested that publications on the issue were "usually caught in exaggeration." To explain, Armand suggested a hypothetical situation to his readers, of the ambassadors to Japan or Annam – the French protectorate of Central Vietnam – visiting France and, upon their return, informing the citizens of their countries of a "widespread and pernicious habit" prevalent in France: "they drink usually wine and other fermented beverages, including eau-de-vie, kirsch, absinthe; enraged by these detestable drugs, they end up losing their reason completely, and they soon fall into physical and moral degradation, characterized by stupor and brutishness, called by the scholars of this country, alcoholic intoxication or *delirium tremens*. Their children are only little monsters, idiots through this hereditary vice; the entire population, degraded, damaged, and decrepit, tends towards a general degeneration, and even in the destruction of the species, which soon, it must be believed, will have disappeared from this piece of the earth called Europe." Armand further explained that such biased reports on the situation of absinthe in France would, naturally, influence how France was viewed in these countries: "By reading such a report in the *Gazette* of Peking, of Yeddo [the former name of Tokyo], or of Hue, you would shrug your shoulders out of pity, about the words of these superficial travellers, who, to make a great effect, hasten to draw conclusions from the particular to the general, and [who] make an exception the rule. However, this is the trap that most of the narrators, or compilers fell into, who spoke about the smoking of opium."[109] While this hypothetical account was meant to attack those who wrote sensationalist reports about opium in China, Japan, or Indochina, Armand's retelling of how a fictional ambassador from one of these countries might describe the consumption of absinthe in France is strikingly reminiscent of the accounts prevalent in France at the time! While writing a clear pastiche, he covered most of the points that absinthe opponents feared the overconsumption of the green fairy would lead to in France.

While direct parallels between opium and absinthe addiction nominally counteracted the theory of absinthe's uniqueness, they nevertheless positioned absinthe as a drink apart. Howard Padwa pointed out that Thomas de Quincey, in his famous 1821 *Confessions of an English Opium Eater*,[110] depicted alcohol and opium as "diametric opposites,"[111] a belief that, if perhaps not openly voiced, is certainly present in these nineteenth- and early twentieth-century accounts. Yet opium was seen by many as similar to absinthe, and such comparisons depicted absinthe as plainly different – and more dangerous – than any other comparable beverage. This framing of absinthe as the opium of the West was clearly intended as a warning, to keep French people from turning to the drink: in addition to absinthism's severe physical and mental consequences, and the allegedly uncharacteristic crimes committed by consumers, drinkers had to fear racial degradation in every sip. In an imperialistic world defined by a strict racial hierarchy, reports, using the construct of the opium of the West, turning French citizens into the Chinese other, implicitly argued that absinthe drinkers voluntarily stepped back from their position of leadership. Unsaid in these comments is the fear that, if too many individuals voluntarily underwent this alleged racial degradation, France as a nation might be forced to step back too.

Death by Absinthe in the Colonies

Absinthism was believed to be fatal in France, but even more so in France's colonial empire. An article published in the *Journal de Genève* in July 1908 discussed the dangers of absinthe, ending with the following anecdote: "They asked General Drude, on his return from Africa, what the most terrible enemy he had had to fight in Morocco was. He answered without hesitation: 'Absinthe.'"[112] The French general Antoine Drude had led French troops in precolonial Morocco after the bombardment of Casablanca in August 1907. This idea of absinthe being France's most fearsome foe in the colonies was widespread from the 1850s – possibly as early as the 1840s – onward. The famous French author Gustave Flaubert composed a short entry on absinthe in his unfinished *Dictionary of Received Ideas*, posthumously published in 1913. His aphoristic entry on absinthe simply said: "Extra-violent poison: one glass and you are dead. The journalists drink it while they write their articles. Has killed more soldiers than the Bedouins."[113] Flaubert's comments were obviously ironic – he clearly did not believe that one glass of absinthe killed consumers, nor that all journalists wrote under its influence. There is therefore no reason to believe that he was any less ironic in his statement about the number of people killed by absinthe. However, while Flaubert's short entry on absinthe might have ridiculed this idea, many authors seem to have taken this claim seriously.

The point of origin for both the diagnosis of absinthism and the idea of absinthe being the opium of the West seems to have been Auguste Motet's 1859 dissertation. Consequently, Motet is often taken as the starting point for the absinthe panics in France. The idea of a colossal fatality of absinthe drinkers in France's colonies, however, preceded Motet, and might have influenced him in this assessment. By the time he wrote his dissertation, the connection of death and absinthe under the Algerian sun was already established. According to Motet himself, the French, "not content with poisoning themselves at home, went to take their murderous potion to their colonies in Africa [i.e., in Algeria]."[114] During the 1860s, in parallel with the medical disputes about absinthism, there were increasingly strident claims that absinthe had killed more French people in Algeria during the military conquest and the early colonization of the region than the climate, diseases, and the weapons of the resisting colonized populations combined.

The action of the climate, the foreign diet, and the various exotic diseases in the colonies were all seen to have graver effects on European bodies when combined with absinthe drinking, which was also believed to predispose European bodies to these diseases.[115] Medical experts found it difficult to distinguish authoritatively between symptoms of absinthism and Europeans suffering from the various threats posed by the environments of these colonies. Doctor Michel Lévy, for example, stated in 1862 that absinthe had "been one of the destructive scourges of Algeria, where its effects are recorded intermixed with those of non-acclimatization."[116]

It was widely believed that absinthe had two different active ingredients: alcohol of a poor quality and essences that gave the drink its distinct taste and look. Due to this division, the deadliness of absinthe was often differentiated – if sometimes awkwardly – from other forms of alcohol in the source material. This can be seen in the 1862 *Manual of Practical Algerian Agriculture* by Émile Cardon, in which he stated: "Strong liquors, eau-de-vie, absinthe especially, are very dangerous in Africa [in Algeria]; strong liquors have killed more people than fevers, absinthe has killed more soldiers than the Arab bullets."[117] Here, the fatal consequences of strong liquors were detached from those of absinthe – even though absinthe had been counted amongst the strong liquors in the first part of the same sentence – and absinthe was presented as having caused large numbers of military casualties. Due to the climate, non-acclimatization, and fears about adulteration of the drink,[118] absinthe consumption in the colonies was regularly presented as having fatal consequences. This was exacerbated by rumours about absinthe in the colonies being adulterated, which lasted until its prohibition. Paul Remlinger mentioned in a 1912 article that aniseed had been added to "alcohol of the lowest quality," "veritable German rubbish," in precolonial Morocco, in order to fraudulently produce some sort of absinthe or anisette.[119]

To nineteenth-century readers, the fatality of absinthe in the colonies must have seemed alarming. Pierre Marbaud wrote in 1860 that a very large – if unspecified – number of the earliest French settlers in Algeria had succumbed to fever caused by their absinthe consumption: "From all the individuals who were sent us in this stormy time, barely 200 remained in Algeria; all the others were killed by absinthe fever, or have gradually returned to France."[120] This, in turn, was understood as a weakening – or even a defeat – of France's position in the colonies. While the role of absinthe in the deaths of those early settlers remains vague in Marbaud's quote, other authors were more specific in their descriptions of the lethal consequences of absinthe overconsumption.

The earliest mention found while researching this book of absinthe being, for French settlers in Algeria, more deadly than – or as deadly as, in this specific case – the climate, disease, or resistance from the colonized was composed for a short note in the journal *Akhbar: Journal d'Algérie* in December 1845, which will be discussed in detail below.[121] This idea seems to have been taken up by Alexandre François Baudet-Dulary, a country doctor by his own definition, who published in 1856 the second extended edition of his book *Popular Hygiene*.[122] In this second edition, Baudet-Dulary added the following statement about absinthe: "The soldier will not forget that excesses of all kinds are fatal after [a] great fatigue, more fatal under a foreign, hot climate, subject to epidemics. In Algeria, absinthe has killed more men than the iron and fire of the Arabs."[123] Baudet-Dulary's account firmly placed these deaths among the military, and he conformed with the contemporary anti-absinthe discourse discussed above by blaming "excesses" for the fatalities. However, in the publications of many other authors, abuse or excess was not explicitly mentioned and it is therefore not entirely clear whether it was the abuse of absinthe or its mere consumption that was seen to be the threat.

Some of these formulations were in comparison with the resistance to the French war of conquest by the Algerian population, usually in the shape of a direct reference to their weapons, or, less often, to the martial qualities of the "Arabs." As such, the feared consequences of absinthe consumption should also be seen as a denigration of the Algerian fighters or of the quality of their weaponry. In these following examples, "Africa" should always be read as Algeria. French authors stated that absinthe killed "more men than the lead of the Arabs" (in 1858);[124] slew "more Europeans than the sword of Abd-el-Kader" in Algeria (in 1859);[125] killed "in Africa more soldiers than the bullets of Abd-el-Kader" (in 1862),[126] "more soldiers than the Arab bullets" (in 1862),[127] more people "than the Arabs" (in 1864),[128] "more soldiers in Algeria than Arab bullets" (in 1867);[129] that it made "more victims than the Arab bullets ever made" (in 1867);[130] that it killed "more Europeans than the lead of the Arabs" (in 1868);[131] that it decimated "our African army *more* than the bullets of the Arabs" (in 1868);[132] that it killed "in Algeria, more French soldiers than the bullets of the Arabs" (in 1876)[133] and "more of our soldiers than the lead of the Arabs" (in 1887).[134] The Abd-el-Kader mentioned in these comparisons is the very same depicted as drinking a glass of absinthe with sultan Abdul Hamid II in the "Future Monument of Peace" by Absinthe Rivoire (Fig. 3.4)!

Interestingly, this formulation was also adapted to other geographic contexts. The Swiss theological journal *Schweizerischer Kirchenzeitung*, for example, published in 1873 an article on the lives of Swiss soldiers, in which the unnamed author suggested that "brandy, beer, wine, and absinthe turn far more soldiers pale and cold than the Prussians could shoot with all their needle rifles."[135] While this author was clearly influenced by the earlier comments on the effects of absinthe in Algeria, this hypothetical passage is overall less confrontational, as Switzerland was not at war with Prussia at the time of its composition: it was a hypothetical comparison, meant as a warning about the apparently questionable state of the Swiss army.

Absinthe was similarly compared to various deadly diseases and the climate. In this context, it should be noted that the claim of absinthe killing more French soldiers and settlers in Algeria than diseases – especially during the initial military conquest – is absurd. In his 1998 book *Disease and Empire*, the historian Philip D. Curtin showed that in the 1860s, the death rates for French troops in Algeria of malaria were four times as high as those for British troops in India.[136] These comparisons between the fatalities of absinthe and diseases are even more striking if one considers that many of them were made by members of the French medical profession. It was proposed that absinthe "kills more surely than pernicious fever" in Algeria (in 1862);[137] that it "has killed more men in Algeria than the war and the climate" (in 1873);[138] that it "had harvested in Algeria more victims than fever and Arab bullets" (in 1877);[139] that it made "more victims than bullets and cholera combined" (in 1889);[140] that it "has made more victims than bullets and fevers together [in Algeria and Tonkin]" (in 1890);[141] and that it was "more fatal to the human race than the plague and cholera" (in 1896).[142] In a 1910 presentation, the French doctor Paul Houdeville similarly stated: "And yet, how many victims has she [absinthe] made, much more than the climate or the fevers! In Africa, during the conquest of Algeria, she has killed more of our soldiers than the bullets of Abd-el-Kader."[143]

These formulations are so similar that they all seem to quote the same original source, yet no actual written source is ever referenced, which points to this concept of the deadliness of absinthe being a popular claim, present in anti-absinthe narratives and taken up as fact by these authors. The question of who came up with this bizarre formulation is not usually addressed by these nineteenth- and early twentieth-century sources. In the few sources that do, the formulation is credited to some unnamed army doctor or general. The French doctor Th. Fauré, for example, referred in his 1867 book to a "saying by I do not know what military doctor, a saying filled with truth: 'Absinthe has killed more soldiers in Algeria than Arab bullets.'"[144] The same year, Clément Ollivier, also a doctor, explained that he had "heard a trustworthy surgeon

Absinthe! fléau qui, en Afrique, a tué plus de soldats que les balles des Arabes et la fièvre. (Maréchal Bugeaud.)

Figure 6.1
Drawing of two tables at which sit three men in various stages
of drunkenness from absinthe, with the caption: "Absinthe,
a scourge which, in Africa, has killed more soldiers than Arab
bullets and the fever. (Maréchal Bugeaud.)"

repeat that in Algeria absinthe made more victims than the Arab bullets ever made."[145] In his 1864 book, on the other hand, the French professor of chemistry Jean Girardin suggested that "one of our African generals [i.e., a French general in Algeria] said that absinthe killed more of his people than the Arabs."[146] The only specific person mentioned as the origin of this saying seems to have been Maréchal Thomas-Robert Bugeaud. Éphrem Aubert suggested in 1910 that Bugeaud, who had been governor-general of Algeria between 1841 and 1847 – and who was, possibly, responsible for banning absinthe in the French army in Algeria – had allegedly first said it regarding alcohol in general. According to Aubert, "it is derived from the testimony of Mr Donot, teacher at Boukanéfis (in the department of Oran). 'Alcohol kills more men than the sword,' said Maréchal Bugeaud.'"[147] Bugeaud was also depicted as the source of this saying – this time specifically about absinthe – in an 1889 sketch, which can be seen in Fig. 6.1.

While the earliest comparisons can be traced back to the 1850s, the height of their popularity stems from the 1860s and 1870s. By the 1850s, however, there had already been a basis for this belief about the extreme fatality of absinthe in Algeria, as can be inferred from the absinthe bans of the 1840s and 1850s. On either 23 or 25 December 1844,[148] the Francophone newspaper *Akhbar: Journal d'Algérie* published a short note on four French officers, "including two health [officers], [who] have just been sent to France, suffering from mental alienation. The origin of their illness was the abuse of spirits, especially [of] absinthe. The immoderate use made of this spirit in Algeria can be considered a real public calamity. It is difficult to list the many victims it has already claimed. Despite the ravages produced by absinthe (which had to be prohibited at the outposts), the sale of it increased day by day. A single merchant provided 60,000 litres here. We regret that we have no effective remedy to offer for a real and only worsening evil, because absinthe has killed almost as many people as the Arabs."[149] The prohibition of absinthe in the Algerian "outposts" mentioned in this passage is the earliest mention of an absinthe ban I have found during my research. In his 1845 report about his medical voyage through Algeria, the Italian doctor Salvatore Furnari also referred to this passage in *Akhbar*, which led him to the conclusion that the prohibition of alcohol in the Qur'an protected Muslims from the development of mental issues.[150] Finally, on 26 September 1845, the day before the first general prohibition of absinthe was instituted in the French army,[151] the twice-weekly newspaper *L'Algérie* also published a second short note taken from *Akhbar* about the dangers of absinthe.[152]

The historian Nessim Znaien suggested in his 2022 article on alcohol prohibitions in French colonies that a form of anti-alcoholism was constructed in the colonies from the middle of the nineteenth century onward, predating, or at least contemporary to, developments in France. In his argument, Znaien specifically referred to the 1854 article by Jean-Gabriel Cappot, published under the pseudonym of Capo de Feuillide, about the colonization of Algeria.[153] In this article, Cappot deplored the omnipresence of drinking establishments in Algeria, which, he believed, caused drunkenness. Amongst the alcoholic drinks sold in these débits, "absinthe was the most commonly offered there, just as its use was the most universally widespread." After his claim that the French settlers in Algeria drank more absinthe than the rest of the world combined, Cappot added that "no one today, no more in Africa than in France, does not know what havoc this drink has wrought on the entire organism of the unfortunates, who were designated by the nickname of *absinthists*. All stumbled and are still stumbling along to death or to idiotic madness, [which is] even worse!"[154]

Alcohol in general – but especially absinthe – was thus framed as negative for the health of French soldiers and settlers in Algeria from the 1840s onwards,[155] with this conviction being so widespread that "no one" – according to Cappot, at least – was unaware of it by 1854. Looking back at this early period, Henri Legrand du Saulle credited French military doctors with sounding the first alarms against absinthe in his 1864 book on *Madness before the Courts*. According to him, French doctors had soon recognized the danger posed by the "deplorable abuse of absinthe" by the French army in Algeria and had tried to stop it: "Military doctors reported the danger; they even preached, on this occasion, holy crusades, but their moral authority was disregarded and their words fell into the void."[156] While their recommendations were not implemented – apart from the prohibitions of selling absinthe within the French army camps – Legrand du Saulle's quote hints at prohibitionist discourses being present in Algeria, amongst military doctors, long before they were ever voiced in mainland France.

The earliest statements about the high fatality rates ascribed to absinthe in colonial contexts – among them the 1844 article in *Akhbar*,[157] Jean-Gabriel Cappot's 1854 article,[158] and Baudet-Dulary's 1856 book[159] – predate the metropolitan focus on the dangers of alcohol in general and absinthe in particular. Michael Marrus explained that "the abuse of alcohol had been virtually unheard of as late as the 1850s" in France. He further explained that the term alcoholism started to be used by French medical experts in the mid-1860s, but that "alcoholism and drunkenness were little discussed as social issues, and seldom judged as being important questions for French society in particular."[160] According to Marrus, an 1886 article in *La Croix* claiming that alcohol caused 2,000 deaths in France annually,[161] was "one of the earliest *cris d'alarme* of the period."[162] In the colonial context of Algeria, however, the first cris d'alarme about the consequences of excessive absinthe drinking can be traced back to the 1840s and 1850s. Hidden behind statements about the deadliness of absinthe is the fear of settlers being outnumbered in the hostile situation that represented the military conquest and the colonial repression of a foreign region. These specific fears about both the French military and the French civilian settler population dying off through their excessive absinthe consumption migrated back to France where they influenced – detached from their clearly colonial context – the anti-absinthe discourse there.

While all these sources depicted absinthe as the main cause of the deaths of French settlers and soldiers in Algeria, Paul-Maurice Legrain suggested in his 1906 book that the real problem was the brutality of French soldiers under the influence of absinthe, in accordance with his theories of absinthe making consumers violent: "You know what alcohol and absinthe have sometimes been able to do with the colonizing soldier; will the black continent ever reveal the secret of the appalling killings coldly carried out in the name of civilization, by innocent actors whose conscience, if it had not been stupefied [by alcohol and absinthe], would have condemned the acts?" Legrain added that he had personally treated returning soldiers and had often had the opportunity "in my service, to collect the confessions of poor people, return- ing from the colonies."[163] Legrain's assessment, in which the absinthe-fuelled French soldiers were the perpetrators of violence against the colonized, and not helpless and dying victims under the thrall of the green fairy, is, however, an exception.

In summary, it can be said that both theories of French consumers turning into the "Oriental other" when under the influence of absinthe, and of French consumers dying from their overconsumption in the colonies, should be seen in the context of nineteenth-century French fears about France's place in a shifting global hierarchy. Nineteenth- and early twentieth-century discourses about absinthe mirrored contemporary fears about France. While the initially Swiss drink absinthe had come to be seen as quintessentially French during the Belle Époque, it was also regularly depicted as a malign force, damaging France's status and hindering the progress of its colonial empire. An analysis of sources from the 1840s and 1850s shows that France's anti-absinthe move- ment probably began from in fears of France being unable to maintain its hold on Algeria, with European settlers – the second group after the French army to be depicted as drinking too much absinthe – either dying, or, through the construct of absinthe being the opium of the West, becoming un-French. In the context of a brutal colonial war of expansion, both were deeply un- desirable, which explains the ferocity of the criticism aimed at the absinthe consumption of settlers by French metropolitan authors.

7

Banning the Opium of the West

Writing a biography of the "king of apéritifs,"[1] as Michael Marrus called absinthe, is a difficult endeavour. Absinthe influenced French life so much that it gave its name to a part of the day and, arguably, to a whole period of the nation's cultural history, while also being mythicized as the most dangerous alcoholic drink to ever exist. It was a strangely malleable drink that could change its nationality, as well as the gender and profession of its inventor, depending on the author of a text. In addition to having had a long and eventful life, having spread across the globe with France's trade, immigrants, and empire, absinthe was also much more than a drink for many. It was a scandal in a glass, it was the "French poison," the opium of the West. Simultaneously, drinking absinthe was also a shared moment of everyday joy and the hour of absinthe was an elaborate, colourful, and stimulating ritual of sociability that endured the absinthe panics of the 1890s. Just as Kolleen Guy showed in the matter of champagne, absinthe had become an "embodiment of the national spirit" in France.[2]

The singling out of absinthe as France's great enemy can be traced to the fact that most French medical and psychiatric experts of the late nineteenth and early twentieth centuries differentiated between the acceptable hygienic beverages of wine, beer, and cider, and other, unacceptable kinds of alcohol, between drunkenness and alcoholism, and, finally, between the diagnoses of alcoholism and absinthism. The differences between absinthe and water, coffee, and wine were depicted in Fig. 7.1, published in *Le Monde illustrée* in 1866. While the artist differentiated between the effects of moderate use and the abuse of water, coffee, and wine, he only depicted one consequence – a miserable prison cell housing a barely human figure – for the absinthe drinker.

Figure 7.1
Drawing depicting the good and bad consequences of the
consumption of water, coffee, wine, and absinthe.

Absinthe was generally believed – mainly by medical and psychiatric experts, but also by members of the various temperance movements – to produce very different effects to common alcohol in drinkers. Absinthe was believed to not only cause physical and mental issues for drinkers, and the degeneration of future generations, but to endanger the existence of the country – and of its colonial empire – itself. Opponents of the drink presented absinthe as a deadly epidemic, sweeping across France and France's empire, which can be seen in the 1865 book by the French journalist Alfred Sirven, who believed that absinthe "kills surely more than the most voracious epidemics."[3]

While absinthe abuse was usually framed as the problem of specific groups that behaved inappropriately, from the perspective of middle-class authors, there were, nevertheless, voices who believed absinthe drinking to be a problem afflicting all classes equally. In 1902, Witold Lemanski described absinthe as a "social leveller" when referring to the physical and mental consequences of its consumption, suggesting that "the Hour of the Parrot levels all social inequalities; in all classes of society they rush, with an equally insane fury, towards these terrible poisons, which engender, worse than death, moral and physical decay."[4] In this assessment of absinthe as a danger to all consumers, irrespective of class, Lemanski echoed fears of the French temperance discourse. An example of this can be found in the monthly newspaper *L'Alcool*, which suggested in an 1896 article by the French journalist Gustave Geffroy that "the green hour of absinthe strikes at the same time on the clock of the elegant café, [and] at the window of the wine merchant's shop."[5]

As the nineteenth century progressed, the voices against absinthe became louder, trying to convince people not to drink it, calling for the institution of bans, and attempting to attribute guilt for the popularity of absinthe. Anecdotes and jokes, whose punchline was that absinthe, after careful preparation, should better be thrown out than consumed, can be found in several reports.[6] Those deemed guilty for absinthe's popularity, in nineteenth- and early twentieth-century explanations, ranged from the New Woman to the working classes, from bohemians to the colonized, from French settlers to absinthe producers. In 1888, the French journalist Georges Maillard wrote about an acquaintance of his, a man in his thirties, who had died of his excessive absinthe consumption. Maillard attributed guilt not necessarily to his acquaintance, but to absinthe manufacturers: "May the first distiller who invented this formidable liqueur be cursed forever! He certainly did not believe he was giving humanity such a fatal present; it was death that he injected into the veins of an entire population." The anger – aimed presumably at Dr

Ordinaire, but expanded to encompass all absinthe producers – was palpable in Maillard's article: "And this crime of poisoning the people is committed every day and in all neighbourhoods. A whole corporation of assassins lives by selling madness and murder to an entire population, and this is tolerated!"[7] Just as absinthe was singled out from among all alcoholic drinks as being particularly dangerous, absinthe manufacturers were singled out from all alcohol producers. An article published in the *New York Times* in 1915, after the institution of France's absinthe ban, suggested that the people of Pontarlier felt "considerably aggrieved at the suppression of the absinthe traffic while the bouilleurs de cru (persons distilling crude alcohol from their own grapes and apples without paying an excise tax, nominally for their own consumption) are still permitted to flood the country with inferior spirits." In this, the *New York Times* suggested that both absinthe lovers and absinthe critics agreed: "The out-and-out prohibitionists, like the absinthe producers, consider it ridiculous to suppress absinthe and not to restrict the production of vile alcohol."[8]

On 16 August 1914, the French minister of the interior, Louis Malvy, proposed a ban on absinthe, and on 7 January 1915, the French president Raymond Poincaré issued a decree prohibiting the sale of absinthe, with potential offenders facing the closure of their débits as well as tax penalties.[9] Finally, on 16 March 1915, the "creation, sale, transportation, and importation of absinthe" was banned by the French government,[10] and this ban was simultaneously introduced in France's colonies, from Algeria[11] to Indochina.[12] The ban also included the so-called "similaires d'absinthe." These drinks that were deemed comparable to absinthe were anise-based aperitifs, which turned milky after water had been added – and that "manufacturers had hoped to substitute for the now forbidden absinthe," as Prestwich explained.[13] After a cantonal ban on absinthe in the cantons of Vaud and Geneva, absinthe opponents had argued in 1907 for a national ban on "all beverages which, under any name, represent an imitation of the liqueur absinthe," out of fear that unscrupulous distillers would try to circumvent the absinthe ban by selling it under a different name.[14] The ban on these "similaires d'absinthe" in France was revoked on 17 July 1922, which led to the production of various anisettes and pastis by former absinthe distilleries.[15] A ban on "similaires d'absinthe" was, however, reinstituted under Vichy France in 1940 and lasted until 1951.[16]

In the colonies, at least, the prohibition of absinthe was eventually interpreted as having been in vain. A 1941 *Manual for Use of Troops Employed Overseas* by the French Ministry of War described alcoholism, together with malaria, as "one of the main factors of mortality among Europeans in our colonies." The sociability of the "hour of absinthe," intrinsically linked for so many French observers to the drink itself, could, it appears, also be created through the consumption of other drinks: "The isolation and the heat, the lack of distractions often lead him [the European] to seek companionship, which he finds in the café, where he also encounters the deadly alcohol in a wide variety of forms. At other times, the European isolated in a post, returns to his lodgings after a tiring day; he drinks first to quench his thirst and gradually takes on habits of intemperance. One could hope that the prohibition of the sale of absinthe would bring a remedy to alcoholism in our colonies: it is not so, whiskey has replaced the green drink."[17]

In neighbouring Switzerland, cantonal bans were instituted in Vaud and Geneva before the green fairy was finally banned from its native country in 1908. Leading up to the decision, the head of the Swiss government – the Federal Council – agreed that it was reasonable to ban the consumption, but was unwilling, due to economic concerns, to restrict the production. This outraged the opponents of absinthe, who deplored the lack of ethical consideration of the Federal Council in an official reply in 1907. In this reply, they accused the Swiss government of accepting that absinthe continued to "mentally and physically harm the Italian, the Argentinian, or the North American," as long as Swiss people were safe.[18] After the institution of the national ban of both consumption and production in Switzerland, the absinthe industry in the Val-de-Travers collapsed, with fourteen distilleries closing and 200 people losing their jobs.[19] An additional 600 farmers in the Val-de-Travers had, at that point, lived from the cultivation of the various herbs needed for the distillation process.[20] The manufacture of absinthe did not end with this ban, however, but was, from that point, done in secret.[21] From 1908, reports about illegally produced absinthe and absinthe smuggling,[22] as well as about prosecutions of café owners, who had been trying to circumvent the prohibition,[23] can be found in various Swiss newspapers from the Romandie. Despite such proof of absinthe's illegal afterlife, the Swiss social scientist Hermann Fahrenkrug depicted the ban in a 1995 article – i.e., a decade before it was lifted – as a case study of how a formerly very popular form of alcohol "almost totally disappeared."[24]

Similarly, after 1915, the absinthe distilleries in France were closed,[25] with these distilleries[26] and the farms growing the various herbs needed for the distillation of absinthe receiving compensation.[27] As in Switzerland, those not strictly keeping to the ban in France were prosecuted. A 1917 article in *The*

Times explained that there were heavy fines for those caught selling absinthe, giving the specific example of the "proprietor of the well-known Mollard restaurant outside the Gare Saint Lazare," in Paris. This proprietor had been caught with 838 bottles of a specific absinthe and ordered to pay "163 fines of £40 each [i.e., £6,520]," as well as £1500 in revenue dues: "Altogether the fines amounted to nearly £8,000."[28] Absinthe producers and sellers from both France and France's colonial empire were taken to court for breaking the ban. For a 2019 student thesis, Celia Faux analyzed 176 closures of débits de boissons ordered by the various local courts of appeal for the sale of absinthe between March 1915 and February 1916. Faux observed a concentration of court cases on the Mediterranean coast of both France and Algeria. Fifty-three closures had been instituted in Nimes, and twenty-eight in Algiers, compared to only six in Paris. Faux's research thus suggests that, despite the hour of absinthe often being depicted as a particularly Parisian phenomenon in the sources and the secondary literature, absinthe might have had more of an illegal afterlife in the South of France and in Algeria than in Paris itself.[29]

In March 2005, the Swiss government decided to lift Switzerland's ban on absinthe, with the French Senate following in April 2011. Switzerland's decision came one hundred years after the so-called "absinthe murders" in August 1905, which French newspapers reported on at the time.[30] This event has been interpreted by many twentieth- and twenty-first-century researchers as the starting point of a global wave of absinthe prohibitions. Even within the context of Europe, however, this narrative is questionable, as a ban on the manufacture, sale, and distribution of absinthe had been decided on in Belgium in February 1903.[31] Yet it is undoubtedly true that the Swiss "absinthe murders" played a role in how absinthe came to be perceived globally in the twentieth century.

On 28 August 1905, a man by the name of Jean Lanfray murdered his wife and two daughters in Commugny in the Swiss canton of Vaud. Most of the secondary literature suggests that Lanfray was an alcoholic, drinking one or several glasses of absinthe each day, in addition to several litres of wine and glasses of other highly alcoholic drinks.[32] On 29 August, the *Gazette de Lausanne* published a short note on this triple murder, which explained that a Jean Lanfrey (*sic*) had been arrested. He was described as a thirty-one-year-old day labourer of French origin, but born and raised in Commugny. The previous day he had shot his twenty-five-year-old French wife and his two little daughters – five and two years old – after an argument about money, in which his wife threatened to return to her parents in Annecy, France. After the murders, Lanfray tried to shoot himself, but only broke his jaw. The only mention of alcohol in this initial report was that "L. was a drinker and debauched."[33] Absinthe was thus not present in this initial report.

The same year a Swiss doctor with the name of Burnand introduced the topic to readers of the French protestant journal *Foi et Vie*, stating that "on 30 August 1905, all Swiss newspapers told, on the 3rd page, under the title of 'family drama,' a sinister story." Quoting from a report in the *Journal de Genève*, Burnand explained that Lanfray's wife had threatened to leave him "because of his conduct, because Lanfrey [*sic*] was addicted to absinthe." Burnand, clearly influenced in his assessment by the wider medical anti-absinthe discourse present in both France and Switzerland at the time, explained that this incident "was only a news item, sadly banal, hardly bloodier than the tragic series of absinthe crimes. Yet it horrified all of Switzerland." Burnand hoped that because of this intense horror felt after Lanfray's actions, a ban on absinthe might be instituted, so that both the problem and its solution might originally stem from Switzerland.[34]

On 24 and 26 February 1906, the *Gazette de Lausanne* reported on Lanfray's court case, which took place in Nyon. Part of Lanfray's defence was a psychiatric report by a doctor, Albert Mahaim, director of the psychiatric institute of Cery in the canton of Vaud. Three months after the crime, Lanfray had been brought to Cery where "he was able to de-alcoholize himself." There, he was, according to Mahaim, a "good worker, not quarrelsome." Mahaim specialized in cases of drunkenness and, the journalist added, suggested something that "the population of Commugny immediately understood," namely that absinthe "was the cause of the crime. It was she who gave Lanfray the fury with which he acted. Alcohol and absinthe made Lanfray what he became. Today, Lanfray is cured; at the time of the crime, he was in a state of serious alcoholism which prevented him from appreciating the significance of his actions."[35] Both intense fury and loss of conscience were believed to be indicative of crimes committed under the influence of absinthe.

Showing that absinthe was still linked to the habits of the French military at the turn of the century, Lanfray's history with absinthe had started during his military service in Annecy. According to him, he only occasionally drank it, as it caused him to experience losses of memory. After a fight with his father in 1900, Lanfray and his wife moved from Commugny to Geneva, where he worked for a beer merchant, and it was there that he started to drink absinthe again. Doctor Mahaim further explained that "if Lanfray says he acted in cold blood at the time of his crime, it is because he does not realize the state of rage that alcohol had put him into. Absinthe is a dangerous poison … This fit of rage can only be explained by the fact that Lanfray had been drinking absinthe for a long time." Lanfray drank "enormously," but not only absinthe, as "he took up to 4 litres of wine a day, plus many absinthes, marc [i.e., a Swiss grape eau-de-vie], etc." Other witnesses of the court case painted a slightly different picture: one of intense alcohol consumption, but not of an *extra-ordinary* alcohol consumption. Francis Rochaix, the owner of the café in Commugny, in which Lanfray had been drinking, was asked whether Lanfray drank too much. Rochaix "acknowledges that Lanfray drank absinthe, but it cannot be said that he drank more than others. 'He drank like everyone else.' (Laughter [in the court room])."[36] Interpreting Lanfray's absinthe drinking as the source of his crime and his consumption as ordinary amongst his contemporaries in Commugny might have further increased fears about absinthe's impact on drinkers.

In a 2000 article on the absinthe ban for *Traverse: Zeitschrift für Geschichte*, Charles Heimberg questioned whether Lanfray had consumed absinthe that day. Early on, the Swiss press was informed that Lanfray regularly drank absinthe, which influenced their reporting, yet according to Heimberg's research, Lanfray had not consumed any absinthe on the day of the murder. Lanfray thus might have been one of these cases of chronic absinthism, where violence was attributed to absinthe even though the culprit had not consumed absinthe immediately before the crime. Quoting an article published in *Le Courrier de Genève* on 3 September 1905, Heimberg referred to this understanding of absinthe's long-term effects: "People will object that Lanfray had not drunk any absinthe on the afternoon of the crime: he had only consumed, it is said, a litre of wine with a few drinking companions. But it is recognized that his favourite liquor was absinthe; his nervous system was impregnated with it; the wine will have been only the last cause, the electric spark which set fire to the loaded torpedo, and which provoked those fits of criminal fury during which the wretch massacred without pity, without the slightest scruple, with a dry eye, with a calm heart, the beings who must have been dearest to him."[37] While it might be true that Lanfray had not consumed any absinthe that day, one of the witnesses in his 1906 court case, Albert Buclin, nevertheless testified that, on the day of the murder, Lanfray had been drinking since morning. The murder was committed at about six o'clock in the evening and "at half-past five he swallowed two *omnibuses*."[38] Absinthe was sometimes called "la correspondence à Charenton." On her blog, Marie-Claude Delahaye further ex plained that absinthe was also occasionally known as a "direct train or an Omnibus to Charenton."[39]

The question about what had caused Lanfray's drunkenness on that 28 August 1905 cannot be definitively answered. The only thing that is certain is that he consumed large amounts of alcohol other than absinthe that day. Mahaim's suggestion that the murder was one of diminished responsibility, due to Lanfray's consumption of absinthe, somewhat chimed with the jury, who ended up being divided on the question of his responsibility. Despite this, Lanfray was found guilty and condemned to life in prison.[40] On the evening of the verdict, 26 February 1906, Lanfray hanged himself in his cell.[41]

Even though Lanfray had been found guilty, Mahaim's defence of violence committed under the influence of absinthe resonated with the broader public. "Public opinion immediately seized upon the cause of the crime: absinthe," explained the journalist reporting on Lanfray's court case.[42] Indeed, the inhabitants of Commugny started a "double petition" against the sale of absinthe, collecting both the signatures of men and women living in the canton of Vaud. 34,423 men – a majority of those able to vote in the canton – signed the petition. An even more remarkable 48,053 signatures could be found on the women's petition,[43] with women signing despite not having the right to vote in 1908. In a 1908 article, the Swiss journalist Paul Pictet included a passage from this petition, in which several of these women from the canton of Vaud openly stated that they feared for their lives due, apparently, to the absinthe consumption of the men around them.[44] These women were, to come back to Thierry Fillaut's 2015 categorization, both potential victims and paragons in the wider absinthe discourse – not drinking and actively trying persuade others to stop drinking, out of fear for their own lives.[45] The prohibition of absinthe was decided on 5 July 1908, with the ban taking effect on 7 October 1910.

Swiss women were only allowed to vote at the cantonal level in Vaud in 1959 – the first canton to introduce this level of women's suffrage – and at the national level in 1971. Indeed, the women of Commugny were the first in Switzerland to take part in a local election on 19 April 1959. Upon that occasion, the *Journal de Genève* published an article with the title "The Women of Commugny and the Absinthe Ban," in which these two events were directly linked. According to the unnamed journalist, "in 1905, moved by a terrible tragedy due to alcoholism," the women of Commugny "launched a petition aimed at banning absinthe in the territory of Vaud, a ban that was extended to the territory of the Confederation [the Confoederatio Helvetica, i.e., Switzerland]."

The journalist admitted that the ban had not completely worked, as absinthe continued to be sold under different names, yet "the courageous initiative of the women of Commugny achieved its goal; no more dreadful dramas caused by the 'green fairy' have been reported; the number of homes ruined by the abuse of this liquor has rapidly diminished and it can be said that absinthe no longer causes drama in Switzerland." These facts, the journalist concluded, were "worth recalling" at this historic moment, "when the women of Commugny, the first in Switzerland, acted as citizens, fifty-four years after the first manifestation of their civic spirit."[46]

Both the case itself and Switzerland's swift path to prohibit absinthe was taken up by the French temperance movement. The absinthe panic felt in France at that time was not started by the tragedy of Commugny, but Lanfray's crime coincided with what many felt: France was, because of absinthe, "in danger of death by alcohol," explained the psychiatrist Emmanuel Régis in 1912.[47] According to Regis, half-measures would not help against this, which led him to recommend the "absolute, radical abolition of the manufacture and circulation of absinthe and aperitifs," which, he feared, was impossible in France, due to the high economic stakes of the absinthe industry.[48] The question of the prohibition of absinthe was hotly debated in France and, starting in 1908, the French Senate discussed the intricacies of the danger posed to France by absinthe over a period of several years.[49]

The various French temperance societies were united in their fight against absinthe. Amongst these societies, the Union française antialcoolique, founded by Paul-Maurice Legrain in either 1894 or 1895,[50] was the most radical. While the majority of the French temperance movements did not aim their criticism at so-called hygienic beverages, only at "industrial alcohol,"[51] the Union française antialcoolique recommended the total abstinence from all forms of alcohol.[52]

In 1905, several of these temperance societies united in the Ligue nationale contre l'alcoolisme,[53] which launched a petition that very year calling for the prohibition of absinthe.[54] The Ligue's goal was to "tolerate wine and 'hygienic drinks' [in order] to fight against absinthe, considered the most formidable agent of alcoholism," according to Dominique Khalifa's 2016 article.[55] This led to the French wine industry supporting the temperance movement's efforts against absinthe, but as Prestwich succinctly put it, the 1915 ban proved to be a "a pyrrhic victory" for these movements. This conscious singling out of absinthe – and the success of the ban – masked France's wider problem with alcoholism.[56]

The 1915 absinthe ban proved to be the pinnacle of the French temperance movement. The secondary literature usually presents a narrative in which there were no measures taken in France against absinthe before the early twentieth century.[57] However, this is only true if one disregards France's colonial empire. According to Znaien, the secondary literature on the history of absinthe often presented the 1915 ban as being the result of cooperation between the wine industry and metropolitan doctors belonging to the wider temperance movement. He suggested that the colonial contexts should be considered, claiming that "despite the lasting opposition of certain deputies, Algeria is the first territory to ban absinthe. The liquor is officially [banned] from 1911."[58] The 1911 prohibition of absinthe in Algeria – valid from 1 January 1912 – that Znaien refers to in this passage, was, however, a limitation of the alcohol content allowed in absinthe. The decree specifically banned the stocking and sale of "absinthe or similar drinks," which had "an alcohol content of less than 55 degrees," not all absinthe.[59] This was due to the conviction that absinthe with a lower alcohol content was of a lower overall quality. Absinthe with a higher alcohol content was still allowed and widely enjoyed in Algeria after this 1911 prohibition. While I agree with Znaien's focus on the importance of the colonial developments, such measures – including, for example, the 1907 limitation of grams of essences contained in absinthe in France[60] – should not be read as absinthe bans.

This 1911–12 measure was also not perceived as a ban on absinthe in Algeria at the time. The *Annales Africaines* published an article on the absinthe ban in Morocco in May 1914, in which this ban was described as a "radical measure," that was, however, "generally approved." It went on to quote an article published in the Algerian newspaper *Petit Oranais* by a journalist called Raoul Besson, who "expressed doubts on its effectiveness," saying that people would just drink other equally strong and potentially harmful forms of alcohol. If the 1912 regulation had been perceived as a ban in Algeria, such hypothetical musings must have been odd for readers of the *Petit Oranais*.[61]

It is, however, undoubtedly true that prohibitions of absinthe in the French army in colonial contexts predated the 1915 absinthe ban. The relative ineffectiveness of the bans from the 1840s and 1850s in Algeria can be explained through the special role that absinthe played in French army life, the absence of other alcoholic alternatives, soldiers believing absinthe to be medicinal, and soldiers being able to buy absinthe elsewhere. These bans in Algeria were, however, not the only ones. An article published in *Le Gaulois* in August 1885 mentioned that the "sale of absinthe has just been banned in Tonkin by

General de Courcy," i.e., by Henri Roussel de Courcy, who had been appointed protector of the neighbouring colony of Annam in July 1885. "You may have read this in all the newspapers," the author assured the readers of *Le Gaulois*.[62] From the absinthe bans of the 1840s in the French military in Algeria, to the 1914 ban in Upper Senegal,[63] there existed a tradition of singling absinthe out as exceptionally harmful and of prohibiting its sale and use in France's colonies before the 1915 absinthe ban in metropolitan France.

When discussing the potential ban of absinthe in the years before 1915 in France, however, French authors did not refer to the early colonial examples implemented by their own army in the 1840s and 1850s. Instead, they compared France to other nations that had already acted upon the dangers allegedly posed by absinthe. The French doctor Joseph Saliège wondered in 1911 about answers to France's alcohol problem: "There is no doubt that the real solution, the only [solution] that can definitely put an end to the intoxication of the race, would be the absolute prohibition of the sale and manufacture of alcohols with essences (absinthe, anisette, etc.). The measure, at first, seems a bit too radical; it frightens and, yet, it is the only efficient [measure], for it is this [measure] that those countries which have tried seriously to solve the problem have relied on: Norway, Texas, the Swiss Cantons."[64] Once the prohibition of absinthe had been introduced in Morocco in 1914, this too was compared with other nations that had introduced bans. In a May 1914 article published in the *Journal de médecine et de chirurgie pratiques*, "the fight against alcoholism" in Morocco was discussed. Based on an alleged omnipresence of absinthe, Resident General Hubert Lyautey had, "by a decree of the Sultan [Youssef ben Hassan]," prohibited "the introduction, manufacture, distribution, and sale of absinthe" in the French protectorate in Morocco. Due to Lyautey's measures, the article concluded, "Morocco is now as advanced as Switzerland and the other countries, which have declared war on alcohol and especially on absinthe. Here [in France] we prefer opening hospitals and asylums for the insane to touching the democratic little glass."[65]

The anti-absinthe discourse in France focused on the crimes committed by absinthe drinkers and the dangers its consumption posed to future generations who were understood to inherit the medical complications of their absinthe-drinking parents, especially their absinthe-drinking mothers. While partaking in the green hour was used to attack all kinds of women – women from the working classes, fashionable women, those fighting for more rights, and more – it was above all the perception that they behaved unbecomingly and endangered both their existing children and those yet unborn that were discussed in the sources. They were depicted as immoderate. Many believed that the potential racial degeneration caused by the spread of the hour of absinthe could only really be regulated by moderation. It was *intemperance* that was often understood to be the problem. This belief was counteracted, however, by the theory of chronic absinthism, through which even moderate consumption could be defined as a threat.

Many French doctors and psychiatrists nevertheless believed that the lack of moderation that they observed amongst the working classes of the French population, both in metropolitan France and in the colonies, led to all kinds of addictions, not just absinthe. The consumption of absinthe was contextualized as spreading from victorious French soldiers to the bourgeoisie, from the bourgeoisie and the artists to the working classes, from men to women (and from women to children), from the colonizers to the colonized, always – with the exception of the initial step from the soldier to the bourgeois – with the socially "lower" group imitating the behaviour of the "higher" one. All groups – the bourgeoisie now included – were described as wanting to gain something by copying the behaviour of these others: glory in the case of the bourgeoisie, freedom in the case of women, glamour and leisure in the case of French working-class men, and civilization in the case of the colonized.

The vilification of the absinthe consumption of marginalized groups – by medical and psychiatric experts as well as by the temperance movement – was a precursor to the prohibition of all absinthe consumption, and the very first phase of this vilification concerned not the consumption of the bohème, women, or workers, but absinthe drinking in Algeria. The first cris d'alarme about the absinthe overconsumption in Algeria, amongst the military and the civilian population – and concrete bans based on these fears – predated the medico-psychiatric condemnation of the drink in France. Fears developed in the specific context of a brutal colonial encounter were uncritically taken up by metropolitan doctors and psychiatrists and incorporated into their theories of the drink in France itself. The diagnosis of absinthism has its roots in concerns about misbehaving settlers and weak soldiers, both groups failing France's aims of building a global empire. Detaching absinthe from its colonial history limits our understanding of the important role that French settlers – their fears, needs, and wishes – played in this aspect of France's social and cultural life in the nineteenth and early twentieth centuries. So much of the vocabulary and the imagery of the green fairy, used in publications by both absinthe opponents and absinthe enthusiasts, is coloured by France's colonial experiences and soaked with prejudice against the colonized populations. Life in France's colonial empire was inextricably linked to the consumption of absinthe, as can be observed, for example, through postcards showing prominent Absinthe Rivoire adverts at the 1906 Colonial Exposition in Marseille (Fig. 7.2).

Calling absinthe the opium of the West or the biggest danger to French settlers in the colonies did not just add Orientalist colour to these publications, it transmitted deep-set fears of racial degeneration – in this context of the strict racial hierarchy of France's colonial empire – and of settler minorities, surrounded by hostile masses of suppressed people. The prohibition of absinthe and the hour of absinthe – and of the "similaires d'absinthe" between 1915 and 1922, and 1940 and 1951 – had an impact on life in France in the twentieth century. As France still has to face up fully to its colonial past, deconstructing the influence that life in Algeria had on this development is necessary. Today, many myths about absinthe remain. Once the bans were lifted in the early 2000s, many people had, as Michael Montagne suggested in 2013, high "expectations of a unique intoxication" upon their first contact with the drink.[66] While this twenty-first-century absinthe – a flavoursome, highly alcoholic drink – could never live up to its scandalous reputation, I am confronted with the same questions about people going blind or mad from its consumption whenever I talk to people about my interest in its history.

Many of these contemporary myths surrounding absinthe were first propagated by various anti-absinthe or temperance movements between the 1870s and 1915 – which, I would argue, were based on earlier writings regarding the behaviour of French soldiers and settlers in Algeria – yet they are still very much alive in the consciousness of twenty-first-century consumers. With all the prohibitions on absinthe lifted, the green fairy is again widely consumed, with absinthe bars found in cities worldwide. Yet, due to the many myths surrounding it, many experience a deeper interest in absinthe. Accordingly, today's absinthe industry sells more than just the drink. In the Val-de-Travers, for example, one can visit the museum Maison de l'Absinthe in Môtiers and buy absinthe paraphernalia – ranging from posters and books to absinthe sausages, biscuits, and chocolates – as well as tour the various absinthe distilleries. Advertisements for different contemporary absinthe brands play with the potential for danger and the many scandalous myths from the past. While absinthism is no longer an accepted diagnosis, people feel like they are playing with fire when consuming the drink. Absinthe is still viewed as unique.

44 - Marseille - Exposition Coloniale - Côté des Attractions (Le Ballon captif)

Figure 7.2
Postcard of a hot air balloon displaying an advert for Absinthe
Rivoire, floating over buildings depicting France's colonies
at the Exposition Coloniale in Marseille in 1906.

Much remains to be studied. What is clear is that the history of absinthe cannot be fully understood without looking at what happened in France's colonies – its popularity started with Algeria; the first bans were introduced in Algeria; many of the prejudices against overconsumption were first applied to French soldiers and settlers in colonial contexts; the idea of absinthe as a murderous brew became particularly urgent when surrounded by masses of the colonized who were at once believed to have a particular predilection towards the drink and to know no moderation. Similarly, the warnings about French drinkers losing their Frenchness through their absinthe consumption must be seen against the backdrop of France's colonial endeavours. Fears of losing the colonies – above all Algeria – due to the absinthe consumption of settlers deeply shaped the anti-absinthe discourse in France.

Drinking absinthe was, in many respects, a celebration of colonial aggression in metropolitan France, and both a piece of home and of French identity for settlers, who fiercely defended themselves and their drink of choice from accusations of immoderation and irrationality coming from the homeland. I stated in the introduction that the history of absinthe can be triangulated by looking at Switzerland, France, and France's colonial empire, particularly Algeria. Looking only at France – or at France and Switzerland – and treating Algeria as an afterthought, only tells half the story of the rise and fall of absinthe, this most notorious of drinks.

Notes

Introduction

1 Marrus, "Social Drinking," 124.
2 Sterling Heilig, "The Green Hour in Paris," *Sun [New York Sun]*, 19 August 1894, 10; Camille Defrance, "L'alcoolisme en Algérie," *Le Progrès de Bel-Abbès: Journal de l'arrondissement de Sidi-Bel-Abbès*, 26 May 1895, 1. See also Hein, Lobbedey, and Neumärker, "Absinth," 2717.
3 Le Bras, "Le vin est la plus saine et la plus hygiénique des boissons," para. 6.
4 Guy, "Culinary Connections," 230.
5 Prestwich, "Temperance in France," 302.
6 Monselet, *Montmartre à Séville*, 16. All translations into English are mine.
7 Lanier, *Absinthe*, 20. Others placed the growth of these débits in the mid-1870s and 1880s. Marrus, "Social Drinking," 129; Lalouette, "Débits de boissons," 131.
8 Barrows, "Parliaments of the People," 88.
9 Lachenmeier et al., "Absinthe, Absinthism and Thujone," 33.
10 Nourrisson, *Crus et cuites*, 154; Haine, *World of the Paris Café*, 4.
11 Marrus, "Social Drinking," 124; Quétel and Simon, "Aliénation alcoolique en France," 518; Le Bras, "Boire pour se soigner," 416.
12 Many of these accounts will be discussed in the book. See, for example, Narrey, *Amours faciles*, 157–8; Daviller, "Alcool et alcoolisme," 45; Heilig, "Green Hour," 10; Jean, "A Paris," *Le Rappel Algérien*, 2 September 1909, 1.
13 Padwa, *Social Poison*, 17.
14 Nourrisson, "Origines de l'antialcoolisme," 500.

15 Marrus, "Social Drinking," 119; Prestwich, *Drink*, 21.

16 Prestwich, "Temperance in France," 303, 309; Haine, *World of the Paris Café*, 97. For a history of the term "boisson hygiénique," see Le Bras, "Le vin est la plus saine et la plus hygiénique des boissons," paras 9–14.

17 Mayet, *Vin de France*, 64.

18 Rochard, "Alcool," 874. The same quote can also be found here: Rochard, *Traité d'hygiène*, 716.

19 Prestwich, *Drink*, 54.

20 Lemoine, *Traité d'hygiène militaire*, 238–9.

21 Lalouette, "Consommation," 289.

22 Picard, *Dangers*, 20.

23 The absinthe expert Marie-Claude Delahaye compared the consumption of absinthe in 1874 with that of 1910: according to her, the consumption was at 7,000 hectolitres in 1874 and at 360,000 hectolitres in 1910. The same number for 1910 can be found in Phil Baker's book and in Dominique Khalifa's article. The numbers provided by Barnaby Conrad and Padosch et al. in their respective publications are slightly lower. Conrad suggested in his 1988 book that in 1912, 221,897 hectolitres of absinthe were drunk in France, while Padosch et al. wrote of 239,492 hectolitres in 1913. Delahaye, "Grandeur et décadence," 478; Conrad, *Absinthe*, 6; Baker, *Dedalus Book of Absinthe*, 128; Padosch, Lachenmeier, and Kröner, "Absinthism," 4; Khalifa, "Vices et vertus," 73.

24 Eidgenössischer Initiativausschuss gegen den Absinth, *Absinthverbot in der Schweiz*, 11.

25 Marrus, "Social Drinking," 115.

26 Rénon, *Maladies populaires*, 289.

27 Hazemann, "Homicides," 7.

28 Padwa, *Social Poison*, 131; Black, *Drugging France*, 282.

29 Baker, *Dedalus Book of Absinthe*, 8. See also Conrad, *Absinthe*, 127; Vuillaume, "Toxicomanie et addiction," 106; Niemeyer, "Fée verte," para. 6.

30 "Prohibition de l'absinthe au Congo," 161–2.

31 "Suppression de l'absinthe en Belgique," 40.

32 Znaien, "Généalogie coloniale," 45.

33 Schaffner, "Absinthe Prohibition," 562.

34 Bauer, "Visiting the 'Green Fairy,'" 4.

35 Terril, "Dudes, Decadence, and Degeneracy," 1.

36 Padosch, Lachenmeier, and Kröner, "Absinthism," 4; Bauer, "Visiting the 'Green Fairy,'" 4.

37 "La lutte contre l'alcoolisme," 365–6; "L'absinthe proscrite," *Annales africaines: Revue hebdomadaire de l'Afrique du Nord*, 15 May 1914, 238.

38 "Interdiction de l'absinthe dans le Haut-Sénégal," 958–9.

39 Padosch, Lachenmeier, and Kröner, "Absinthism," 4; Bauer, "Visiting the 'Green Fairy,'" 4.

40 Lalouette, "Consommation," 294.

41 Heilig, "Green Hour," 10.

42 "Foreign Intelligence. France," *Times*, 17 September 1864, 10.

43 In 1886, for example, ten years before France officially colonized Madagascar, absinthe seems to have been present there. Lanessan, *Expansion coloniale de la France*, 363–4.

44 Lemire, *Indo-Chine*, 38. See also Bauvallet, "Alcoolisme chronique," 81; "Tonquin," *Times*, 13 March 1884, 10.

45 Irmgard Bauer mentioned in her 2020 article that absinthe had been used as payment for local workers in French Polynesia. Bauer, "Visiting the 'Green Fairy,'" 3.

46 Kermorgant, "Alcoolisme," 332, 337.

47 In 1885, for example, absinthe seems to have been quite commonly consumed in Vienna. See "Vienna Today," *Times*, 5 September 1885, 4.

48 Hein, Lobbedey, and Neumärker, "Absinth," 2717. See also Baker, *Dedalus Book of Absinthe*, 15; Bauer, "Visiting the 'Green Fairy,'" 3.

49 Georgeon, *Au pays du raki*, 159.

50 Souguenet, *Route de Timmimoun*, 103.

51 "France Has Her Little India," *Times*, 25 March 1861, 8.

52 Decroos, "Réglementation," 33–4.

53 Legrain, *Éléments de médecine mentale*, 219.

54 Aubert, *Alcoolisation de la France*, 14. Emphasis in the original.

55 Houdeville, *Comment préserver*, 13. See also anonymous, *Petit manuel du ligueur*, 11; Saliège, "Rapport," 165; Ruyssen, "Tempérance," 137.

56 Paul de Saint-Victor, "Théatres," *La Presse*, 30 December 1860, 1–2.

57 Thanks to the French historian of alcohol, Stéphane Le Bras, who helped me with the translation of this term.

58 Saint-Victor, "Théatres," 2.

59 Padwa, *Social Poison*, 33; 57.

60 G. Grandin, "Nouvelles Locales," *Journal du Cher: Politique, littéraire, industriel*, 10 January 1861, 3. See also "Faits Divers," *Feuille de Provins: Journal de l'arrondissement*, 26 January 1861, 3.

61 Lemanski, *Hygiène du colon*, 122.

62 See also A. Froemer, "La Maison Pernod et l'histoire de l'absinthe," *Le Pan-théon de l'industrie: Revue hebdomadaire internationale illustrée des expositions et des concours*, 5 October 1884, 353–4.

63 Lemanski, *Hygiène du colon*, 122–3.

64 Schneider, "Toward the Improvement of the Human Race," 269.

65 Pick, *Faces of Degeneration*, 21. See also Harsin, "Gender, Class, and Madness," 1057.

66 Nye, "Degeneration and the Medical Model," 21. See also Black, *Drugging France*, 9.

67 Nourrisson, "Origines de l'antialcoolisme," 501. On the interlinking of fears about birth rates and absinthe specifically, see Prestwich, "Temperance in France," 307.

68 Mayet, *Vin de France*, 75.

69 Lierre, *Question de l'absinthe*, 6–7.

70 Berthoud, "Fée verte."

71 Heimberg, "Comment renouveler."

72 Prestwich, "Temperance in France."

73 Due to their highly technical nature, some of these publications could not be used for this book, which aims at a general audience. See, for example, Vogt, "Absinthium"; Vogt and Montagne, "Absinthe"; Gimpel et al., "Absinth"; Smith, "Absinthe Attacks"; Luauté, "Absinthisme"; Lachenmeier, "Absinth. Geschichte einer Thujon- oder Alkoholabhängigkeit"; Cole, *Buveurs d'absinthe*.

74 See, for example, Lajer-Burcharth, "Modernity"; MacLeod, "Marie Corelli and Fin-de-Siècle Francophobia"; DeBoer, "Flavour of Absinthe"; Earle, "Green Eyes"; Rekand, "Absinthe, the Nervous System and Painting"; Young, "Heroic Indolence"; Hatch, "Green with Madness"; Diaz, "Ivresse des poètes"; Wilson-Bareau, "Manet's Absinthe Drinker."

75 See, for example, Faux, "She Makes a Beast of Man"; Borja, "Absinthe"; Altamirano, "Intoxicating Women"; Overkempe, "Following the Fairy."

76 See, for example, Delahaye, *Histoire de la fée verte*; Delahaye, *Muse des poètes*; Delahaye, *Absinthe, Son Histoire*; Delahaye, *Affiches*; Delahaye, *Absinthe au féminin*.

77 Delachaux, *Absinthe*.

78 Noël, *Nouvelles confidences sur l'absinthe*.

79 On the practice of medical self-experimentation with psychotropic drugs in nineteenth-century France, see Black, *Drugging France*, 64–116.

80 See, for example, Geffroy, "Bonne Absinthe," 128; Lierre, *Question de l'absinthe*, 37–8.

81 Jean Lanfray, a labourer in Switzerland, murdered his family in August 1905 while drunk, which caused outrage and panic, as people blamed absinthe for his actions.

82 Anet, "War against Absinthe," 189.

Chapter One

1 Guy, *When Champagne Became French*, 17.

2 On the concept of louche, see Bickel, Ellis, and Resnick, "Examining the Temperature Dependence of Louche Formation in Absinthe."

3 "Les manifestations," *Le Radical*, 20 February 1899, 3; Ribouleau, *À travers l'hygiène*, 164; Marc de Brus, "La vie au grand air," *La Liberté*, 5 February 1902, 3–4; "A notre grande salle," *L'Écho de Maréville* 157 (1906), 4; Charles-Henry Hirsch, "Fin d'aventure," *Le Journal*, 14 February 1910, 3. See also Haine, *World of the Paris Café*, 96; Lachenmeier et al., "Absinthe: A Review," 368.

4 Brus, "Vie au grand air," 3. See also Lachenmeier et al., "Absinthe: A Review," 368.

5 Arnould, *Nouveaux éléments d'hygiène*, 636.

6 Bauer, "Visiting the 'Green Fairy,'" 2. For a slightly different definition of these three categories, see Heidrich and Liggenstorfer, "Absinthe-Herstellung," 65.

7 Gasnier, "Affiches publicitaires," part 1, 48.

8 Lévy, *Traité d'hygiène*, 52.

9 On this last point, see Sterling Heilig, "The Green Hour in Paris," *Sun [New York Sun]*, 19 August 1894, 10; Livon, "Absinthe," 18; Monier, *Causeries*, 236–7; "L'absinthe et ses dangers," 373; Arnould, *Nouveaux éléments d'hygiène*, 636–7.

10 "Report on: Macé," 1076–7.

11 Motet, "Considérations générales," 15.

12 For more on these two methods, see Heidrich and Liggenstorfer, "Absinthe-Herstellung," 66; Faux, "She Makes a Beast of Man," 11.

13 This article had been copied from an earlier article in the *New Orleans Delta*. The *New Orleans Delta* in turn had apparently taken its information from the "Paris correspondent of a New York paper, the *World*."

14 "Measuring Civilization," *Indiana State Sentinel*, 10 April 1861, 4. Emphasis in the original.

15 Bergeret, *Alcoolisme*, 192.

16 Eidgenössischer Initiativausschuss gegen den Absinth, *Absinthverbot in der Schweiz*, 3. Prestwich, "Temperance in France," 302.

17 Morache, *Traité d'hygiène militaire*, 704. Emphasis in the original.

18 Motet, "Considérations générales," 15.

19 Morache, *Traité d'hygiène militaire*, 704.

20 Chapuis, "Absinthe réhabilitée," 517.

21 Lemoine, *Traité d'hygiène militaire*, 238.

22 Prestwich, "Temperance in France," 304–5.

23 Lemoine, *Traité d'hygiène militaire*, 238. See also Eidgenössischer Initiativausschuss gegen den Absinth, *Absinthverbot in der Schweiz*, 4.

24 Pinaud, "Alcoolisme chez les arabes," 26.

25 "Measuring Civilization," 4. The same formulation can be found in an article on the "Pernicious Effects of Absinthe," written by Louis Figuier in 1862. In his 1896 book on the *Dangers of the Abuse of Alcoholic Drinks*, Dominique Thierrin explains that verdigris was used to give absinthe "the desired green colour." Figuier, "Effets pernicieux," 337; Thierrin, *Dangers*, 23–4.

26 Langle, "Cafés et débits," paras 139, 142.

27 Morache, *Traité d'hygiène militaire*, 704. Emphasis in the original. See also Baudrimont, *Dictionnaire*, 31; Monin, *Hygiène de l'estomac*, 37.

28 Burns, *Temperance Dictionary*, 4; "Absinthe," *British Medical Journal*, 17 April 1869, 353; "Chine et Indo-Chine," *Le Temps*, 22 June 1885, 2; Viry, *Manuel d'hygiène militaire*, 175. Others believed that copper oxides were used to colour the drink. Bard, *Algérie en 1854*, 23.

29 Figuier, "Effets pernicieux," 337–8.

30 Jules Hayaux, "L'absinthe au Maroc: Interview d'un diplomate," *Le Rappel*, 2 February 1914, 1.

31 "Tribunaux," *La Croix de Genève: Organe des colonies suisses en France*, 31 January 1899, 2.

32 Hayaux, "Absinthe au Maroc: Interview d'un diplomate," 1.

33 Tissandier, *Merveilles de la photographie*, 103–4, n1. See also Waldthausen, "Reflection," 349.

34 Cazin, *Traité pratique*, 6, n1. Emphasis in the original.

35 Blakesley, *Four Months in Algeria*, 99. Emphasis in the original. See also Rogers, *Winter in Algeria*, 322; Pouchet, *Leçons*, 296.

36 Livon, "Absinthe," 19.

37 Casanova, "Intoxications chroniques," 19–20.

38 Triboulet and Mathieu, *Alcool et alcoolisme*, 190. Emphasis in the original.

39 Laborde, "Alcool et sa toxicité."

40 Directly after this, the same passage was printed that appeared in Livon's text five years later. "Alcoolisme" (Encyclopédie d'hygiène et de médecine publique), 637.

41 Triboulet and Mathieu, *Alcool et alcoolisme*, 190.

42 Rivière, "Plantes," 291.

43 Hayaux, "Absinthe au Maroc: Interview d'un diplomate," 1.

44 Hutton, "Myth," 63. See also Cotton, "Vincent van Gogh," 77; Bauer, "Visiting the 'Green Fairy,'" 3.

45 Choulette, *Observations pratiques*, 32–4.

46 Baudrimont, *Dictionnaire*, 31. Emphasis in the original.

47 Cargill, "Myth of the Green Fairy," 91.

48 Despite suggesting this, Strang et al. acknowledged that the damage done by absinthe was also due to its alcohol content. Strang, Arnold, and Peters, "Absinthe," 1591.

49 Lachenmeier and Nathan-Maister, "Systematic Misinformation," 258.

50 Herrmann, "Indeterminate Pharmacology," 203.

51 Earle, "Green Eyes," 692; Cargill, "Myth of the Green Fairy," 88; Lachenmeier and Nathan-Maister, "Absinthe and Tobacco," 218; D'Ulivo, "Solution to the Absinthe Challenge," 4011; Bauer, "Visiting the 'Green Fairy,'" 4.

52 Monin, *Alcoolisme*, 171. Monin repeated almost the same phrase in his 1890 book. Monin, *Misères nerveuses*, 145.

53 Wahl, *Crime*, 91. See also Hugh, "Absinthe Hour," 195.

54 Eugène Pelletan, "La moderne Babylone. Lettre d'un provincial en tournée à Paris," *Journal de Beaugency: Écho de la Beauce et de la Sologne*, 2 August 1863, 3–4.

55 Pignel, *Conducteur*, 159.

56 On boukha, see Studer, "Under the Influence."

57 A. Froemer, "La Maison Pernod et l'histoire de l'absinthe," *Le Panthéon de l'industrie: Revue hebdomadaire internationale illustrée des expositions et des concours*, 5 October 1884, 353–4. Emphasis in the original.

58 Berthoud, "Fée verte," 639.

59 Lanier, *Absinthe*, 8–9.

60 Berthoud, "Fée verte," 639–40. See also Jack Turner, "Green Gold: The Return of Absinthe," *New Yorker*, 13 March 2006, 38–44, here 40.

61 Baker, *Dedalus Book of Absinthe*, 104–5. Others give the time of his flight as the early 1790s. Lanier, *Absinthe*, 9; Lachenmeier et al., "Absinthe, Absinthism and Thujone," 33.

62 Lanier, "Bittersweet Taste," 282; Fahrenkrug, "What Happened to the 'Fée

Verte,'" 272; Luauté, Saladini, and Benyaya, "Toxicité neuropsychiatrique,"
498; Lachenmeier et al., "Absinthe, Absinthism and Thujone," 33.

63 Liggenstorfer, "Ursprung des Absinthe," 23.

64 Delahaye, "Grandeur et décadence," 475–6.

65 Stocker, "Absinth," 32; "L'histoire de l'absinthe, à Couvet," *Le conteur vaudois:
Journal de la Suisse romande* 28, no. 2 (1890) : 1–2.

66 Berthoud, "Fée verte," 640.

67 Liggenstorfer, "Ursprung des Absinthe," 24.

68 Chapuis, "Absinthe réhabilitée," 517. A very similar description of Mère Henriod can be found in Jean-Jacques Charrère's article. Jean-Jacques Charrère,
"La saga de l'absinthe interdite. Part 2," *Journal de Genève*, 11 July 1994, 12.

69 Adams, *Hideous Absinthe*, 20.

70 Berthoud, "Fée verte," 640.

71 "L'histoire de l'absinthe, à Couvet," 1.

72 Delahaye, "Grandeur et décadence," 475–6; Lanier, "Bittersweet Taste," 282.

73 Young, "Heroic Indolence," 249.

74 Lanier, *Absinthe*, 9.

75 Delahaye, "Grandeur et décadence," 475–6; Bihl-Willette, *Tavernes*, 197.

76 Chapuis, "Absinthe réhabilitée," 517.

77 Bauer, "Visiting the 'Green Fairy,'" 2.

78 Lanier, *Absinthe*, 9; Baker, *Dedalus Book of Absinthe*, 105.

79 Gasnier, "Affiches publicitaires," part 1, 49.

80 Berthoud, "Fée verte," 640–1.

81 Froemer, "Maison Pernod," 353.

82 Villon, "Absinthe," 149.

83 See, for example, Stocker, "Absinth," 32.

84 "L'histoire de l'absinthe, à Couvet," 1.

85 J. Guillemaud, "L'absinthe," *Le Caviste. Organe officiel de la Chambre syndicale
des cavistes et liquoristes de Paris*, 2 January 1900, 2. Capitalization in the
original.

86 Froemer, "Maison Pernod," 353.

87 Bonneff and Bonneff, *Marchands de folie*, 166–7. Capitalization in the original.

88 Guillemaud, "Absinthe," 2. Capitalization in the original.

89 Froemer, "Maison Pernod," 353. See also Villon, "Absinthe," 149.

90 Stocker, "Absinth," 32.

91 Liggenstorfer, "Ursprung des Absinthe," 24.

92 Froemer, "Maison Pernod," 353. See also Villon, "Absinthe," 149; Bonneff and
Bonneff, *Marchands de folie*, 167.

93 Advert for White Knights, *Times*, 15 September 1819, 4.

94 Terril, "Dudes, Decadence, and Degeneracy," 3.

95 Delahaye, *Absinthe, son histoire*, 53–5; Baker, *Dedalus Book of Absinthe*, 105; Gasnier, "Affiches publicitaires," part 1, 49.

96 Lachenmeier et al., "Absinthe: A Review," 366.

97 Villon, "Absinthe," 149.

98 Froemer, "Maison Pernod," 353.

99 "Un ancien remède," *Le Petit fanal Oranais*, 14 April 1901, 1.

100 Hugh, "Absinthe Hour," 195.

101 Liggenstorfer, "Ursprung des Absinthe," 23.

102 Gustave Petitpierre, *Souvenirs et généalogie des familles Sandoz et Borel-Jaquet. Dossier particulier Borel-Girard. Aux archives de l'Etat, Neuchâtel*, as quoted in Berthoud, "Fée verte," 640.

103 Lachenmeier et al., "Absinthe, Absinthism and Thujone," 33; Cotton, "Vincent van Gogh," 76.

104 Charrère, "Saga," 12.

105 "La nationalité de l'absinthe," *Le conteur vaudois: Journal de la Suisse romande* 46, no. 30 (1908): 3.

106 Adams, *Hideous Absinthe*, 21. See also Faux, "She Makes a Beast of Man," 10.

107 Guy, *When Champagne Became French*, 17.

108 Nourrisson, *Crus et cuites*, 159.

109 Heilig, "Green Hour," 10.

110 Lalouette, "Consommation," 298–9.

111 W. Nick, "Le colon algérien," *Le Petit Bouira: Journal républicain*, 9 February 1895, 1.

112 Prestwich, *Drink*, 80.

113 Hugh, "Absinthe Hour," 195.

114 See, for example, Heilig, "Green Hour," 10.

115 Martin, *Manuel d'hygiène*, 203–4; Baudet-Dulary, *Hygiène populaire*, 38; Monin, *Alcoolisme*, 174.

116 Bauer, "Visiting the 'Green Fairy,'" 3.

117 Heilig, "Green Hour," 10.

118 Marit, *Hygiène de l'Algérie*, 374.

119 Saxton, "Before Addiction," 32.

120 Gasnier, "Affiches publicitaires," part 1, 69.

121 Mayet, *Vin de France*, 75.

122 "Foreign Intelligence. France," *Times*, 17 September 1864, 10. Emphasis in the original.

123 Sterling Heilig, "France's Green Devil," *Evening Star*, 22 December 1906, 2.

124 Owens and Nathan, *Little Green Book*.

125 Monselet, *Montmartre à Séville*, 17. Emphasis in the original.

126 See, for example: "Absinthe," *Lancet*, 17 August 1907, 464–5.

127 Villacrose, *Vingt ans en Algérie*, 151.

128 Monselet, *Montmartre à Séville*, 17.

129 Nourrisson, "Consommation alcoolique," 57.

130 Delahaye, *Histoire de la fée verte*, 93–4. Yves Chapuis also compared the ceremony of preparing absinthe to that of preparing tea in Muslim countries. Chapuis, "Absinthe réhabilitée," 518.

131 Nourrisson, "Consommation alcoolique," 57.

132 "The Ravages of the War," *Times*, 6 September 1870, 8.

133 J.F. O., "The State of Paris," *Times*, 7 April 1871, 8. Emphasis in the original.

134 Lanier, *Absinthe*, 18.

135 Castellane, *Souvenirs*, 167. Emphasis in the original.

136 Lemanski, *Hygiène du colon*, 105–6.

137 Jean de Montmartre, "L'apéritif national," *Le Radical*, 28 December 1898, 2.

138 Geffroy, "Paysage d'alcool," 111.

139 Moreau, *Liqueur d'absinthe*, 13. Emphasis in the original.

140 On this, see also Prestwich, *Drink*, 12.

141 Moreau, *Liqueur d'absinthe*, 13.

142 Monselet, *Montmartre à Séville*, 18–19. See also Montmartre, "Apéritif national," 2.

143 Heilig, "France's Green Devil," 2.

144 Lemanski, *Hygiène du colon*, 105.

Chapter Two

1 Frégier, *Absinthisme*, 5. Capitalization in the original.

2 Jean-Jacques Charrère, "La saga de l'absinthe interdite. Part 3," *Journal de Genève*, 18 July 1994, 12; Baker, *Dedalus Book of Absinthe*, 107.

3 Conrad, *Absinthe*, 90; Hutton, "Myth," 63; Lachenmeier et al., "Absinthe, Absinthism and Thujone," 33.

4 The toxicologist Donald Barceloux mentioned in 2012 that French soldiers in Algeria received rations not of absinthe, but of "wormwood-containing wine as an antipyretic" between 1844 and 1847. Barceloux, *Medical Toxicology*, 761.

5 Conrad, *Absinthe*, 90; Fahrenkrug, "What Happened to the 'Fée Verte,'" 272–3; Hein, Lobbedey, and Neumärker, "Absinth," 2717; Baker, *Dedalus Book of*

Absinthe, 107; Hutton, "Myth," 63; Lachenmeier et al., "Absinthe: A Review," 366; Owens and Nathan, *Little Green Book*; Cotton, "Vincent van Gogh," 76; Pizzorno and Murray, *Textbook*, 591; Saxton, "Before Addiction," 31.

6 Bauer, "Visiting the 'Green Fairy,'" 2.

7 Baker, *Dedalus Book of Absinthe*, 107.

8 Langle, "Cafés et débits," para. 148; Delahaye, *Absinthe, son histoire*, 84; Baker, *Dedalus Book of Absinthe*, 107; Delahaye, *Affiches*, 72; Adams, *Hideous Absinthe*, 20; Lachenmeier et al., "Absinthe, Absinthism and Thujone," 33; Niemeyer, "Fée verte," para. 2; Pizzorno and Murray, *Textbook*, 591.

9 Delahaye, *Histoire de la fée verte*, 60; O'Reilly, "Absinthe Makes the Tart Grow Fonder," 111; Conrad, *Absinthe*, 6, 90; Hutton, "Myth," 63; Padosch, Lachenmeier, and Kröner, "Absinthism," 3; Niemeyer, "Fée verte," para. 2; Lachenmeier et al., "Absinthe, Absinthism and Thujone," 33.

10 Delachaux, *Absinthe*, 35; Baker, *Dedalus Book of Absinthe*, 107; Delahaye, *Absinthe, son histoire*, 84; Delahaye, *Affiches*, 72; Noël, *Nouvelles confidences sur l'absinthe*, 113; Nourrisson, "Fines herbes," 439; Bröckers, "Absinthe als Treibstoff der Moderne," 27; Adams, *Hideous Absinthe*, 4; Owens and Nathan, *Little Green Book*.

11 Delahaye, *Histoire de la fée verte*, 73; Delahaye, *Absinthe, son histoire*, 84; Jack Turner, "Green Gold: The Return of Absinthe," *New Yorker*, 13 March 2006, 38–44, 40.

12 Studer, "Green Fairy in the Maghreb," 494. See also Studer, "Same Drink," 23. I have uncritically referred to absinthe rations as a narrative shortcut in one of my other publications, which was, however, not specifically on the history of absinthe. See Studer, "Remembrance of Drinks Past," 171.

13 Armand, *Algérie médicale*, 474, 445.

14 Ibid., 474, 479.

15 Viry, *Manuel d'hygiène militaire*, 173. See also Laveran, *Traité d'hygiène militaire*, 288; Rochard, *Traité d'hygiène*, 897. I have discussed these wine and coffee rations in my article on coffee in colonial Algeria. See Studer, "Without Coffee."

16 "Algérie," *Journal de Genève*, 10 January 1845, 1.

17 "Courrier du Soir," *L'Indépendant de la Moselle*, 29 October 1845, 1.

18 "Faits Divers," *L'Algérie: Courrier d'Afrique, d'Orient et de la Méditerranée*, 2 November 1845, 4.

19 "Courrier d'Afrique," *La Semaine: Encyclopédie de la presse périodique*, 2/9 November 1845, 47.

20 Rossignol, *Traité élémentaire*, 373.

21 Didiot, *Code des officiers*, 525; Viry, "Hygiène militaire," 263; Salle, *Gelures et insolations*, 61. See also Anselmier, *Empoisonnement*, 27.

22 Guba, *Taming Cannabis*, 69.

23 Figuier, "Effets pernicieux," 343–4.

24 Guba, *Taming Cannabis*, 189.

25 Quetin, *Guide*, 249–50, n1. Emphasis in the original.

26 Viry, *Manuel d'hygiène militaire*, 176.

27 Burns, *Temperance Dictionary*, 4; "Measuring Civilization," *Indiana State Sentinel*, 10 April 1861, 4.

28 Armand, *Algérie médicale*, 445, n1. See also Armand, *Médecine et hygiène*, 445, n1.

29 Hennequin, *Conquête de l'Algérie*, 47.

30 Varin, *Algérie*, 22.

31 Laveran, *Traité d'hygiène militaire*, 294.

32 Morache, *Traité d'hygiène militaire*, 706. See also Raynaud, "Alcoolisme en Algérie," 68.

33 "Chine et Indo-Chine," *Le Temps*, 22 June 1885, 2; Tout-Paris, "Un proscrit," *Le Gaulois*, 22 August 1885, 1.

34 Charvériat, *Huit jours en Kabylie*, 201, n1; Monin, *Misères nerveuses*, 145.

35 Lierre, *Question de l'absinthe*, 62.

36 Prochaska, *Making Algeria French*, 206; Stoler, *Carnal Knowledge*, 82.

37 Dunwoodie, "Assimilation," 64.

38 Figuier, "Effets pernicieux," 343–4.

39 "En 1850, Édouard Pernod venait fabriquer son absinthe à Lunel," *Midi Libre*, 7 June 2020, accessed 2 April 2023, https://www.midilibre.fr/2020/06/07/en-1850-edouard-pernod-venait-fabriquer-son-absinthe-a-lunel,8920775.php.

40 On the history of this epidemic, see Delaporte, *Disease and Civilization*; Kudlick, "Learning from Cholera."

41 This was reported in *The Times* in early April 1832. "French Papers," *Times*, 3 April 1832, 1. Emphasis in the original.

42 Thévenot, *Traité*, 362.

43 See, for example, Lierre, *Question de l'absinthe*, 61.

44 Whin-Hurst, "The Drinking of Absinthe," *Times*, 17 August 1907, 13. See also "L'Absinthe à l'Académie," *Le Petit Midi*, 3 January 1897, 2; Walker, "Effects of Absinthe," 568; "Absinthe," *Lancet*, 17 August 1907, 464–5.

45 There were also accounts of French soldiers in Algeria, specifically during the war against Abd-el-Kader, being forced to mix absinthe and urine in order to

survive. See "The Paris Papers," *Times*, 8 October 1845, 6; Berteuil, *Algérie française*, 273.

46 Viry, "Hygiène militaire," 262–3.

47 Charvériat, *Huit jours en Kabylie*, 201–2, n1; Lucienne, *Leçons d'anti-alcoolisme*, 44; Griveau, *Alcoolisme*, 95; Decroos, "Réglementation," 27.

48 Aubert, *Alcoolisation de la France*, 14–15, n1. Emphasis in the original.

49 Conrad, *Absinthe*, 90.

50 Hutton, "Myth," 63.

51 "Absinthe," *Times*, 26 April 1872, 10.

52 Dagen, "History of Malaria and Its Treatment," 8.

53 Cohen, "Malaria and French Imperialism," 26; Prochaska, *Making Algeria French*, 89.

54 Castellane, *Souvenirs*, 167.

55 See, for example, Sirven, *Abrutis*, 18–19.

56 Anselmier, *Empoisonnement*, 25–6.

57 Blanc, *Soldats et colons*, 13.

58 Pagès, *Hygiène pour tous*, 281–2. Emphasis in the original.

59 Ravenez, *Vie du soldat*, 176.

60 See, for example, Duvernois, *Algérie*, 248; Bernard, *Algérie qui s'en va*, 119.

61 Saxton, "Before Addiction," 31.

62 Prestwich, "Temperance in France," 302; Delahaye, *Histoire de la fée verte*, 73; Conrad, *Absinthe*, 6, 90; Baker, *Dedalus Book of Absinthe*, 107; Bihl-Willette, *Tavernes*, 197; Padosch, Lachenmeier, and Kröner, "Absinthism," 3; Lachenmeier et al., "Absinthe, Absinthism and Thujone," 33; Owens and Nathan, *Little Green Book*; Pizzorno and Murray, *Textbook*, 591.

63 "Absinthe" (26 April 1872), 10.

64 Sterling Heilig, "France's Green Devil," *Evening Star*, 22 December 1906, 2.

65 Very similar narratives exist around Orangina, whose popularity allegedly also only began in France after it was publicly consumed by soldiers returned from the "successful" war in Algeria in the late 1950s and early 1960s. Ghozland, *Un siècle de réclames*, Affiches 191–4; "French Branding Story: Orangina Marks 75 Years of Ad Fizz," *Independent*, 16 July 2011, accessed 19 February 2023, https://www.independent.co.uk/life-style/food-and-drink/french-branding-story-orangina-marks-75-years-of-ad-fizz-2314796.html.

66 Haine, *World of the Paris Café*, 95.

67 Noël, *Nouvelles confidences sur l'absinthe*, 113.

68 Adams, *Hideous Absinthe*, 4.

69 Moreau, *Liqueur d'absinthe*, 13.

70 Anselmier, *Empoisonnement*, 26.

71 Tout-Paris, "Un proscrit," 1.

72 Anselmier, *Empoisonnement*, 26–7.

73 "Foreign Intelligence. France," *Times*, 17 September 1864, 10.

74 Delahaye, "Grandeur et décadence," 476; Adams, *Hideous Absinthe*, 20; Owens and Nathan, *Little Green Book*; Bauer, "Visiting the 'Green Fairy,'" 2.

75 Saliège, "Rapport," 154. As absinthe is feminine in French, it was also regularly called "Queen Absinthe." See, for example, Mayet, *Vin de France*, 64. This royal vocabulary was also used by opponents of the drink, shown by Emma Walker calling absinthe the "queen of poisons" in 1906. Walker, "Effects of Absinthe," 568.

76 Chapuis, "Absinthe réhabilitée," 518–19.

77 Delahaye, *Absinthe, son histoire*, 88; Hein, Lobbedey, and Neumärker, "Absinth," 2717; Adams, *Hideous Absinthe*, 20; Nourrisson, *Crus et cuites*, 142.

78 Eidgenössischer Initiativausschuss gegen den Absinth, *Antwort*, 11–12.

79 Roux, *Étude*, 42. Emphasis in the original. See also Casanova, "Intoxications chroniques," 76.

80 Dubuisson and Vigouroux, *Responsabilité pénale*, 358.

81 Morache, *Traité d'hygiène militaire*, 706.

82 See, for example, Jules Hayaux, "L'absinthe au Maroc," *Le Rappel*, 8 February 1914, 1.

83 Pichon, *Maladies de l'esprit*, 354. Emphasis in the original. See also Dubut de Laforest, *Pathologie sociale*, 454, n1.

84 Griveau, *Alcoolisme*, 95. For a very similar statement, see "L'Absinthe à l'Académie," 2.

85 Delahaye, *Absinthe, son histoire*, 96–7.

86 Viré, *Algérie*, 91–2.

87 Monselet, *Montmartre à Séville*, 16.

88 Viré, *Algérie*, 91–2.

89 Régis, *Constantine*, 10–11; Baudel, *Un an à Alger*, 21; Bernard, *Algérie qui s'en va*, 79.

90 "Une famille boufariquoise à l'heure de l'absinthe en 1855," *L'Afrique du Nord illustrée: Journal hebdomadaire d'actualités nord-africaines*, 30 December 1934, 4.

91 Marcotte de Quivières, *Deux ans en Afrique*, 21.

92 Thierry-Mieg, *Six semaines en Afrique*, 294, n1. Emphasis in the original.

93 Bynum, "Chronic Alcoholism," 162. Warren Walker informer the readers of his 1982 article that "cases of human spontaneous combustion continued to be reported throughout the nineteenth century." Walker, "Lost Liquor Lore," 20.

94 Fallot, *Par-delà la Méditerranée*, 29.

95 Anoymous, *Souvenirs d'Afrique, 1854–1855*, 163.

96 Galtier-Boissière, *Anti-alcoolisme en histoires vraies*, 89.

97 See, for example, Houdeville, *Comment préserver*, 13.

98 Delahaye, *Absinthe, son histoire*, 92.

99 Casanova, "Intoxications chroniques," 19.

100 Foix, "En Algérie," 141.

101 Aubert, *Œuvre*, 15–16.

102 M., "Bulletin," 153.

103 Charvériat, *Huit jours en Kabylie*, 201, n1.

104 Villacrose, *Vingt ans en Algérie*, 353.

105 Lierre, *Question de l'absinthe*, 62; Bailly, *Études sur l'Algérie*, 158–9.

106 Capo de Feuillide, "De la colonisation algérienne," *La Presse*, 21 July 1854, 2. He repeated the same phrase in his 1856 book. Cappot, *Algérie française*, 38–9.

107 Triboulet and Mathieu, *Alcool et alcoolisme*, 190.

108 Rouby, "Alcoolisme," 240–1; Triboulet and Mathieu, *Alcool et alcoolisme*, 190, n1.

109 Raynaud, "Alcoolisme en Algérie," 67.

110 Beaufumé, *Abus des liqueurs alcooliques*, 4–5.

111 See, for example, Rémy, *Lettres d'un voyageur*, 5; Carteron, *Voyage en Algérie*, 213; Evans, *Last Winter in Algeria*, 276; Bourde, *A travers l'Algérie*, 221–2; Régis, *Constantine*, 10–11; Grad, *Études de voyage*, 12; Baudel, *Un an à Alger*, 181; Donnet, *En Sahara*, 66.

112 See, for example, Cappot, *Algérie française*, 39; Thierry-Mieg, *Six semaines en Afrique*, 294–5, n1.

113 Rouby, "Alcoolisme," 239.

114 Ibid., 242.

115 Raynaud, "Alcoolisme en Algérie," 68.

116 Cooke, *Conquest and Colonisation*, 80. Emphasis in the original.

117 See, for example, Raynaud, "Alcoolisme en Algérie," 67.

118 W. Nick, "Le colon algérien," *Le Petit Bouira: Journal républicain*, 9 February 1895, 1. For a similar argument about France's West African colonies, see Vibert, *Qestions brûlantes*, 408.

119 "Bulletin," *Le Courrier de Tlemcen*, 14 October 1883, 1. For other reactions by

French settlers to Charles Ferry's statement, see "La colonisation algérienne,"
La Tafna: Journal de l'arrondissement de Tlemcen, 19 December 1883, 1;
Personne. "Bulletin," *Le Courrier de Tlemcen*, 21 December 1883, 1; Meynié,
Juifs en Algérie, 281; "De Paris à Biskra," *Le Républicain de Constantine*,
10 October 1889, 1–2.

120 Ageron, *Histoire de l'Algérie contemporaine*, 17–72, para. 145.

121 Bergot, *Algérie*, 2–3. Capitalization in the original.

122 Davis, "Desert 'Wastes' of the Maghreb"; Shaker, "The Beginning and Historisation of Decline Theories."

123 Jean de Blida, "La Verte," *La Tafna: Journal de l'arrondissement de Tlemcen*,
16 May 1894, 1.

124 On this idea of an inherent healthiness of a public consumption of alcohol,
see also Padwa, *Social Poison*, 18.

125 Treille, *Principes*, 160.

126 Bonain, *Européen sous les tropiques*, 244.

127 "Absinthe," *Times*, 26 April 1872, 10.

128 On the history of Port Said, see Elgezy, "A Memory Debate."

129 "Absinthe," *Times*, 26 April 1872, 10.

130 Saliège, "Rapport," 155.

131 Bonain, *Européen sous les tropiques*, 244.

Chapter Three

Chapter title from Jean de Montmartre, "L'apéritif national," *Le Radical*,
28 December 1898, 2.

1 Ibid.

2 Schultz, "Celebration and Censure," 19.

3 Barnao, "Leisure Time and 'Alcoholic Interactions,'" 293.

4 Montmartre, "Apéritif national," 2.

5 Strang, Arnold, and Peters, "Absinthe," 1590.

6 Saxton, "Before Addiction," 24.

7 Mayet, *Vin de France*, 72; Sterling Heilig, "The Green Hour in Paris," *Sun
[New York Sun]*, 19 August 1894, 10.

8 Alfred Delvaud, "L'île de Calypse," *Figaro*, 24 August 1862, 4–5. This same
quote can also be found in Delvaud, *Histoire anecdotique*, 248.

9 "Absinthe," *Times*, 4 May 1868, 12.

10 Marrus, "Social Drinking," 124.

11 Monselet, *Montmartre à Séville*, 16–19.

12 Angelo de Sorr, "Les professeurs d'absinthe," *Figaro*, 14 June 1859, 2. See also Anonymous, *Algérie et la lettre de l'empereur*, 43; Kock, *Buveurs d'absinthe*, 115; F. Rado, "Les Trichines," *La Bohème*, 15 April 1866, 2–3.

13 "Absinthe" (4 May 1868), 12.

14 Mikael Suni, "Alcoolisme et absinthisme," *La Dépêche: Journal de la démocratie* (6 April 1895): 1.

15 Frey, *Méthode pour prolonger la vie*, 53. Emphasis in the original.

16 Baker, *Dedalus Book of Absinthe*, 7.

17 Bauer, "Visiting the 'Green Fairy,'" 2.

18 Huisman, Brug, and Mackenbach, "Absinthe," 739.

19 Prestwich, "Temperance in France," 302.

20 Delvaud, "Île de Calypse," 4. Also in Delvaud, *Histoire anecdotique*, 248–9. See also Montmartre, "Apéritif national," 2.

21 Legrand du Saulle, *Étude médico-légale sur les épileptiques*, 135.

22 Heilig, "Green Hour," 10.

23 Demartini, "Culture des cafés," 56.

24 See, for example, "Foreign Intelligence: France," *Times*, 17 September 1864, 10; "Absinthe" (4 May 1868), 12; Heilig, "Green Hour," 10.

25 Jean, "A Paris," *Le Rappel Algérien*, 2 September 1909, 1.

26 See, for example, Evans, *Last Winter in Algeria*, 276.

27 Jean, "A Paris," 1.

28 "Alcohol Drinking Doubles in France," *New York Times*, 23 July 1925, 4.

29 Lucienne, *Leçons d'anti-alcoolisme*, 44.

30 "L'absinthe," *Journal de Genève*, 21 June 1908, 1.

31 Eidgenössischer Initiativausschuss gegen den Absinth, *Absinthverbot in der Schweiz*, 12; Eidgenössischer Initiativausschuss gegen den Absinth, *Antwort*, 6.

32 Hugh, "Absinthe Hour," 195.

33 "L'absinthe" (21 June 1908): 1.

34 Hazemann, "Homicides," 12.

35 Mayet, *Vin de France*, 72.

36 Heilig, "Green Hour," 10.

37 Ibid.

38 Sterling Heilig, "France's Green Devil," *Evening Star*, 22 December 1906, 2.

39 Lebovitz, *Drinking French*, 98.

40 Heilig, "France's Green Devil," 2.

41 "Absinthe and Its Victim," *New York Times*, 15 October 1887, 4.

42 Rouby, "Alcoolisme," 240–1.

43 Delvaud, "Île de Calypse," 4. Emphasis in the original. Also in Delvaud, *Histoire anecdotique*, 249.

44 "Absinthe" (4 May 1868), 12.

45 Goudeau, *Paris qui consomme*, 93.

46 Baker, *Dedalus Book of Absinthe*, 23, 7; Lee and Balick, "Absinthe," 218.

47 Cotton, "Vincent van Gogh," 76.

48 Decroos, "Réglementation," 34–5.

49 See, for example, Galtier-Boissière, *Anti-alcoolisme en histoires vraies*.

50 Decroos, "Réglementation," 35.

51 Niemeyer, "Fée verte," para. 7.

52 Saxton, "Before Addiction," 28.

53 Delahaye, *Absinthe au féminin*, 33.

54 Nourrisson, "Fines herbes," 439.

55 Young, "Heroic Indolence," 248.

56 Narrey, *Amours faciles*, 157–8. See also Mayet, *Vin de France*, 66.

57 Legrand du Saulle, *Folie*, 541. See also Arnold, "Absinthe," 112; Gambelunghe and Melai, "Absinthe," 186; Cargill, "Myth of the Green Fairy," 88.

58 Bauer, "Visiting the 'Green Fairy,'" 2.

59 Padosch, Lachenmeier, and Kröner, "Absinthism," 1–2; Cotton, "Vincent van Gogh," 76.

60 DeBoer, "Flavour of Absinthe," 50; Padosch, Lachenmeier, and Kröner, "Absinthism," 1–2.

61 DeBoer, "Flavour of Absinthe," 50.

62 Padosch, Lachenmeier, and Kröner, "Absinthism," 1–2; Cotton, "Vincent van Gogh," 76.

63 DeBoer, "Flavour of Absinthe," 50.

64 Huisman, Brug, and Mackenbach, "Absinthe," 739.

65 Arnold, "Vincent van Gogh"; Lanier, *Absinthe*, 12–13; DeBoer, "Flavour of Absinthe," 50; Blumer, "Illness of Vincent van Gogh"; Cargill, "Myth of the Green Fairy," 89; Cotton, "Vincent van Gogh."

66 Delahaye, "Grandeur et décadence," 476.

67 Black, *Drugging France*, 105.

68 Earle, "Green Eyes," 694.

69 Motet, "Considérations générales," 16–17.

70 See, for example, "Absinthe" (4 May 1868), 12.

71 Lancereaux's clearest criticism of absinthe can be found in an 1880 article

published in the *Bulletin de l'Académie de médecine*. Here, Jacquet presumably refers to either Lancereaux's 1878 book or his 1880 article. Lancereaux, *Alcoolisme*; Lancereaux, "Absinthisme aigu."

72 Jacquet, *Alcool*, 725. Emphasis in the original.

73 Monin, *Alcoolisme*, 172. Emphasis in the original. See also Colin, *Ouvrage de vulgarisation*, 280.

74 Daviller, "Alcool et alcoolisme," 45.

75 Monin, *Alcoolisme*, 171–2.

76 Rude, *Tout Paris au café*, 71–2.

77 "The Charms of Absinthe," *New York Times*, 19 October 1884, 5. See also Lanier, *Absinthe*, 15–16.

78 DeBoer, "Flavour of Absinthe," 50.

79 Heilig, "France's Green Devil," 2.

80 Denommé, "Note Concerning the Death of George Sand," 261.

81 Heilig, "France's Green Devil," 2.

82 See, for example, Monin, *Misères nerveuses*, 145; Steeg, *Dangers*, 99; Arnould, *Nouveaux éléments d'hygiène*, 639; Guinard, *Enseignement*, 225–6; Rénon, *Maladies populaires*, 288; Remlinger, "Progrès de l'alcoolisme," 751.

83 Montmartre, "Apéritif national," 2.

84 Galtier-Boissière, *Anti-alcoolisme en histoires vraies*, 72.

85 See, for example, Eidgenössischer Initiativausschuss gegen den Absinth, *Absinthverbot in der Schweiz*, 16.

86 "Comment l'alcool peut tuer un peuple," *La Presse*, 2 August 1921, 2.

87 Lucien Victor-Meunier, "Le Minotaure," *Le Rappel*, 20 December 1897, 1.

88 Earle, "Green Eyes," 693.

89 Monin, *Alcoolisme*, 172. Emphasis in the original.

90 Motet, "Considérations générales," 16–17.

91 Monin, *Alcoolisme*, 171–2.

92 Daviller, "Alcool et alcoolisme," 45.

93 Howard, "Advertising Industry," 428. See also Schultz, "Celebration and Censure," 19.

94 Howard, "Advertising Industry," 430.

95 Nourrisson, *Crus et cuites*, 147.

96 Conrad, *Absinthe*, 90.

97 Howard, "Advertising Industry," 429.

98 Gasnier, "Affiches publicitaires," part 2, 43–4.

99 Bernard, "Alcoolisme et antialcoolisme," 612.

100 Tsikounas, "Quand l'alcool fait sa pub," 100.

101 For more on Paul-Maurice Legrain, see Patricia Prestwich's 1997 article on him: Prestwich, "Paul-Maurice Legrain."

102 Legrain, *Éléments de médecine mentale*, 407.

103 Hazemann, "Homicides," 14.

104 *L'Afrique du Nord illustrée*, 7 December 1912, 54.

105 *L'Afrique du Nord illustrée*, 10 October 1912, 26.

106 *L'Afrique du Nord illustrée*, 2 November 1912, 4.

107 *L'Afrique du Nord illustrée*, 26 April 1913, 7.

108 Charles Mayet, "Le vin de France," *Le Temps*, 28 February 1894, 2.

109 Howard, "Advertising Industry," 429–30.

110 Prestwich, "Temperance in France," 303. Emphasis in the original.

111 Delahaye, *Absinthe au féminin*, 12.

112 Mayet, "Vin de France," 2. See also Prestwich, "Temperance in France," 303.

113 In her book on the depiction of absinthe-drinking women in adverts and art, Marie-Claude Delahaye shows two of these adverts. Delahaye, *Absinthe au féminin*, 73, 83.

114 Skibicki, "Victimes de stéréotypes," 226.

115 "L'absinthe" (21 June 1908), 1.

116 Delahaye, *Affiches*, 48. See also Delahaye, *Absinthe au féminin*, 91.

117 See, for example, Andrew and Kanya-Forstner, *France Overseas*, 41.

118 Delahaye, *Affiches*, 54.

119 Ibid., 102.

120 Legrain, *Éléments de médecine mentale*, 404.

121 Anet, "War against Absinthe," 189.

Chapter Four

1 Marrus, "Social Drinking," 115.

2 Borja, "Absinthe," 42.

3 Fillaut, "Alcoolisme et antialcoolisme," paras 18–22.

4 Frégier, *Absinthisme*, 10.

5 Villacrose, *Vingt ans en Algérie*, 364; Legrain, "Guerre à l'apéritif," 31.

6 Cappot, *Algérie française*, 39.

7 Fillaut, "Alcoolisme et antialcoolisme," para. 23.

8 See, for example, "Absinthe," *Times*, 4 May 1868, 12.

9 Prestwich, "Female Alcoholism," 322.

10 Lalouette, "Consommation," 295; Fillaut, "Alcoolisme et antialcoolisme," para. 4.

11 Ruyssen, "Tempérance," 137.

12 Eidgenössischer Initiativausschuss gegen den Absinth, *Absinthverbot in der Schweiz*, 12.

13 See also Stocker, "Absinth," 36.

14 Marrus, "Social Drinking," 126.

15 Prestwich, "Female Alcoholism," 324.

16 "Measuring Civilization," *Indiana State Sentinel*, 10 April 1861, 4.

17 "Absinthe Drunkenness," 242.

18 Garnier, *Folie à Paris*, 32.

19 Delahaye, *Absinthe, son histoire*, 120.

20 L., "Un poison bien français," 5.

21 Balesta, *Absinthe et absintheurs*, 54.

22 Goudeau, *Paris qui consomme*, 96.

23 Geffroy, "Bonne Absinthe," 128.

24 On working-class women socializing over glass of absinthe after work, see also Delahaye, *Absinthe au féminin*, 68.

25 Geffroy, "Bonne Absinthe," 129–30.

26 Sterling Heilig, "The Green Hour in Paris," *Sun [New York Sun]*, 19 August 1894, 10.

27 Haine, *World of the Paris Café*, 181–2.

28 Marrus, "Social Drinking," 126.

29 Heilig, "Green Hour," 10. Emphasis in the original.

30 Lalouette, "Débits de boissons," 133.

31 Delahaye, *Absinthe au féminin*, 43.

32 Lalouette, "Débits de boissons," 133.

33 L., "Un poison bien français," 5.

34 Lucienne, *Leçons d'anti-alcoolisme*, 44.

35 Niemeyer, "Fée verte," para. 3.

36 Delahaye, *Absinthe au féminin*, 50. See also ibid., 8, 61; Altamirano, "Intoxicating Women," 1.

37 Delahaye, *Absinthe au féminin*, 55.

38 Fillaut, "Alcoolisme et antialcoolisme," para. 17.

39 Pick, *Faces of Degeneration*, 92.

40 Gordon, "French Psychiatry and the New Woman," 161.

41 Altamirano, "Intoxicating Women," 1–2.

42 Terril, "Dudes, Decadence, and Degeneracy," 2.

43 Nourrisson, *Crus et cuites*, 164.

44 Lalouette, "Débits de boissons," 132.

45 Haine, *World of the Paris Café*, 185.

46 "Absinthe" (4 May 1868), 12. See also Marrus, "Social Drinking," 131; Haine, *World of the Paris Café*, 184.

47 Villacrose, *Vingt ans en Algérie*, 45; Bernard, *Algérie qui s'en va*, 177.

48 Barrows, "Parliaments of the People," 89.

49 Fillaut, "Alcoolisme et antialcoolisme," para. 11.

50 Bernard, "Alcoolisme et antialcoolisme," 611; Barrows, "Parliaments of the People," 89, 94; Harris, *Murders and Madness*, 247; Tsikounas, "Quand l'alcool fait sa pub," 99.

51 For a reaction to the relaxation of these rules in general, see Dastre, "Lutte contre l'alcoolisme," 692.

52 Ross, "Serving Sex," 289.

53 Fillaut, "Alcoolisme et antialcoolisme," paras 18–22.

54 This sketch shows a woman on a bicycle, riding past a group of men, during the "hour of absinthe." *La Vie en culotte rouge: Journal littéraire et artistique paraissant tous les dimanches*, 29 October 1911, 15.

55 Heilig, "Green Hour," 10.

56 Jean de Blida, "La Verte," *La Tafna: Journal de l'arrondissement de Tlemcen*, 16 May 1894, 1.

57 Lanier, "Bittersweet Taste," 285; Lanier, *Absinthe*, 7; Liggenstorfer, "Thujon," 53; Montagne, "Drugs on the Internet," 509.

58 Monin, *Alcoolisme*, 174.

59 Padosch, Lachenmeier, and Kröner, "Absinthism," 11; Cargill, "Myth of the Green Fairy," 88.

60 Raynaud, "Alcoolisme en Algérie," 67.

61 Bonneff and Bonneff, *Marchands de folie*, 156.

62 Delahaye, *Absinthe au féminin*, 64.

63 Fillaut, "Alcoolisme et antialcoolisme," paras 18–22.

64 Afanasyeva, "Pratiques," para. 4.

65 Fillaut, "Alcoolisme et antialcoolisme," para. 16.

66 Nourrisson, "Origines de l'antialcoolisme," 502.

67 Ibid.; Fillaut, "Alcoolisme et antialcoolisme," para. 32.

68 Afanasyeva, "Pratiques," para. 4.

69 Fillaut, "Alcoolisme et antialcoolisme," para. 2. Capitalization in the original.

70 Heilig, "Green Hour," 10.

71 Galtier-Boissière, *Anti-alcoolisme en histoires vraies*, 72.

72 Prestwich, "Female Alcoholism," 327.

73 Heilig, "Green Hour," 10.

74 "Society Women's Drinking," *Sun [New York Sun]*, 14 January 1900, 5.

75 Faux, "She Makes a Beast of Man," 15; Borja, "Absinthe," 42.

76 Adams, *Hideous Absinthe*, 39.

77 Davray, *Amour à Paris*, 90.

78 Haine, *World of the Paris Café*, 191.

79 Haine, "Absinthe," 165. In his 1996 book, Haine discussed the large presence of sex workers in Parisian cafés after 1870. Haine, *World of the Paris Café*, 188.

80 Marcailhou d'Aymeric, *Manuel hygiénique*, 17.

81 Monin, *Alcoolisme*, 173.

82 Haine, "Absinthe," 165.

83 Feydeau, *Alger*, 124.

84 Bernard, *Algérie qui s'en va*, 289.

85 Koziell, "Hygiène de quelques quartiers d'Alger," 23; Saliège, "Rapport," 155; Remlinger, "Progrès de l'alcoolisme," 748; Ceccaldi, *Pays de la poudre*, 28, 115–16.

86 Duchesne, *Prostitution dans la ville d'Alger*, 83. Emphasis in the original.

87 Geffroy, "Bonne Absinthe," 130.

88 Heilig, "Green Hour," 10.

89 Lalou, *Contribution*, 236, n1. The same quote was also mentioned by Emma Walker in 1906: Walker, "Effects of Absinthe," 568.

90 Dastre, "Lutte contre l'alcoolisme," 696–7.

91 For a source discussing the consumption of alcohol in general by French working-class women, see "Alcohol Drinking Doubles in France," *New York Times*, 23 July 1925, 4.

92 Ribouleau, *À travers l'hygiène*, 164.

93 Hazemann, "Homicides," 13.

94 Decroos, "Réglementation," 35.

95 Camp, *Charité privée*, 204.

96 Faux, "She Makes a Beast of Man," 17.

97 Harris, *Murders and Madness*, 243.

98 Granier, *Femme criminelle*, 18.

99 Feydeau, *Alger*, 124; Bernard, *Algérie qui s'en va*, 289.

100 Mayet, *Vin de France*, 69–70.

101 Lierre, *Question de l'absinthe*, 26–7.

102 Heilig, "Green Hour," 10.

103 Schwarz, "Society, Physicians, and the Corset," 553.

104 Steele, *Corset*, 75.

105 Lanier, *Absinthe*, 28.

106 Bauer, "Visiting the 'Green Fairy,'" 3.

107 Iskin, "Popularising New Women," 101.

108 Charles Mayet, "Le vin de France," *Le Temps*, 28 February 1894, 2; Mayet, *Vin de France*, 75.

109 Geffroy, "Bonne Absinthe," 129–30.

110 Devoisins, *Femme et l'alcoolisme*, 23–4.

111 Reynolds, "Vélo-Métro-Auto," 84. Ellen Gruber Garvey explained that bicycling became accessible to women in the 1890s, with the development of the bicycle with two wheels of the same size. Gruber Garvey, "Reframing the Bicycle," 66.

112 Pasteur, *Femmes à bicyclette*, 14.

113 Lemanski, *Hygiène du colon*, 171.

114 Ibid., 171–2.

115 See, for example L., "Un poison bien français," 5.

116 "Alcohol Drinking Doubles in France," *New York Times*, 23 July 1925, 4.

117 Delahaye, *Absinthe au féminin*, 60.

118 For this development in other countries, see Park, "Sport, Dress Reform and the Emancipation of Women"; Hallenbeck, *Claiming the Bicycle*.

119 Pasteur, *Femmes à bicyclette*, 11; Gruber Garvey, "Reframing the Bicycle," 66.

120 Reynolds, "Vélo-Métro-Auto," 84–5.

121 Ibid., 87–8.

122 Georges Conrad, "Bicyclistes," *Don Juan: Bi-hebdomadaire littéraire, artistique et illustré*, 15 July 1897, 4.

123 While Réïra does not appear to be an Arabic name, Auclert might have meant to write Ra'isa.

124 Auclert, *Femmes arabes*, 227–9.

Chapter Five

1 M., "Propos de table," 9–10.

2 Jacquet, *Alcool*, 718.

3 Prestwich, *Drink*, 81.

4 Haine, *World of the Paris Café*, 91.

5 See, for example, Musset, "Entre salubrité, conservation et goût," 80.

6 Mayet, *Vin de France*, 66.

7 M., "Propos de table," 10.

8 Haine, *World of the Paris Café*, 101.

9 Lucienne, *Leçons d'anti-alcoolisme*, 44.

10 Hazemann, "Homicides," 12–13.

11 Ibid., 10–11.

12 Ibid., 13.

13 Langle, "Cafés et débits," para. 149.

14 Hutton, "Myth," 62.

15 Baker, *Dedalus Book of Absinthe*, 124.

16 Brunon, *Alcoolisme ouvrier en Normandie*, 6.

17 Dubois, "Combat contre l'alcoolisme," 14–15. See also Marrus, "Social Drinking," 124, n46.

18 Young, "Heroic Indolence," 250, n80. See also Haine, *World of the Paris Café*, 97; Faux, "She Makes a Beast of Man," 66.

19 Prestwich, "Temperance in France," 302; Adams, *Hideous Absinthe*, 5.

20 Several sources mentioned the absinthe consumption of French working-class men in colonies. Anselmier, *Empoisonnement*, 11; Casanova, "Intoxications chroniques," 19; Viré, *Algérie*, 93; Foix, "En Algérie," 141.

21 Decroos, "Réglementation," 17.

22 Raynaud, "Alcoolisme en Algérie," 68.

23 Esparbès, *Légion étrangère*, 59–60, 266. See also Comor, "Plaisirs des légionnaires," 38.

24 Sterling Heilig, "The Green Hour in Paris," *Sun [New York Sun]*, 19 August 1894, 10.

25 Baker, *Dedalus Book of Absinthe*, 125.

26 Goudeau, *Paris qui consomme*, 95. Emphasis in the original.

27 Langle, "Cafés et débits," para. 149.

28 Eidgenössischer Initiativausschuss gegen den Absinth, *Absinthverbot in der Schweiz*, 15–16.

29 Bauer, "Visiting the 'Green Fairy,'" 3.

30 Descieux, *Influence de l'état moral*, 15–16.

31 Marrus, "Social Drinking," 124; Quétel and Simon, "Aliénation alcoolique en France," 518; Le Bras, "Boire pour se soigner," 416.

32 Thierrin, *Dangers*, 55. Emphasis in the original.

33 Camp, *Paris bienfaisant*, 191.

34 Young, "Heroic Indolence," 250.

35 Harris, *Murders and Madness*, 245.

36 Fillaut, "Alcoolisme et antialcoolisme," para. 1.

37 Nourrisson, "Origines de l'antialcoolisme," 498.

38 "French National Curse Suppressed," *Times*, 3 April 1915, 7.

39 Georges Maillard, "L'alcoolique," *Le Pays: Journal quotidien, politique, littéraire et commercial*, 8 August 1888, 2.

40 Pascal, *Petit botaniste*, 143.

41 Lee and Balick, "Absinthe," 218. See also Nourrisson, "Origines de l'antialcoolisme," 495.

42 Rochard, *Traité d'hygiène*, 856.

43 Hazemann, "Homicides," 13.

44 Heilig, "Green Hour," 10. Emphasis in the original.

45 Marrus, "Social Drinking," 132.

46 Ibid., 130.

47 "Alcohol Drinking Doubles in France," *New York Times*, 23 July 1925, 4.

48 French Supplement to the Lancet, 341.

49 "Alcohol Drinking Doubles in France," 4. The eight-hour working day was introduced in France in 1919. Souamaa, "Loi des huit heures," 28.

50 "Alcohol Drinking Doubles in France," 4.

51 Jacquet, *Alcool*, 718.

52 Brunon, *Alcoolisme ouvrier en Normandie*, 13.

53 Daviller, "Alcool et alcoolisme," 45. Emphasis in the original.

54 Stocker, "Absinth," 37.

55 Barrows, "After the Commune," 208.

56 Barrows, Room, and Verhey, *Social History of Alcohol*, 219.

57 Camp, *Paris bienfaisant*, 191.

58 Poiré, *Tunisie française*, 133.

59 Ceccaldi, *Pays de la poudre*, 77.

60 Delahaye, *Histoire de la fée verte*, 57.

61 See, for example Rouby, "Alcoolisme," 239.

62 Conrad, *Absinthe*, 116–17.

63 Paul Duché, "La République s'amuse," *L'Express du Midi*, 24 December 1896, 1.

64 "Le député de Pontarlier. Un muftis à la Chambre," *L'Express du Midi*, 24 December 1896, 1.

65 Marc, "Menus Propos," *La Dépêche algérienne*, 25 May 1898, 3.

66 Feydeau, *Alger*, 73–4.

67 L., "Un poison bien français," 5.

68 Poiré, *Tunisie française*, 39.

69 Remlinger, "Progrès de l'alcoolisme," 750.

70 Feydeau, *Alger*, 124; Bernard, *Algérie qui s'en va*, 289.

Notes to pages 133-40

215

71 See, for example, Galland, "Excursion," 15.

72 Richardot, *Sept semaines*, 94. Later on in his travel account, Richardot referred again to this settler. Ibid., 266.

73 Pinaud, "Alcoolisme chez les arabes," 27.

74 Guba, *Taming Cannabis*, 189.

75 Duchêne-Marullaz, "Hygiène des musulmans d'Algérie," 65–6.

76 Poiré, *Tunisie française*, 133.

77 Vignon, *France en Algérie*, 410. See also ibid., 481.

78 Jean Carde, "Au pays rouge," *Le Temps*, 16 September 1896, 3.

79 Raynaud, "Alcoolisme en Algérie," 68. See also Charvériat, *Huit jours en Kabylie*, 112.

80 Windham, *Notes in North Africa*, 47. Emphasis in the original.

81 Rohlfs, *Marokko*, 85.

82 See, for example, Dumas, *Français d'Afrique*, 69; Anfreville de la Salle, *Madagascar*, 62.

83 Anonymous, *Algérie et la lettre de l'empereur*, 42–3. Emphasis in the original.

84 "Décret du 15 novembre 1914," 405–6.

85 See, for example, Feydeau, *Alger*, 73–4.

86 Richardot, *Sept semaines*, 94.

87 Prestwich, "Temperance in France," 307.

88 Baker, *Dedalus Book of Absinthe*, 124. See also Earle, "Green Eyes," 701.

89 Camp, *Ancêtres de la Commune*, 5.

90 Camp, *Convulsions de Paris*, VII. See also Barrows, "After the Commune," 208.

91 Figuier, "Effets pernicieux," 336; Girardin, *Considération*, 25; Maillard, "Alcoolique," 2; Lucienne, *Leçons d'anti-alcoolisme*, 44.

92 Decroos, "Réglementation," 29.

93 "L'absinthe en Angleterre," 93; Anonymous, *Petit manuel du ligueur*, 11.

94 Hazemann, "Homicides," 10.

95 Lierre, *Question de l'absinthe*, 37–8.

96 Ben-Noun, "Drinking Wine to Inebriation in Biblical Times."

97 Wahl, *Crime*, 91.

98 See, for example, Lanier, *Absinthe*, 12; Padosch, Lachenmeier, and Kröner, "Absinthism," 4; Huisman, Brug, and Mackenbach, "Absinthe," 740.

99 Legrain, "Guerre à l'apéritif," 30–1. Emphasis in the original.

100 See, for example, Pinaud, "Alcoolisme chez les arabes," 27.

101 Walmsley, *Sketches of Algeria*, 10–11.

102 "French National Curse Suppressed," 7.

103 Legrain, "Guerre à l'apéritif," 31.

104 Eidgenössischer Initiativausschuss gegen den Absinth, *Absinthverbot in der Schweiz*, 14. Emphasis in the original.

105 Hazemann, "Homicides," 8–9.

106 Ibid., 19–20.

107 L., "Homicides commis par les absinthiques," 62.

108 Laurent, "Revue des thèses," 111–12.

109 L., "Homicides commis par les absinthiques," 62–3.

110 Hazemann, "Homicides," 111–12.

111 Eidgenössischer Initiativausschuss gegen den Absinth, *Absinthverbot in der Schweiz*, 8.

112 Laurent, "Revue des thèses," 112.

113 L., "Un poison bien français," 4–5.

114 Monin, *Alcoolisme*, 140–1.

115 "French National Curse Suppressed," 7.

116 Hamon, *Déterminisme et responsabilité*, 159–60.

117 Daniel, "Il faut tuer cette dangereuse révolutionnaire," 33–4. Emphasis in the original.

118 Haine, *World of the Paris Café*, 115.

119 Harris, *Murders and Madness*, 243.

120 Ibid., 254.

121 "Crimes de l'absinthe," 63.

122 "Entêtement mortel," 143–4.

123 "Les crimes de l'absinthe," *La Presse illustrée*, 21 October 1883, 2.

124 *La Presse illustrée*, 21 October 1883, 1, accessed 16 August 2023, https://gallica.bnf.fr/ark:/12148/bd6t5106004b/f1.item.

125 L., "Un poison bien français," 4.

126 Legrain, *Éléments de médecine mentale*, 335.

127 Hazemann, "Homicides," 104.

128 Ibid., 112.

129 Pinaud, "Alcoolisme chez les arabes," 27.

Chapter Six

1 Legrain, *Éléments de médecine mentale*, 333; M., "Propos de table," 10.

2 Haine, *World of the Paris Café*, 11.

3 For more on Magnan's life and theories, see Dowbiggin, "Back to the Future"; Eadie, "Absinthe, Epileptic Seizures and Valentin Magnan."

4 Magnan/Fillassier, *Alcoholism and Degeneracy*, 368.

5   Prestwich, "Temperance in France," 305.

6   Eidgenössischer Initiativausschuss gegen den Absinth, *Absinthverbot in der Schweiz*, 17.

7   Guba, *Taming Cannabis*, 119.

8   Capo de Feuillide, "De la colonisation algérienne," *La Presse*, 21 July 1854, 2.

9   Bynum, "Chronic Alcoholism," 162. On Magnus Huss's definition of chronic alcoholism, see, for example, Bernard, "Alcoolisme et antialcoolisme," 618–19.

10 Motet, "Considérations générales," 17.

11 Ibid., 14.

12 Eidgenössischer Initiativausschuss gegen den Absinth, *Absinthverbot in der Schweiz*, 6.

13 Monin, *Alcoolisme*, 174–5. See also L., "Un poison bien français," 4.

14 Pictet, "Suisse," 346.

15 Eidgenössischer Initiativausschuss gegen den Absinth, *Antwort*, 15.

16 Lachenmeier et al., "Absinthe, Absinthism and Thujone," 34.

17 L., "Un poison bien français," 4.

18 This can be seen, for example, in popular descriptions of Jean Lanfray, who murdered his family in Commugny, Switzerland, in August 1905.

19 "Measuring Civilization," *Indiana State Sentinel*, 10 April 1861, 4. See also Marit, *Hygiène de l'Algérie*, 374; Anselmier, *Empoisonnement*, 7–8.

20 Magnan/Fillassier, *Alcoholism and Degeneracy*, 371.

21 Monin, *Alcoolisme*, 174–5. See also Prestwich, "Temperance in France," 308; Baker, *Dedalus Book of Absinthe*, 128.

22 "L'Absinthisme," *Journal de Genève*, 2 April 1893, 3.

23 Monin, *Alcoolisme*, 175; Mikael Suni, "Alcoolisme et absinthisme," *La Dépêche: Journal de la démocratie*, 6 April 1895, 1; Colin, *Ouvrage de vulgarisation*, 281. See also Conrad, *Absinthe*, 101; Hutton, "Myth," 62, Terril, "Dudes, Decadence, and Degeneracy," 7.

24 Magnan, "Accidents déterminés," 227–32.

25 Magnan, *Étude expérimentale et clinique sur l'alcoolisme*, 37–8.

26 Magnan, "Comparative Action," 411. See also Magnan and Fillassier, "Alcoholism and Degeneracy," 371.

27 Goldstein, "Hysteria Diagnosis," 210–11.

28 Ibid., 221.

29 Black, *Drugging France*, 156–7.

30 M., "Propos de table," 10. The same formulation of absinthe being "epilepsy in bottles" can also be found in a 1906 publication by Paul-Maurice Legrain. Legrain, *Éléments de médecine mentale*, 333.

31 Wahl, *Crime*, 91.

32 Ribouleau, *À travers l'hygiène*, 163–4.

33 Figuier, "Effets pernicieux," 346.

34 Motet, "Considérations générales," 13. See also "Measuring Civilization," 4.

35 Anselmier, *Empoisonnement*, 11–12.

36 Magnan/Fillassier, *Alcoholism and Degeneracy*, 369.

37 Ibid., 372.

38 Ibid.

39 Sterling Heilig, "France's Green Devil," *Evening Star*, 22 December 1906, 2.

40 Lierre, *Question de l'absinthe*, 26–7. See also Moreau, *Liqueur d'absinthe*, 26.

41 Marcé, "Sur l'action toxique de l'essence d'absinthe." See also Marcé, *Traité pratique*, 606.

42 Legrand du Saulle, *Étude médico-légale sur les épileptiques*, 123.

43 Raynaud, "Alcoolisme en Algérie," 67.

44 Guyot, *Question de l'alcool*, 82.

45 Ibid., 109–10.

46 Ibid., 106–7.

47 Ernst, *Dictionnaire universel d'idées*, 3. Emphasis in the original. Other examples of absinthe being called the opium of the West can be found in the following sources: Picard, *Dangers*, 20; Picard, "Boissons alcooliques," 337; anonymous, *Guide sentimental*, 49; Pierre Robbe, "L'alcool et la bicyclette," *Le Vélo: Journal quotidien de la vélocipédie, de l'automobile et de tous les sports*, 9 April 1899, 3. An article written by Thomas Grimm and published in November 1871 described absinthe as the "European opium." Thomas Grimm, "Les buveurs d'absinthe," *Le Petit Journal*, 12 November 1871, 1.

48 Legrand du Saulle, *Folie*, 540.

49 Stocker, "Absinth," 35.

50 Derks, *History of the Opium Problem*, 385.

51 Pascal, *Petit botaniste*, 143.

52 Laupts, *Perversions et perversité sexuelles*, 362.

53 Paul de Saint-Victor, "Théatres," *La Presse*, 30 December 1860, 1–2.

54 Descours-Gatin, *Quand l'opium finançait la colonisation en Indochine*, 9, 25.

55 Derks, *History of the Opium Problem*, 394.

56 Black, *Drugging France*, 28.

57 Ibid., 63.

58 Derks, *History of the Opium Problem*, 407; Padwa, *Social Poison*, 32.

59 Derks, *History of the Opium Problem*, 383.

60 Scheltema, "Opium Question," 213.

61 Santi, *Entérite chronique paludéenne*, 175.

62 Proschan, "Syphilis, Opiomania, and Pederasty," 622.

63 Régis, "Préface," ii. See also Padwa, *Social Poison*, 69.

64 E.G., "Nos petites habitudes," *Le conteur vaudois: Journal de la Suisse romande* 3 (1865): 3.

65 Moreau, *Liqueur d'absinthe*, 7.

66 Padwa, *Social Poison*, 32.

67 Prestwich, "Temperance in France," 303.

68 Motet, "Considérations générales," 13–14.

69 Nourrisson, *Crus et cuites*, 11.

70 Figuier, "Effets pernicieux," 336.

71 Bouchardat and Junod, *Eau-de-vie*, 75.

72 Bergeret, *Alcoolisme*, 193–4.

73 Daviller, "Alcool et alcoolisme," 47.

74 Jobard, *Nouvelle économie sociale*, 416.

75 Marx, "Zur Kritik der Hegel'schen Rechts-Philosophie," 72. Emphasis in the original.

76 Gorges, *Revue de l'exposition universelle*, 224.

77 Druhen, *Tabac*, 20; Honoré de Barsac, "Boutades Économiques," *Le Figaro*, 30 July 1871, 2; Réclus, *Géographie*, 244; Suni, "Alcoolisme et absinthisme," 1; Barbey d'Aurevilly, *Ridicules du temps*, 229–30.

78 Jean de Nivelle, "L'hérédité fatale," *Le Soleil*, 28 October 1882, 1.

79 Quidam, "Les Empoisonneurs," *Le Figaro*, 15 June 1883, 1.

80 "Alcoolisme – Répression," 499.

81 Jacques Bonhomme, "Morphinomanie," *La Petite Presse*, 22 November 1891, 1.

82 Tailhade, *Noire Idole*, 6–7.

83 This article was the reprint of an article written by the same author for the journal *La Tunisie Française*.

84 See my article on teaism for an analysis of the diagnosis in twentieth-century Tunisia: Studer, "Was trinkt der zivilisierte Mensch?"

85 R. de la. Porte, "L'abus du thé pire que l'abus de l'opium," *L'Eveil de l'Indo-chine*, 14 May 1933, 6.

86 "Measuring Civilization," 4.

87 "L'absinthe" (*Journal de Genève*, 21 June 1908): 1.

88 Aubert, "Alcool et alcoolisme," 28. Emphasis in the original.

89 Solmon, *Essai*.

90 Frégier, *Absinthisme*, 7.

91 Guba, *Taming Cannabis*, 103.

92 Pierre Robbe, "Carnet du Jour," *Le Vélo: Journal quotidien de la vélocipédie, de l'automobile et de tous les sports*, 9 January 1897, 2–3.

93 Wade, "Going Berserk," 9.

94 Robbe, "Carnet du Jour," 2.

95 See, for example, "Un coup de rasoir," *Le Petit Parisien*, 8 January 1897, 1–2; "Mystérieux attentat," *Le Radical*, 10 January 1897, 3.

96 Robbe, "Carnet du Jour," 2–3.

97 Pouchet, *Leçons*, 806.

98 Thierrin, *Dangers*, 23.

99 Ibid., 55. Emphasis in the original.

100 Gorges, *Revue de l'exposition universelle*, 224.

101 Daviller, "Alcool et alcoolisme," 46.

102 Adams, *Hideous Absinthe*, 194. See also Maxime Rasteil, "Le procès de l'absinthe," *Le Réveil bônois*, 26 February 1897, 1.

103 On the history of this "anti-Jewish absinthe," see Durieu, *Juifs algériens*, 106, 143, 151, 321; Darmenjian, *Antijudaïsme*, 245–57, paras 9, 10; Fieni, *Decadent Orientalisms*, 78.

104 Lierre, *Question de l'absinthe*, 12–13. Emphasis in the original.

105 Eidgenössischer Initiativausschuss gegen den Absinth, *Antwort*, 13.

106 Delauney, *Staouéli*, 83–4.

107 Remlinger, "Progrès de l'alcoolisme," 751.

108 St de H., "La Ligue nationale contre l'alcoolisme," *La Croix*, 9 May 1907, 4.

109 Armand, *Traité*, 538–9. Emphasis in the original.

110 Quincey, *Confessions*.

111 Padwa, *Social Poison*, 25.

112 "Une bonne affaire," *Journal de Genève*, 2 July 1908, 1.

113 Flaubert, *Dictionnaire des idées reçues*, 3.

114 Motet, "Considérations générales," 8.

115 See, for example, Loir, "Conditions sanitaires," 112.

116 Lévy, *Traité d'hygiène*, 52. See also Moreau, *Liqueur d'absinthe*, 35–6.

117 Cardon, *Manuel d'agriculture*, 75–6.

118 See, for example, Baudicour, *Colonisation de l'Algérie*, 138; Choulette, *Observations pratiques*, 112–13; Blakesley, *Four Months in Algeria*, 99; Marit, *Hygiène de l'Algérie*, 374; Anselmier, *Empoisonnement*, 27–8; C., "Eucalypsinthe," 119; Morache, *Traité d'hygiène militaire*, 704–5; Viry, "Hygiène militaire," 262.

119 Remlinger, "Progrès de l'alcoolisme," 749.

120 Marbaud, *Coup d'œil*, 23.

121 "Algérie," *Journal de Genève*, 10 January 1845, 1.

122 This quote was not included in the first edition of *Popular Hygiene*, which was published in 1852 in Rouen.

123 Baudet-Dulary, *Hygiène populaire*, 69.

124 Duvernois, *Algérie*, 248.

125 Blakesley, *Four Months in Algeria*, 99.

126 Figuier, "Effets pernicieux," 346.

127 Cardon, *Manuel d'agriculture*, 75–6.

128 Girardin, *Considération*, 25.

129 Fauré, *Causeries populaires*, 44.

130 Ollivier, *Influence*, 183.

131 Chonnaux-Dubisson, *Rachitisme*, 13.

132 Meunier, *Causeries du docteur*, 208. Emphasis in the original.

133 Riant, *Alcool et tabac*, 84.

134 Bouchardat, *Traité d'hygiène*, 296.

135 "Das Soldatenleben," 485.

136 Curtin, *Disease and Empire*, 144.

137 Marit, *Hygiène de l'Algérie*, 374.

138 Soubeiran, *Hygiène élémentaire*, 105.

139 C., "Eucalypsinthe," 119.

140 Monin, *Alcoolisme*, 171.

141 To this, Monin added: "blessed be the day (one might say) when the Fairy with green eyes will confine herself to the déclassés and brewery girls!" Monin, *Misères nerveuses*, 145–6.

142 Steeg, *Dangers*, 14.

143 Houdeville, *Comment préserver*, 13.

144 Fauré, *Causeries populaires*, 44.

145 Ollivier, *Influence*, 183.

146 Girardin, *Considération*, 25.

147 Aubert, *Œuvre*, 15.

148 It is given as 23 December in Furnari and as 25 December in the *Journal de Genève*. Furnari, *Voyage médical*, 331; "Algérie" (10 January 1845): 1.

149 As quoted in the *Journal de Genève*. The same passage can also be found in *L'Algérie* in January 1845. "Abus des liqueurs alcooliques," *L'Algérie: Courrier d'Afrique, d'Orient et de la Méditerranée*, 6 January 1845, 2; "Algérie" (10 January 1845): 1.

150 Furnari, *Voyage médical*, 331.

151 Rossignol, *Traité élémentaire*, 373.

152 "Faits Divers," *L'Algérie: Courrier d'Afrique, d'Orient et de la Méditerranée*, 26 September 1845, 4.

153 Znaien, "Généalogie coloniale," 52.

154 Feuillide, "Colonisation algérienne," 2. Emphasis in the original.

155 See also: Martin, *Manuel d'hygiène*, 204.

156 Legrand du Saulle, *Folie*, 542.

157 "Algérie" (10 January 1845): 1.

158 Feuillide, "Colonisation algérienne," 2.

159 Baudet-Dulary, *Hygiène populaire*, 69.

160 Marrus, "Social Drinking," 117–18.

161 Le Moine, "Alcool. Suppression des crimes et des impôts par l'alcool," *La Croix*, 26 January 1886, 1.

162 Marrus, "Social Drinking," 118.

163 Legrain, *Éléments de médecine mentale*, 233.

Chapter Seven

1 He specified that absinthe was the "king of apéritifs from the mid-1880s." Marrus, "Social Drinking," 124.

2 Guy, *When Champagne Became French*, 1.

3 Sirven, *Abrutis*, 17.

4 Lemanski, *Hygiène du colon*, 122. Capitalization in the original.

5 Geffroy, "Paysage d'alcool," 109.

6 See, for example, Geffroy, "Bonne Absinthe," 130; Oudaille, "Commandements de l'hygiène," 145; "L'histoire de l'absinthe, à Couvet," *Le conteur vaudois: Journal de la Suisse romande* 28, no. 2 (1890): 1–2; Lemanski, *Hygiène du colon*, 90; Testis, "L'heure … de l'Absinthe?," *Le Réveil de Mascara*, 16 June 1906, 1–2.

7 Georges Maillard, "L'alcoolique," *Le Pays: Journal quotidien, politique, littéraire et commercial*, 8 August 1888, 2.

8 "Absinthe Ban Ineffective," *New York Times*, 17 January 1915, 8.

9 Langle, "Cafés et débits," para. 168.

10 Delahaye, "Grandeur et décadence," 487; Fillaut, "Lutte contre l'alcoolisme," para. 1; Faux, "She Makes a Beast of Man," 20.

11 "18 novembre 1915 (deux arrêts)," 69.

12 "L'absinthe en Indochine," *Les Annales coloniales: Journal semi-quotidien*, 10 February 1917, 2.

13 Prestwich, "Temperance in France," 318.

14 Eidgenössischer Initiativausschuss gegen den Absinth, *Antwort*, 3.

15 Nourrisson, *Crus et cuites*, 143–4; Gasnier, "Affiches publicitaires," part 1, 75.

16 Delahaye, "Grandeur et décadence," 487–8.

17 Ministère de la guerre, *Manuel à l'usage des troupes employées Outre-mer*, 248–9.

18 Eidgenössischer Initiativausschuss gegen den Absinth, *Antwort*, 11.

19 Senn, "Wo Spott und Absinth blühen," 14.

20 Liggenstorfer, "Ursprung des Absinthe," 25.

21 Senn, "Wo Spott und Absinth blühen," 14.

22 "Contrebande," *Journal de Genève*, 17 May 1909, 2; "Une grosse affaire d'absinthe," *Gazette de Lausanne*, 22 July 1924, 4.

23 See, for example, "L'absinthe," *Journal de Genève*, 26 July 1908, 5.

24 Fahrenkrug, "What Happened to the 'Fée Verte,'" 271.

25 Delahaye, "Grandeur et décadence," 487.

26 Nourrisson, *Crus et cuites*, 143.

27 Borja, "Absinthe," 53.

28 "Nearly £8,000 in Fines for Selling Absinthe," *Times*, 15 January 1917, 7.

29 Archives Nationales, Paris, BB/18/6844: List of liquor-store closures after the absinthe ban, Paris, February 1916, as quoted in: Faux, "She Makes a Beast of Man," 38–9.

30 See, for example, "Le crime de Commugny," *La Prospérité*, 17 March 1906, 3; "Lettre de Suisse. Le mouvement antialcoolique," *Le Temps*, 12 March 1907, 1–2.

31 "Belgique," *Journal de Genève*, 5 February 1903, 3.

32 Lanier, *Absinthe*, 36; DeBoer, "Flavour of Absinthe," 49; Cotton, "Vincent van Gogh," 77; Terril, "Dudes, Decadence, and Degeneracy," 9.

33 "Triple assassinat," *Gazette de Lausanne*, 29 August 1905, 3.

34 Burnand, "Suisse contre l'absinthe," 717–18.

35 "Le crime de Commugny," *Gazette de Lausanne*, 24 February 1906, 2.

36 Ibid., 2.

37 Heimberg, "Comment renouveler," 97.

38 "Le crime de Commugny" (24 February 1906), 2. Emphasis in the original.

39 Delahaye, "Une correspondance pour Charenton."

40 "Le crime de Commugny," *Gazette de Lausanne*, 26 February 1906, 2–3.

41 Cotton, "Vincent van Gogh," 77; Saxton, "Before Addiction," 180.

42 "Le crime de Commugny" (24 February 1906), 2.

43 Heimberg, "Comment renouveler," 97–8. The 1959 article in the *Journal de Genève* gave the numbers of 34,375 men and 48,057 women. "Les femmes de Commugny et l'interdiction de l'absinthe," *Journal de Genève*, 5 May 1959, 2.

44 Pictet, "Suisse," 345–6. See also Eidgenössischer Initiativausschuss gegen den Absinth, *Absinthverbot in der Schweiz*, 15.

45 Fillaut, "Alcoolisme et antialcoolisme," paras 18–22.

46 "Les femmes de Commugny et l'interdiction de l'absinthe," 2.

47 Régis, "Préface," i.

48 Ibid., xi.

49 See Poulle, "Rapport Supplémentaire."

50 Marrus, "Social Drinking," 119; Durouchoux, "Associations," 43; Fillaut, "Alcoolisme et antialcoolisme," para. 16.

51 Fedoul and Jacquet, "Histoire," para. 5.

52 Ibid., para. 8.

53 Durouchoux, "Associations," 43.

54 Fillaut, "Alcoolisme et antialcoolisme," para. 12.

55 Khalifa, "Vices et vertus," 73.

56 Prestwich, "Temperance in France," 301.

57 Langle, "Cafés et débits," para. 167.

58 Znaien, "Généalogie coloniale," 43–4.

59 "Le commerce de l'absinthe en Algérie," *Journal de médecine et de chirurgie pratiques*: 767. See also "Le commerce de l'absinthe en Algérie" (*La Province médicale*), 10.

60 Jacquet, *Alcool*, 242.

61 "L'absinthe proscrite," *Annales africaines: Revue hebdomadaire de l'Afrique du Nord*, 15 May 1914, 238.

62 Tout-Pari, "Un proscrit," *Le Gaulois*, 22 August 1885, 1. See also "Chine et Indo-Chine," *Le Temps*, 22 June 1885, 2.

63 "Interdiction de l'absinthe dans le Haut-Sénégal," 958–9.

64 Saliège, "Rapport," 155.

65 "La lutte contre l'alcoolisme," 365–6.

66 Montagne, "Drugs on the Internet," 508.

Bibliography

"18 novembre 1915 (deux arrêts)." *Revue algérienne, tunisienne et marocaine de législation et de jurisprudence* 32 (1916): 69–74.

"Absinthe." *British Medical Journal* 1, no. 433 (17 April 1869): 353.

"Absinthe." *Lancet*, 17 August 1907, 464–5.

"Absinthe Drunkenness." *Scientific American* 4, no. 16 (20 April 1861): 242.

Adams, Jad. *Hideous Absinthe: A History of the Devil in a Bottle*. London/New York: Tauris Parke Paperbacks, 2008.

Afanasyeva, Victoria. "Pratiques de mobilisation des femmes pour la cause antialcoolique en France: militantes, enseignantes, femmes de plume (1873–1903)." *Genre & Histoire* 19 (Spring 2017). Accessed 3 March 2023. https://journals.open edition.org/genrehistoire/2736.

Ageron, Charles-Robert. *Histoire de l'Algérie contemporaine, 1871–1954*. Vol. 2. Paris: Presses Universitaires de France, 1979. Accessed 26 March 2023. https://www. cairn.info/histoire-de-l-algerie-contemporaine-2—9782130356448-page-17.htm.

"Alcoolisme." In *Encyclopédie d'hygiène et de médecine publique*, edited by Jules Rochard, 610–38. Vol. 2. Paris: Lecrosnier et Babé, 1890.

"Alcoolisme – Répression." In *Rapports et délibérations. Conseil général de la Vienne*, 496–506. Poitiers: Imprimerie A. Masson, 1900.

Altamirano, Skye Tarrah. "Intoxicating Women of the Belle Époque: Absinthe's Influence on Painted Depictions of Women during the Bohemian Golden Age." Master's thesis, University of California, Irvine, 2021.

Andrew, Christopher M., and Alexander S. Kanya-Forstner. *France Overseas: The Great War and the Climax of French Imperial Expansion*. London: Thames and Hudson, 1981.

Anet, H. "The War against Absinthe on the Continent." *Economic Review* 17, no. 2 (April 1907): 189–92.

Anfreville de la Salle, Léon d'. *A Madagascar*. Paris: Plon-Nourrit et Cie, 1902.

Anonymous. *L'Algérie et la lettre de l'empereur*. Paris: Librairie de Firmin Didot Frères, 1863.

Anonymous. *Guide sentimental de l'étranger dans Paris. Par un parisien*. Paris: Calmann Lévy, 1878.

Anonymous. *Petit manuel du ligueur. Par un professeur de l'Université de Toulouse*. Toulouse: Imprimerie et Librairie Édouard Privat, 1902.

Anonymous. *Souvenirs d'Afrique, 1854–1855, par le Dr X*. Lille: Imprimerie de Lefebvre-Ducrocq, 1868.

Anselmier, Victor. *De l'empoisonnement par l'absinthe*. Paris: Imprimerie de J. Claye, 1862.

Armand, Adolphe. *L'Algérie médicale: Topographie, climatologie, pathogénie, pathologie, prophylaxie, hygiène, acclimatement et colonisation*. Paris: Librairie de Victor Masson, 1854.

– *Médecine et hygiène des pays chauds et spécialement de l'Algérie et des colonies*. Paris: Challamel Ainé, 1859.

– *Traité de climatologie générale du Globe: Étude médicale sur tous les climats*. Paris: G. Masson, 1873.

Arnold, Wilfred Niels. "Absinthe." *Scientific American* 260, no. 6 (June 1989): 112–17.

– "Vincent van Gogh and the Thujone Connection." *Journal of the American Medical Association* 260, no. 20 (25 November 1988): 3042–4.

Arnould, Jules. *Nouveaux éléments d'hygiène*. Paris: J.-B. Baillière et Fils, 1902.

Aubert, Éphrem. "L'alcool et l'alcoolisme." *L'Alcool: Journal mensuel. Bulletin de la Société contre l'usage des boissons spiritueuses* (January 1904): 28–9.

– *L'alcoolisation de la France: Pour que la France vive*. Paris: Éditions Bossard, 1920.

– *Une œuvre de régénération sociale et du salut national*. Paris: E. André Fils, 1910.

Auclert, Hubertine. *Les femmes arabes en Algérie*. Paris: Société d'Éditions Littéraires, 1900.

Bailly, Étienne. *Études sur l'Algérie en 1855 pendant un voyage exécuté par M. Bailly*. Paris: Imprimerie Félix Malteste et Cie, 1868.

Baker, Phil. *The Dedalus Book of Absinthe*. Sawtry: Daedalus, 2001.

Balesta, Henri. *Absinthe et absintheurs*. Paris: L. Marpon, 1860.

Barbey d'Aurevilly, Jules. *Les ridicules du temps*. Paris: Éd. Rouveyre et G. Blond, 1883.

Barceloux, Donald G. *Medical Toxicology of Drug Abuse: Synthesized Chemicals and Psychoactive Plants*. Hoboken: Wiley, 2012.

Bard, Joseph. *L'Algérie en 1854: Itinéraire général de Tunis à Tanger. Colonisation. Paysages. Monuments. Culte. Agriculture. Statistique. Hygiène. Industrie. Commerce. Avenir.* Paris: L. Maison, 1854.

Barnao, Charlie. "Leisure Time and 'Alcoholic Interactions': Rites, Norms and Action Strategies amongst Young Drinkers." In *Mapping Leisure across Borders*, edited by Fabio Massimo Lo Verde, Ishwar Modi, and Gianna Cappello, 291–310. Newcastle upon Tyne: Cambridge Scholars Publishing, 2013.

Barrows, Susanna. "After the Commune: Alcoholism, Temperance, and Literature in the Early Third Republic." In *Consciousness and Class Experience in Nineteenth-Century Europe*, edited by John M. Merriman, 205–18. New York: Holmes and Meier, 1979.

– "'Parliaments of the People': The Political Culture of Cafés in the Early Third Republic." In *Drinking Behaviour and Belief in Modern History*, edited by Susanna Barrows and Robin Room, 87–97. Berkeley/Los Angeles/Oxford: University of California, 1991.

Barrows, Susanna, Robin Room, and Jeffrey Verhey. *The Social History of Alcohol: Drinking and Culture in Modern Society.* Berkeley: Alcohol Research Group, 1987.

Baudel, M.-J. *Un an à Alger: Excursions et souvenirs.* Paris: Ch. Delagrave, 1887.

Baudet-Dulary, Alexandre François. *Hygiène populaire: Simples moyens de ménager et de fortifier la santé, par un vieux médecin de campagne.* Paris: J.-B. Baillière, 1856.

Baudicour, Louis de. *La colonisation de l'Algérie: Ses éléments.* Paris: Jacques Lecoffre et Co., 1856.

Baudrimont, Ernest. *Dictionnaire des altérations et falsifications des substances alimentaires médicamenteuses et commerciales, avec l'indication des moyens de les reconnaître.* Paris: Asselin et Cie, 1882.

Bauer, Irmgard L. "Visiting the 'Green Fairy': Absinthe-Tourism – A Potential Challenge for Travel Medicine?" *Travel Medicine and Infectious Disease* 37 (2020): 1–6.

Bauvallet, Henri-Célestin. "Alcoolisme chronique et paralysie générale progressive: Étude clinique." Medical thesis, University of Bordeaux, 1911.

Beaufumé, François Eugène. *De l'abus des liqueurs alcooliques comme cause de dégénérescence physique et morale des peuples et des moyens d'y remédier.* Paris: Dentu, 1871.

Ben-Noun, Liubov. "Drinking Wine to Inebriation in Biblical Times." *Israel Journal of Psychiatry and Related Sciences* 39, no. 1 (2002): 61–4.

Bergeret, Louis François Étienne. *L'alcoolisme. Dangers et inconvénients. De l'abus des boissons alcooliques. Dangers et inconvénients pour les individus, la famille*

et la société. Moyens de modérer les ravages de l'ivrognerie. Paris: J.-B. Baillière
  et Fils, 1870.

Bergot, Raoul. *L'Algérie telle qu'elle est.* Paris: Albert Savine, 1890.

Bernard, Henri. "Alcoolisme et antialcoolisme en France au XIXe siècle (autour
  de Magnus Huss)." *Histoire, Économie et Société* 3, no. 4 (1984): 609–28.

Bernard, Marius. *L'Algérie qui s'en va.* Paris: E. Plon, Nourrit, et Cie, 1887.

Berteuil, Arsène. *L'Algérie française. Histoire, mœurs, coutumes, industrie, agriculture.* Vol. 2. Paris: Dentu, 1856.

Berthoud, Dorette. "La 'fée verte': pour une histoire de l'absinthe." *Schweizerische
  Zeitschrift für Geschichte* 19, no. 3 (1969): 638–61.

Bickel, Jessica E., Anna Ellis, and Andrew Resnick. "Examining the Temperature
  Dependence of Louche Formation in Absinthe." *ACS Omega* 6 (2021): 17674–9.

Bihl-Willette, Luc. *Des tavernes aux bistrots. Une histoire des cafés.* Lausanne:
  Éditions l'Âge de l'Homme, 1997.

Black, Sara E. *Drugging France: Mind-Altering Medicine in the Long Nineteenth
  Century.* Montreal: McGill-Queen's University Press, 2022.

Blakesley, Joseph Williams. *Four Months in Algeria: With a Visit to Carthage.*
  Cambridge: Macmillan, 1859.

Blanc, Gratia. *Soldats et colons: Scènes de la vie algérienne.* Paris: Verboeckhoven
  et Cie, 1869.

Blumer, Dietrich. "The Illness of Vincent van Gogh." *American Journal of Psychiatry* 159, no. 4 (April 2002): 519–26.

Bonain, Adolphe. *L'Européen sous les tropiques: Causeries d'hygiène coloniale
  pratique.* Paris: Henri Charles-Lavauzele, 1907.

Bonneff, Léon, and Maurice Bonneff. *Marchands de folie.* Paris: Marcel Rivière &
  Cie, 1913.

Borja, John. "Absinthe, Alcoholism, and the Asylum in France, 1870–1918." *Yale
  Historical Review* (6 February 2021). Accessed 2 March 2023. https://yalehistorical
  review.ghost.io/absinthe-alcoholism-and-the-asylum-in-france-1870-1918/.

Bouchardat, Apollinaire, and Henri Junod. *L'eau-de-vie, ses dangers. Conférences
  populaires.* Paris: Ch. Meyrueis et Cie/Germer-Baillière, 1863.

Bouchardat, Apollinaire. *Traité d'hygiène publique et privée, basée sur l'étiologie.*
  Paris: Ancienne Libraire Germer Baillière et Cie, 1887.

Bourde, Paul. *A travers l'Algérie: Souvenirs de l'excursion parlementaire.* Paris: G.
  Charpentier, 1880.

Brasher, C.W.J. "Absinthe and Absinthe Drinking in England." *Lancet* (26 April
  1930): 944–6.

Bröckers, Mathias. "Absinthe als Treibstoff der Moderne." In *Absinthe – die Wieder-*

kehr der Grünen Fee: Geschichten und Legenden eines Kulturgetränkes, edited by Mathias Bröckers, Chris Heidrich, and Roger Liggenstorfer, 27–33. Solothurn: Nachtschatten Verlag, 2006.

Brunon, Raoul. *L'alcoolisme ouvrier en Normandie*. Paris: Masson et Cie, 1899.

Burnand. "La Suisse contre l'absinthe." *Foi et vie: Revue de quinzaine* (1905): 715–19.

Burns, James Dawson. *The Temperance Dictionary: Designed to Present a Condensed Record of Facts and Arguments, in Alphabetical Order. On Topics Relevant to the Temperance Movement; Embracing References Historical, Biographical, Biblical, Scientific, Philological, Statistical, etc., etc.* AA-ADU. London: J. Caudwell, 1861.

Bynum, William F. "Chronic Alcoholism in the First Half of the 19th Century." *Bulletin of the History of Medicine* 42, no. 2 (March–April 1968): 160–85.

Camp, Maxime du. *La charité privée à Paris*. Paris: Hachette et Cie, 1885.

– *Les ancêtres de la Commune: L'Attentat Fieschi*. Paris: G. Charpentier, 1877.

– *Les convulsions de Paris: Les prisons pendant la Commune*. Paris: Librairie Hachette et Cie, 1881.

– *Paris bienfaisant*. Paris: Librairie Hachette et Cie, 1888.

Cappot, Jean-Gabriel. *L'Algérie française*. Paris: Henri Plon, 1856.

Cardon, Émile. *Manuel d'agriculture pratique algérienne*. Paris: Revue du Monde Colonial, 1862.

Cargill, Kima. "The Myth of the Green Fairy: Distilling the Scientific Truth about Absinthe." *Food, Culture & Society* 10, no. 1 (2008): 87–99.

Carteron, Charles. *Voyage en Algérie: Tous les usages des Arabes, leur vie intime et extérieure, ainsi que celle des Européens dans la colonie*. Paris: J. Hetzel, 1866.

Casanova, Antoine-Léonard-Charles-Raphael. "Intoxications chroniques par l'alcool, l'absinthe et le vulnéraire: Des signes particuliers qu'elles présentent au point de vue au diagnostic différentiel." Medical Thesis, University of Paris, 1885.

Castellane, Pierre de. *Souvenirs de la vie militaire en Afrique*. Paris: Victor Lecou, 1852.

Cazin, François-Joseph. *Traité pratique et raisonné des plantes médicinales indigènes*. Paris: Labé, 1858.

Ceccaldi, F. *Au pays de la poudre: En campagne avec les "joyeux."* Maroc occidental *(1911–1912)*. Paris: Imprimerie-Librarie Militaire Universelle L. Fournier, 1914.

C., G. "L'eucalypsinthe, succédané de l'absinthe." *Gazette médicale de l'Algérie* (1877): 119.

Chapuis, Yves. "L'absinthe réhabilitée." *Bulletin de l'Académie nationale de médecine* 197, no. 2 (2013): 515–21.

Charvériat, François. *Huit jours en Kabylie: A travers la Kabylie et les questions Kabyles*. Paris: E. Plon, Nourrit et Cie, 1889.

Chonnaux-Dubisson, Louis Auguste Télesphore. *Du Rachitisme*. Amiens: Imprimerie et Libraire Alfred Caron Fils, 1868.

Choulette, Sébastien. *Observations pratiques de chimie, de pharmacie et de médecine légale*. Paris/Strasbourg: G. Baillière and Derivaux, 1860.

Cohen, William Benjamin. "Malaria and French Imperialism." *Journal of African History* 24, no. 1 (1983): 23–36.

Cole, Thomas B. "*Les buveurs d'absinthe* (The Absinthe Drinkers)." *Journal of the American Medical Association* 314, no. 7 (18 August 2015): 652–3.

Colin, Anna. *Ouvrage de vulgarisation: Comment lutter contre la tuberculose et contre l'alcoolisme*. Bourg: Genin & Cie, 1911.

Comor, André-Paul. "Les plaisirs des légionnaires au temps des colonies: l'alcool et les femmes." *Guerres mondiales et conflits contemporains* 2, no. 222 (2006): 33–42.

Conrad, Barnaby III. *Absinthe: History in a Bottle*. San Francisco: Chronicle, 1988.

Cotton, Simon. "Vincent van Gogh, Chemistry and Absinthe." *Education in Chemistry* (May 2011): 75–9.

Cooke, George Wingrove. *Conquest and Colonisation in North Africa: Being the Substance of a Series of Letters from Algeria Published in the "Times," and Now by Permission Collected*. London: W. Blackwood and Sons, 1860.

"Crimes de l'absinthe." *L'Alcool: Journal mensuel. Bulletin de la Société contre l'usage des boissons spiritueuses* 1 (January 1896): 63.

Curtin, Philip D. *Disease and Empire: The Health of European Troops in the Conquest of Africa*. Cambridge: Cambridge University Press, 1998.

Dagen, Morag. "History of Malaria and Its Treatment." In *Antimalarial Agents: Design and Mechanism of Action*, edited by Graham L. Patrick, 1–48. Amsterdam: Elsevier, 2020.

Daniel, Marina. "'Il faut tuer cette dangereuse révolutionnaire': Louise Michel, victime d'une tentative de meurtre au Havre en 1888." *Études Normandes* 55, no. 3 (2006): 27–40.

Darmenjian, Geneviève. *Antijudaïsme et antisémitisme en Algérie coloniale, 1830–1962*. Aix-en-Provence: Presses universitaires de Provence, 2018. Accessed 24 March 2023: https://books.openedition.org/pup/46813.

"Das Soldatenleben, Pflichten und Gefahren für den Schweizer'schen Wehrmann in Lager und Kaserne." *Schweizerischer Kirchenzeitung: Fachzeitschrift für Theologie und Seelsorge* (1873): 485–6.

Dastre, Albert. "La lutte contre l'alcoolisme." *Revue des deux Mondes* 154 (1 July 1899): 692–707.

Daviller. "L'alcool et l'alcoolisme." *Bulletin: Société académique du Bas-Rhin pour le progrès des sciences, des lettres, des arts et de la vie économique* 23 (1889): 39–72.

Davis, Diana K. "Desert 'Wastes' of the Maghreb: Desertification Narratives in French Colonial Environmental History of North Africa." *Cultural Geographies* 11, no. 4 (October 2004): 359–87.

Davray, Jules. *L'amour à Paris*. Paris: Librairie Fort, 1894.

DeBoer, Jason. "The Flavour of Absinthe." *Literature in North Queensland* 28, no. 2 (October 2001): 49–52.

"Décret du 15 novembre 1914." In *Recueil de législation & jurisprudence*, edited by P. Dareste, G. Appert, L. Rotureau-Launay, and A. Marcille, 405–7. Paris: Marchal & Godde, 1915.

Decroos, Pierre. "La réglementation légale de l'absinthe: Étude de législation comparée." Legal thesis, University of Nancy, 1910.

Delachaux, Pierre-André. *L'absinthe: Arôme d'apocalypse*. Hauterive: Éditions Gilles Attinger, 1991.

Delahaye, Marie-Claude. "Grandeur et décadence de la fée verte." *Histoire, Économie et Société* 4 (1988): 475–89.

– *L'absinthe au féminin*. St-Remy-de-Provence: Éditions Équinoxe, 2007.

– *L'absinthe: Histoire de la fée verte*. Paris: Berger-Levrault, 1983.

– *L'absinthe: Les affiches*. Auvers-sur-Oise: Musée de l'Absinthe, 2002.

– *L'absinthe: Muse des poètes*. Auvers-sur-Oise: Musée de l'Absinthe, 2000.

– *L'absinthe: Son histoire*. Auvers-sur-Oise: Musée de l'Absinthe, 2001.

– "Une correspondance pour Charenton." Absinthe Museum, Auvers-sur-Oise, 16 February 2018. Accessed 14 March 2023. http://absinthemuseum.auvers.over-blog.com/2018/02/une-correspondance-pour-charenton.html.

Delaporte, François. *Disease and Civilization: The Cholera in Paris, 1832*. Cambridge: MIT Press, 1986.

Delauney, Émile. *Staouéli. Histoire du monastère, depuis sa fondation, suivi de: une excursion à Oran, Misserghin, Biskra, etc*. Limoges: Eugène Ardant et Cie, 1877.

Delvaud, Alfred. *Histoire anecdotique des cafés et cabarets de Paris*. Paris: E. Dentu, 1862.

Demartini, Anne-Emmanuelle. "La culture des cafés aux XIXe siècle: D'après Susanna Barrows." *Revue de la BNF* 53 (2016): 54–61.

Denommé, Robert T. "A Note Concerning the Death of George Sand." *Romance Notes* 10, no. 2 (Spring 1969): 261–4.

Derks, Hans. *History of the Opium Problem: The Assault on the East, ca. 1600–1950*. Brill: Leiden, 2012.

Descieux, Louis Cyprien. *Influence de l'état moral de la société sur la santé publique*. Paris: Jacques Lecoffre, 1865.

Descours-Gatin, Chantal. *Quand l'opium finançait la colonisation en Indochine:*

L'élaboration de la régie générale de l'opium (1860 à 1914). Paris: L'Harmattan, 1992.

Devoisins, Albert-Joseph. *La femme et l'alcoolisme: Mémoire présenté à la Société française de tempérance pour le concours de 1886*. Paris: Imprimerie G. Rougier et Cie, 1885.

Diaz, José-Luis. "L'ivresse des poètes." *Revue de la* BNF 53 (2016): 102–13.

Didiot, Pierre-Augustin. *Code des officiers de santé de l'armée de terre ou traité de droit administratif, d'hygiène et de médecine légale militaires*. Paris: Victor Rozier, Éditeur, 1863.

Donnet, Gaston. *En Sahara: À travers le pays des Maures nomades*. Paris: L.-Henry May, 1898.

Dowbiggin, Ian. "Back to the Future: Valentin Magnan, French Psychiatry, and the Classification of Mental Diseases, 1885–1925." *Social History of Medicine* 9, no. 3 (December 1996): 383–408.

Druhen, Ignace. *Du tabac, son influence sur la santé et sur les facultés intellectuelles et morales, hygiène des fumeurs*. Besançon: Imprimerie de Dodivers, 1867.

D'Ulivo, Lucia. "Solution to the Absinthe Challenge." *Analytical and Bioanalytical Chemistry* 406 (2014): 4011.

Dubois, René. "Le combat contre l'alcoolisme: Le rôle de l'initiative privée." Legal thesis, University of Paris, 1902.

Dubuisson, Paul, and Auguste Vigouroux. *Responsabilité pénale et folie: Étude médico-légale*. Paris: Félix Alcan, 1911.

Dubut de Laforest, Jean-Louis. *Pathologie sociale. Mademoiselle Tantale. La transfusion du sang. Le gaga. Morphine. Hypnotisme. Fécondation artificielle. Monomanes. Nymphomanes. Tératologie. Le vaccin de la syphilis. Les rayons X et le fluoroscope*. Paris: Paul Dupont, 1897.

Duchêne-Marullaz, Henri. "L'hygiène des musulmans d'Algérie." Medical thesis, University of Lyon, 1905.

Duchesne, Édouard-Adolphe. *De la prostitution dans la ville d'Alger depuis la conquête*. Paris: J.-B. Baillière & Garnier Frères, 1853.

Dumas, Paul. *Les français d'Afrique et le traitement des indigènes*. Paris: Challamel et Cie, 1889.

Dunwoodie, Peter. "Assimilation, Cultural Identity and Permissible Deviance in Francophone Algerian Writing of the Interwar Years." In *Algeria and France 1800–2000: Identity, Memory, Nostalgia*, edited by Patricia M.E. Lorcin, 63–83. Syracuse: Syracuse University Press, 2006.

Durieu, Louis [Pseudonym of Blum, Eugène]. *Les juifs algériens (1870–1901): Études de démographie algérienne*. Paris: Librairie Cerf, 1902.

Durouchoux, Luc. "Les associations de prévention en France." *Après-Demain* 10 (2009): 42–5.

Duvernois, Clément. *L'Algérie, ce qu'elle est, ce qu'elle doit être: Essai économique et politique*. Algiers/Paris: Dubos Frères & Just Rouvier, 1858.

Eadie, M.J. "Absinthe, Epileptic Seizures and Valentin Magnan." *Journal of the Royal College of Physicians of Edinburgh* 39, no. 1 (1 March 2009): 73–8.

Earle, David M. "'Green Eyes, I See You. Fang, I Feel': The Symbol of Absinthe in *Ulysses*." *James Joyce Quarterly* 40, no. 4 (2003): 691–709.

Eidgenössischer Initiativausschuss gegen den Absinth. *Absinthverbot in der Schweiz*. Lausanne: Sekretariat der eigenössischen [eidgenössischen] Initiative gegen den Absinth, 1907.

– *Antwort auf die Botschaft des Bundesrates vom 9. Dezember 1907*. Zürich: J.F. Kobold-Lüdi, 1908.

Elgezy, Ahmed. "A Memory Debate: The Controversial Case of the Lesseps Statue in Port Said." *Égypte/Monde Arabe* 23 (2021): 145–57.

"Entêtement mortel." *L'Alcool: Journal mensuel. Bulletin de la Société contre l'usage des boissons spiritueuses* 9 (September 1898): 143–4.

Ernst, Serge. *Dictionnaire universel d'idées*. Vol. 1. Paris: Alphonse Picard, 1875.

Esparbès, Georges d'. *La Légion étrangère*. Paris: E. Flammarion, 1901.

Evans, H. Lloyd. *Last Winter in Algeria*. London: Chapman & Hall, 1868.

Fahrenkrug, Hermann. "What Happened to the 'Fée Verte': Notes on the Lost Drinking of Absinthe in Switzerland." *Addiction Research* 2, no. 3 (1995): 271–7.

Fallot, Ernest. *Par-delà la Méditerranée: Kabylie, Aurès, Kroumirie*. Paris: E. Plon, Nourrit et Cie, 1887.

Fauré, Th. *Causeries populaires sur l'hygiène et la physiologie*. Marseille: Bérard, 1867.

Faux, Celia Joan. "She Makes a Beast of Man, A Martyr of Woman: Absinthe in France, 1908–1922." Senior Projects, Bard College, 2019. Accessed 7 October 2022. https://digitalcommons.bard.edu/senproj_s2019/175.

Fedoul, Sénia, and Olivier Jacquet. "Une histoire de la qualité sanitaire des vins. Les règlementations à l'épreuve de l'expertise médicale et des pratiques œnologiques." *Territoires du vin* 10 (2019). Accessed 3 March 2023. https://preo.u-bourgogne.fr/territoiresduvin/index.php?id=1754&lang=fr.

Feydeau, Ernest. *Alger: Étude*. Paris: Michel Lévy Frères, 1862.

Fieni, David. *Decadent Orientalisms: The Decay of Colonial Modernity*. New York: Fordham University Press, 2020.

Figuier, Louis. "Sur les effets pernicieux de la liqueur d'absinthe." *L'Année scientifique et industrielle* (1862): 336–46.

Fillaut, Thierry. "Alcoolisme et antialcoolisme en France (1870–1970): Une affaire de genre." In *Boire: Une affaire de sexe et d'âge*, edited by Marie-Laure Déroff and Thierry Fillaut, 15–28. Rennes: Presses de l'EHESP, 2015. Accessed 18 March 2023. https://www.cairn.info/boire-une-affaire-de-sexe-et-d-age—9782810903658-page-15.htm.

– "La lutte contre l'alcoolisme dans l'armée pendant la Grande Guerre. Principes, méthodes et résultats." In *Expériences de la folie: Criminels, soldats, patients en psychiatrie (XIXe – XXe siècles)*, edited by Laurence Guignard, Hervé Guillemain, and Stéphane Tison, 141–52. Rennes: Presses Universitaires de Rennes, 2013.

Flaubert, Gustave. *Dictionnaire des idées reçues*. Paris: Éditions du Boucher, 2002.

Foix. "En Algérie." *L'Alcool: Journal mensuel. Bulletin de la Société contre l'usage des boissons spiritueuses* 2 (February 1899): 141–2.

Frégier, Casimir. *L'absinthisme en face de la loi*. Constantine: Typographie de L. Marle, 1863.

French Supplement to the Lancet, edited by Charles Achard and Charles Flandin (1 March 1919): 341–4.

Frey, Jules. *Méthode pour prolonger la vie: Simples observations*. Paris: E. Lachaud, 1879.

Furnari, Salvatore. *Voyage médicale dans l'Afrique septentrionale ou de l'ophtalmologie considéré dans ses rapports avec les différentes races*. Paris: J.-B. Baillière, 1845.

Galland, Charles de. "Excursion dans la petite Kabylie." In *Association française pour l'avancement des sciences*. Congrès d'Alger 1881, 9–23. Paris: Au secrétariat de l'Association, 1882.

Galtier-Boissière, Émile. *L'anti-alcoolisme en histoires vraies: Lectures, courtes leçons, rédigées conformément aux programmes officiels*. Paris: Librairie Larousse, 1901.

Gambelunghe, Cristiana, and Paola Melai. "Absinthe: Enjoying a New Popularity among Young People?" *Forensic Science International* 130 (2002): 183–6.

Garnier, Paul. *La folie à Paris: Étude statistique, clinique et médico-légale*. Paris: J.-B. Baillière et Fils, 1890.

Gasnier, Richard. "Les affiches publicitaires d'alcool: Images et société (1880–1920)." PhD thesis, University Lumière Lyon 2, 2006.

Geffroy, Gustave. "La bonne Absinthe." *L'Alcool: Journal mensuel. Bulletin de la Société contre l'usage des boissons spiritueuses* 9 (September 1897): 128–30.

– "Paysage d'alcool." *L'Alcool: Journal mensuel. Bulletin de la Société contre l'usage des boissons spiritueuses* 7 (July 1896): 109–11.

Georgeon, François. *Au pays du raki: Le vin et l'alcool de l'empire ottoman à la Turquie d'Erdoğan*. Paris: CNRS Éditions, 2021.

Gimpel, M., Y. Hönersch, H.-J. Altmann, R. Wittkowski, and C. Fauhl-Hassek.

"Absinth. Abschätzung des Thujongehaltes von Absinthgetränken nach historischen Rezepten." *Deutsche Lebenmittel-Rundschau* 10 (2006): 457–63.

Girardin, Jean. *Considération sur l'usage et l'abus de l'eau-de-vie et des autres liqueurs fortes: Économie sociale.* Lille: Imprimerie L. Danel, 1864.

Ghozland, F. *Un siècle de réclames: Les boissons.* Toulouse: Éditions Milan, 1986.

Goldstein, Jan. "The Hysteria Diagnosis and the Politics of Anticlericalism in Late Nineteenth-Century France." *Journal of Modern History* 54, no. 2 (June 1982): 209–39.

Gordon, Felicia. "French Psychiatry and the New Woman: The Case of Dr Constance Pascal, 1877–1937." *History of Psychiatry* 17, no. 2 (2006): 159–82.

Gorges, Édouard. *Revue de l'exposition universelle: Les merveilles de la civilisation.* Paris: F. Santorius, 1855–56.

Goudeau, Émile. *Paris qui consomme. Dessins de Pierre Vidal.* Paris: Henri Beraldi, 1893.

Grad, Charles. *Études de voyage. Vol. II. Les travaux publics en Algérie.* Nancy: Imprimerie Berger-Levrault et Cie, 1883.

Granier, Camille. *La femme criminelle.* Paris: Octave Doin, 1906.

Griveau, Paul. *L'alcoolisme fléau social: Mœurs, législation, droit comparé.* Paris: Marchal et Billard, 1906.

Gruber Garvey, Ellen. "Reframing the Bicycle: Advertising-Supported Magazines and Scorching Women." *American Quarterly* 47, no. 1 (March 1995): 66–101.

Guba, David A. Jr. *Taming Cannabis: Drugs and Empire in Nineteenth-Century France.* Montreal: McGill-Queen's University Press, 2020.

Guinard, Louis. *Enseignement du santorium: Causeries familières sur la tuberculose et l'hygiène faites au sanatorium de Bligny.* Paris: Masson et Cie, 1905.

Guy, Kolleen M. "Culinary Connections and Colonial Memories in France and Algeria." *Food and History* 8, no. 1 (2010): 219–36.

– *When Champagne Became French: Wine and the Making of a National Identity.* London/Baltimore: Johns Hopkins University Press, 2003.

Guyot, Yves. *La question de l'alcool: Allégations et réalités.* Paris: F. Alcan, 1917.

Haine, Scott. "Absinthe." Review of *Hideous Absinthe*, by Jad Adams and *L'absinthe au féminin*, by Marie-Claude Delahaye. *H-France Review* 8 (2008): 162–7.

– *The World of the Paris Café: Sociability among the French Working Class, 1789–1914.* Baltimore: Johns Hopkins University Press, 1996.

Hallenbeck, Sarah. *Claiming the Bicycle: Women, Rhetoric, and Technology in Nineteenth-Century America.* Carbondale: Southern Illinois University Press, 2016.

Hamon, Augustin Frédéric. *Déterminisme et responsabilité*. Paris: Librairie C. Reinwald Schleicher Frères, 1898.

Harris, Ruth. *Murders and Madness: Medicine, Law, and Society in the Fin de Siècle*. Oxford: Oxford University Press, 1991.

Harsin, Jill. "Gender, Class, and Madness in Nineteenth-Century France." *French Historical Studies* 17, no. 4 (Autumn 1992): 1048–70.

Hatch, Christopher. "Green with Madness: Absinthe-Induced Madness and Its Use in the Theatre of the Late 19th and Early 20th Centuries." In *Madness in Plural Contexts: Crossing Borders, Linking Knowledge*, edited by Fátima Alves, Katrina Jaworski, and Stephen Butler, 107–14. Leiden: Brill, 2012.

Hazemann, Robert Henri. "Les homicides chez les absinthiques." Medical thesis, University of Paris, 1897.

Heidrich, Chris, and Roger Liggenstorfer. "Absinthe-Herstellung." In *Absinthe – die Wiederkehr der Grünen Fee: Geschichten und Legenden eines Kulturgetränkes*, edited by Mathias Bröckers, Chris Heidrich, and Roger Liggenstorfer, 65–8. Solothurn: Nachtschatten Verlag, 2006.

Heimberg, Charles. "Comment renouveler l'histoire du mouvement ouvrier: l'exemple de l'interdiction de l'absinthe." *Traverse: Zeitschrift für Geschichte* 7, no. 2 (2000): 95–106.

Hein, Jakob, Lars Lobbedey, and Klaus-Jürgen Neumärker. "Absinth – Neue Mode, alte Probleme." *Deutsches Ärzteblatt* 98, no. 42 (19 October 2001): 2716–24.

Hennequin, Amédée. *La conquête de l'Algérie*. Paris: Charles Douniol, 1857.

Herrmann, Vanessa. "The Indeterminate Pharmacology of Absinthe in Nineteenth-Century Literature and Beyond." In *Psychopharmacology in British Literature and Culture, 1780–1900*, edited by Natalie Roxburg and Jennifer S. Henke, 195–213. Cham: Palgrave Macmillan, 2020.

Houdeville, Paul. *Comment préserver sa santé? Conférence faite par M. le docteur Paul Houdeville à la colonie de santé du Mesnil-Esnard le 29 Mai 1910*. Rouen: Imprimerie Lecerf Fils, 1910.

Howard, Sarah. "The Advertising Industry and Alcohol in Interwar France." *Historical Journal* 51, no. 2 (June 2008): 421–55.

Hugh, H.P. "The Absinthe Hour in Paris." *Ludgate* 3 (December 1896): 195–9.

Huisman, Martijn, Johannes Brug, and Johan Mackenbach. "Absinthe: Is Its History Relevant for Current Public Health?" *International Journal of Epidemiology* 36 (2007): 738–44.

Hutton, Ian. "Myth, Reality and Absinthe." *Current Drug Discovery* 9 (September 2002): 62–4.

"Interdiction de l'absinthe dans le Haut-Sénégal." *Journal de médecine et de chirurgie pratiques: À l'usage des médecins praticiens* 84 (10 December 1913): 958–9.

Iskin, Ruth E. "Popularising New Women in Belle Epoque Advertising Posters." In *A "Belle Epoque"? Women in French Society and Culture 1890–1914*, edited by Diana Holmes and Carrie Tarr, 95–112. New York/Oxford: Berghahn Books, 2007.

Jacquet, Louis. *L'alcool. Étude économique générale: Ses rapports avec l'agriculture, l'industrie, le commerce, la législation, l'impôt, l'hygiène individuelle et sociale.* Paris: Masson et Cie, 1912.

Jobard, Jean-Baptiste-Ambroise-Marcellin. *Nouvelle économie sociale, ou Monautopole industriel, artistique, commercial et littéraire.* Paris: Mathias, 1844.

Kermorgant, Alexandre. "L'alcoolisme dans les colonies françaises." *Bulletin de la Société de pathologie exotique* 2, no. 6 (1909): 330–40.

Khalifa, Dominique. "Vices et vertus: Ivresse de la Belle Époque." *Revue de la BNF* 53 (2016): 70–9.

Kock, Henry de. *Les Buveurs d'absinthe (La Magnétiseuse).* Paris: L. de Potter, 1864.

Koziell, Louis-Joseph-Pierre. "Hygiène de quelques quartiers d'Alger." Medical thesis, University of Bordeaux, 1897.

Kudlick, Catherine J. "Learning from Cholera: Medical and Social Responses to the First Great Paris Epidemic in 1832." *Microbes and Infection* 1 (1999): 1051–7.

Laborde, Jean Baptiste Vincent. "L'alcool et sa toxicité: Les alcools dits supérieurs et d'industrie et les bouquets artificiels." *Gazette médicale de l'Algérie* (1888): 146–8.

"L'absinthe en Angleterre." *L'Alcool: Journal mensuel. Bulletin de la Société contre l'usage des boissons spiritueuses* 6 (June 1896): 93–4.

"L'absinthe et ses dangers." *La Médecine internationale* 12 (December 1899): 373.

Lachenmeier, Dirk W. "Absinth. Geschichte einer Thujon- oder Alkoholabhängigkeit." *Fortschritte der Neurologie-Psychiatrie* 75 (2007): 306–8.

Lachenmeier, Dirk W., and David Nathan-Maister. "Absinthe and Tobacco: A New Look at an Old Problem? (Comment on: Absinthe – Is Its History Relevant for Current Public Health?)." *International Journal of Epidemiology* 37 (2008): 217–18.

– "Systematic Misinformation about Thujone in Pre-Ban Absinthe." *Deutsche Lebensmittel-Rundschau* 6 (2007): 255–62.

Lachenmeier, Dirk W., David Nathan-Maister, Theodore A. Breaux, Jean Pierre Luauté, and Joachim Emmert. "Absinthe, Absinthism and Thujone. New Insight into the Spirit's Impact on Public Health." *Open Addiction Journal* 3 (2010): 32–8.

Lachenmeier, Dirk W., Stephan G. Walch, Stephan A. Padosch, and Lars U. Kröner. "Absinthe: A Review." *Critical Reviews in Food Science and Nutrition* 46, no. 5 (2006): 365–77.

Lajer-Burcharth, Ewa. "Modernity and the Condition of Disguise: Manet's 'Absinthe Drinker.'" *Art Journal* 45, no. 1 (Spring 1985): 18–26.

Lalouette, Jacqueline. "La consommation de vin et d'alcool au cours du XIXe et au début du XXe siècle." *Ethnologie française* 10, no. 3 (July–September 1980): 287–302.

– "Les débits de boissons urbains entre 1880 et 1914." *Ethnologie française* 12, no. 2 (April-June 1982): 131–6.

Lalou, Socrate D. *Contribution à l'étude de l'essence d'absinthe et de quelques autres essences (hysope, tanaisie, sauge, fenouil, coriandre, anis et badiane)*. Paris: C. Naud, 1903.

"La lutte contre l'alcoolisme." *Journal de médecine et de chirurgie pratiques* 85 (10 May 1914): 365–6.

Lancereaux, Étienne. "Absinthisme aigu." *Bulletin de l'Académie de médecine* 9 (1880): 893–901.

– *De l'alcoolisme et de ses conséquences au point de vue de l'état physique, intellectuel, et moral des populations*. Paris: E. Donnaud, 1878.

Lanessan, Jean-Louis de. *L'expansion coloniale de la France: Étude économique, politique et géographique sur les établissements français d'outre-mer*. Paris: F. Alcan, 1886.

Langle, Henry-Melchior de. "Cafés et débits lieu de nouveautés." In *Le Petit Monde des cafés et débits parisiens au XIXe siècle: Évolution de la sociabilité citadine*, edited by Henry-Melchior de Langle, 149–222. Paris: Presses Universitaires de France, 1990. Accessed 21 February 2023. https://www.cairn.info/le-petit-monde-des-cafes-et-debits-parisiens—9782130429913-page-149.htm.

Lanier, Doris. *Absinthe: The Cocaine of the Nineteenth Century*. Jefferson/London: MacFarland & Company, 1995.

– "The Bittersweet Taste of Absinthe in Hemingway's 'Hills Like White Elephants.'" *Studies in Short Fiction* 26, no. 3 (Summer 1989): 279–88.

Laupts [pseudonym of Saint-Paul, Georges]. *Perversions et perversité sexuelles: Tares et poisons*. Paris: Georges Carré, 1896.

Laurent, Émile. "Revue des thèses." Review of *Les homicides commis par les absinthiques*, by Robert Hazemann. *Archives de l'anthropologie criminelle* 13 (1898): 111–12.

Laveran, Alphonse. *Traité d'hygiène militaire*. Paris: G. Masson, 1896.

Lebovitz, David. *Drinking French: The Iconic Cocktails, Apéritifs, and Café Traditions of France, with 160 Recipes*. Berkeley: Ten Speed Press, 2020.

Le Bras, Stéphane. "Boire pour se soigner: Une nouvelle menace pour la santé publique." *Revue Historique* 702 (2022): 399–430.

– "'Le vin est la plus saine et la plus hygiénique des boissons': Anatomie d'une lé-gende (XIXe-XXe siècle)." In *Faux bruits, rumeurs et fake news*, edited by Philippe Bourdin. Paris: Éditions du Comité des travaux historiques et scientifiques, 2021. Accessed 8 December 2022. http://books.openedition.org/cths/15460.

"Le commerce de l'absinthe en Algérie." *Journal de médecine et de chirurgie pratiques* 82 (1 January 1911): 767.

"Le commerce de l'absinthe en Algérie." *La Province médicale* 23 (1912): 10.

Lee, Roberta A., and Michael J. Balick. "Absinthe: La Fée Vert." *Ethnomedicine* 1, no. 3 (May 2005): 217–19.

Legrain, Paul-Maurice. *Éléments de médecine mentale appliqués à l'étude du droit: Cours professé à la Faculté de droit.* Paris: A. Rousseau, 1906.

– "Guerre à l'apéritif." *L'Alcool: Journal mensuel. Bulletin de la Société contre l'usage des boissons spiritueuses* 2 (February 1899): 30–2.

Legrand du Saulle, Henri. *Étude médico-légale sur les épileptiques.* Paris: Y. Adrien Delahaye et Cie, 1877.

– *La folie devant les tribunaux.* Paris: F. Savy, 1864.

Lemanski, Witold. *Hygiène du colon, ou vade-mecum de l'européen aux colonies.* Paris: G. Steinheil, 1902.

Lemire, Charles. *L'Indo-Chine. Cochinchine française. Royaume de Cambodge, Royaume d'Annam et Tonkin.* Paris: Challamel Ainé, 1884.

Lemoine, Georges-Alphonse-Hubert. *Traité d'hygiène militaire.* Paris: Masson et Cie, 1911.

Lévy, Michel. *Traité d'hygiène publique et privée.* Vol. 2. Paris: J.-B. Baillière et Fils, 1862.

Lierre, Henri. *La question de l'absinthe.* Paris: Imprimerie Vallée, 1867.

Liggenstorfer, Roger. "Der Ursprung des Absinthe." In *Absinthe – die Wiederkehr der Grünen Fee: Geschichten und Legenden eines Kulturgetränkes*, edited by Mathias Bröckers, Chris Heidrich, and Roger Liggenstorfer, 23–5. Solothurn: Nachtschatten Verlag, 2006.

– "Thujon – gefährlicher Wirkstoff oder kreativer Antrieb?" In *Absinthe – die Wiederkehr der Grünen Fee: Geschichten und Legenden eines Kulturgetränkes*, edited by Mathias Bröckers, Chris Heidrich, and Roger Liggenstorfer, 53–7. Solothurn: Nachtschatten Verlag, 2006.

Livon, Ch. "Absinthe (Essence d')." In *Dictionnaire de physiologie*, edited by Charles Richet, 13–23. Vol. 1. Paris: Félix Alcan, 1895.

L. "Les homicides commis par les absinthiques." *L'Alcool: Journal mensuel. Bulletin de la Société contre l'usage des boissons spiritueuses* 5 (May 1897): 62–3.

Loir, Adrien. "Les conditions sanitaires et l'hygiène en Tunisie." In *Revue Générale des Sciences Pures et Appliquées: La France en Tunisie*, 106–14. Paris: Georges Carré, 1897.

Luauté, Jean-Pierre. "L'absinthisme: La faute du docteur Magnan." *L'Evolution Psychiatrique* 72 (2007): 515–30.

Luauté, Jean-Pierre, O. Saladini, and J. Benyaya. "Toxicité neuropsychiatrique de l'absinthe. Historique, données actuelles." *Annales Médico-Psychologiques* 163 (2005): 497–501.

Lucienne, V.-S. *Leçons d'anti-alcoolisme: Rédigées conformément au programme des écoles publiques*. Lille: Imprimerie-Libraire Camille Robbe, 1899.

L. "Un poison bien français." *L'Alcool: Journal mensuel. Bulletin de la Société contre l'usage des boissons spiritueuses* (January–February 1897): 3–5.

MacLeod, Kirsten. "Marie Corelli and Fin-de-Siècle Francophobia: The Absinthe Trail of French Art." *English Literature in Transition* 43, no. 1 (2000): 66–82.

Magnan, Valentin. "Accidents déterminés par l'abus de la liqueur d'absinthe." *L'Union médicale* 92, 94 (1864): 227–32; 257–62.

– *Étude expérimentale et clinique sur l'alcoolisme: Alcool et absinthe, épilepsie absin-thique*. Paris: Typographie de Renou et Maulde, 1871.

– "On the Comparative Action of Alcohol and Absinthe." *Lancet* (19 September 1874): 410–12.

Magnan, Valentin, and Alfred Fillassier. "Alcoholism and Degeneracy: Statistics of the Central Service for the Admission of Insane Persons for the Town of Paris and for the Department of the Seine, from 1867–1912." In *Problems in Eugenics. Papers Communicated to the First International Eugenics Conference Held at the University of London, July 24th to 30th, 1912*, 367–78. London: The Eugenics Education Society, 1912.

Marbaud, Pierre. *Coup d'œil sur l'Algérie pendant la crise de 1859–1860 et réflexions sur le décret relatif de la vente des terres domaniales*. Constantine: Imprimerie et Lithographie de Ve Guende, 1860.

Marcailhou d'Aymeric, Alphonse. *Manuel hygiénique du colon algérien*. Algiers: Imprimerie Juillet Saint-Lager, 1873.

Marcé, Louis-Victor. "Sur l'action toxique de l'essence d'absinthe." *Comptes rendus hebdomadaires des séances de l'Académie des sciences* 58 (1864): 628–9.

– *Traité pratique des maladies mentales*. Paris: J.B. Baillière, 1862.

Marcotte de Quivières, Charles. *Deux ans en Afrique*. Paris: Librairie Nouvelle, 1855.

Marit, Jean-Joseph. *Hygiène de l'Algérie: Exposé des moyens de conserver la santé et de se préserver des maladies dans les pays chauds et spécialement en Algérie*. Paris/Algiers: J.-B. Baillière et Fils & Bastide – Dubos Frères – Tissier, 1862.

Marrus, Michael R. "Social Drinking in the *Belle Epoque*." *Journal of Social History* 7, no. 2 (Winter 1974): 115–41.

Martin, A.-E.-Victor. *Manuel d'hygiène: A l'usage des européens qui viennent s'établir en Algérie*. Algiers/Paris: Dubos Frères et Marest, 1847.

Marx, Karl. "Zur Kritik der Hegel'schen Rechts-Philosophie." In *Deutsch-Französische Jahrbücher*, edited by Arnold Ruge, and Karl Marx, 71–85. Paris: Bureau der Jahrbücher, 1844.

Mayet, Charles. *Le vin de France*. Paris: Jouvet et Cie, 1894.

Meunier, Hippolyte. *Les causeries du docteur: Entretiens familiers sur l'hygiène*. Paris: Librairie de L. Hachette et Cie, 1868.

Meynié, Georges. *Les juifs en Algérie*. Paris: Albert Savine, 1888.

Ministère de la guerre. *Manuel à l'usage des troupes employées Outre-mer*. Part 1. Paris: Charles-Lavauzelle & Cie, 1941.

M., J.-B. "Bulletin." *Gazette médicale de l'Algérie* 20 (1889): 153–4.

M., L. "Propos de table." *L'Alcool: Journal mensuel. Bulletin de la Société contre l'usage des boissons spiritueuses* 1 (January 1896): 9–11.

Monier, E. *Causeries sur l'hygiène et causeries scientifiques*. Compiègne: Henry Lefebvre, 1897.

Monin, Ernest. *L'alcoolisme: Étude médico-sociale*. Paris: Octave Doin, 1889.

– *L'hygiène de l'estomac: Guide pratique de l'alimentation*. Paris: Octave Doin, 1895.

– *Misères nerveuses*. Paris: Paul Ollendorff, 1890.

Monselet, Charles. *De Montmartre à Séville*. Paris: Achille Faure, 1865.

Montagne, Michael. "Drugs on the Internet, Part V: Absinthe, Return of the Emerald Mask." *Substance Use and Misuse* 48, no. 7 (2013): 506–13.

Morache, Georges. *Traité d'hygiène militaire*. Paris: J.-B. Baillière et Fils, 1886.

Moreau, Jules-Michel Ferdinand. *De la liqueur d'absinthe et de ses effets*. Paris: F. Savy, 1863.

Motet, Alexandre Auguste. "Considérations générales sur l'alcoolisme, et plus particulièrement des effets toxiques produits sur l'homme par la liqueur d'absinthe." Medical thesis, Faculty of Medicine, Paris, 1859.

Musset, Benoît. "Entre salubrité, conservation et goût: Définir le 'bon vin' en France (1560–1820)." *Revue Historique* 677 (2016): 57–82.

Narrey, Charles. *Les amours faciles*. Paris: Librairie Centrale, 1866.

Niemeyer, Katharina. "'Fée verte' – 'hada verde' – düstere Muse. Absinth in der Boheme des Fin de siècle." *zeitenblicke* 9, no. 3 (23 December 2009). Accessed 22 February 2023. https://www.zeitenblicke.de/2009/3/niemeyer/index_html.

Noël, Benoît. *Nouvelles confidences sur l'absinthe*. Yens sur Morges: Édition Cabédita, 2003.

Nourrisson, Didier. "Aux origines de l'antialcoolisme." *Histoire, économie et société* 4 (1988): 491–506.

– *Crus et cuites: Histoire du buveur.* Paris: Perrin, 2013.

– "La consommation alcoolique en Seine-Inférieure au XIXe siècle." *Annales de Normandie* 1 (1991): 49–73.

– "Les 'fines herbes' du plaisir." *Ethnologie Française* 34, no. 3 (July–September 2004): 435–42.

Nye, Robert Allen. "Degeneration and the Medical Model of Cultural Crisis in the French *Belle Époque*." In *Political Symbolism in Modern Europe: Essays in Honor of George L. Mosse*, edited by Seymour Drescher, David Sabean, and Allan Sharlin, 19–41. New Brunswick/London: Transaction Books, 1982.

Ollivier, Clément. *Influence des affections organiques sur la raison ou pathologie morale.* Paris/Tours: Germer Baillière & Guilland-Verger, 1867.

O'Reilly, Shelley. "Absinthe Makes the Tart Grow Fonder: A Note on 'Wormwood' in Christina Rosetti's 'Goblin Market.'" *Victorian Poetry* 34, no. 1 (Spring 1996): 108–14.

Oudaille. "Les commandements de l'hygiène." *L'Alcool: Journal mensuel. Bulletin de la Société contre l'usage des boissons spiritueuses* 10 (October 1898): 143–5.

Overkempe, T.R. "Following the Fairy: A Socio-Geographical History of Absinthe in Paris from 1850–1890." Master's thesis, Utrecht University, 2021.

Owens, Paul, and Paul Nathan. *The Little Green Book of Absinthe: An Essential Companion with Lore, Trivia, and Classic and Contemporary Cocktails.* New York: Penguin, 2010. Not paginated.

Padosch, Stephan A., Dirk W. Lachenmeier, and Lars U. Kröner. "Absinthism: A Fictitious 19th Century Syndrome with Present Impact." *Substance Abuse Treatment, Prevention, and Policy* 1 (2006): 1–14.

Padwa, Howard. *Social Poison: The Culture and Politics of Opiate Control in Britain and France, 1821–1926.* Baltimore: John Hopkins University Press, 2012.

Pagès, Calixte. *L'hygiène pour tous.* Paris: C. Naud, 1903.

Park, Jihang. "Sport, Dress Reform and the Emancipation of Women in Victorian England: A Reappraisal." *International Journal of the History of Sport* 6, no. 1 (1989): 10–30.

Pascal, André. *Le Petit botaniste de l'enfance, ou leçons sur l'histoire et les usages des plantes les plus utiles à connaître.* Grenoble: Maisonville et Fils, 1864.

Pasteur, Claude. *Les femmes à bicyclette à la Belle Epoque.* Paris: Éditions France-Empire, 1986.

Picard, Eugène. "Boissons alcooliques (Dangers des). Extrait du Manuel d'instruction populaire à l'usage des instituteurs." *Bulletin des sociétés de secours mutuels. Revue des institutions de prévoyance* (1876): 333–42.

– *Dangers de l'abus des boissons alcooliques: Manuel d'instruction populaire à l'usage des instituteurs.* Paris: Imprimerie de E. Donnaud, 1874.

Pichon, Georges. *Les maladies de l'esprit: Délires des persécutions, délire des grandeurs, paralysie générale, épilepsie, dégénérescence, etc., etc. Délires alcoolique et toxique. Morphinomanie, éthéromanie, absinthisme, chloralisme, etc., etc. Études cliniques et médico-légales.* Paris: Octave Doin, 1888.

Pick, Daniel. *Faces of Degeneration: A European Disorder, c. 1848–c. 1918.* Cambridge: Cambridge University Press, 1989.

Pictet, Paul. "Suisse. La prohibition de l'absinthe." *Le Musée social: Annales* 8 (1906): 345–50.

Pignel, Armand. *Conducteur ou guide du voyageur et du colon de Paris à Alger et dans l'Algérie.* Paris/Algiers: Debécourt & Bastite et Brachet, 1836.

Pinaud, Pierre-Alfred-Hippolyte-André-René. "L'alcoolisme chez les Arabes en Algérie." Medical thesis, University of Bordeaux, 1933.

Pizzorno, Joseph E., and Michael T. Murray. *Textbook of Natural Medicine.* St Louis (Missouri): Elsevier, 2013.

Poiré, Eugène. *La Tunisie française.* Paris: E. Plon, Nourrit et Cie, 1892.

Pouchet, Gabriel. *Leçons de pharmacodynamie et de matière médicale.* Paris: Octave Doin, 1901.

Poulle, Guillaume. "Rapport Supplémentaire fait au nom de la Commission chargée d'examiner la proposition de loi de M. de Lamarzelle et un grand nombre de ses collègues tendant à interdire la fabrication et la vente de l'absinthe." *Sénat. Impressions: Projets, propositions, rapports* 232 (11 July 1911): 1–50.

Prestwich, Patricia. *Drink and the Politics of Social Reform: Anti-Alcoholism in France since 1870.* Palo Alto: Society for the Promotion of Science & Scholarship, 1988.

– "Female Alcoholism in Paris, 1870–1920: The Response of Psychiatrists and of Families." *History of Psychiatry* 14, no. 3 (2003): 321–36.

– "Paul-Maurice Legrain (1860–1939)." *Addictions* 92, no. 10 (October 1997): 1255–63.

– "Temperance in France: The Curious Case of Absinth." *Historical Reflections/ Réflexions Historiques* 6, no. 2 (Winter 1979): 301–19.

Prochaska, David. *Making Algeria French: Colonialism in Bône, 1870–1920.* Cambridge/New York: Cambridge University Press, 1990.

"Prohibition de l'absinthe au Congo." *L'Alcool: Journal mensuel. Bulletin de la Société contre l'usage des boissons spiritueuses* 11 (November 1898): 161–2.

Proschan, Frank. "'Syphilis, Opiomania, and Pederasty': Colonial Constructions of Vietnamese (and French) Social Diseases." *Journal of the History of Sexuality* 11, no. 4 (October 2002): 610–36.

Quétel, Claude, and Jean-Yves Simon. "L'aliénation alcoolique en France (XIXe siècle et 1ère moitié du XXe siècle)." *Histoire, Économie et Société* 4 (1988): 507–33.

Quetin, E. *Guide du voyageur en Algérie: Itinéraire du savant, de l'artiste, de l'homme du monde et du colon*. Paris/Algiers: L. Maison & Dubos Frères et Marest, 1848.

Quincey, Thomas de. *Confessions of an English Opium-Eater*. Ware: Wordsworth Classics, 2009.

Ravenez, Eugène-François. *La vie du soldat au point de vue de l'hygiène*. Paris: J.-B. Baillière et Fils, 1889.

Raynaud, Lucien. "L'alcoolisme en Algérie." *L'Alcool: Journal mensuel. Bulletin de la Société contre l'usage des boissons spiritueuses* 5 (10 May 1896): 66–8.

Réclus, Onésime. *Géographie*. Paris: L. Mulo, 1873.

Régis, Emmanuel. "Préface." In *Les opiomanes: Mangeurs, buveurs et fumeurs d'opium. Étude Clinique et Médico-littéraire*, by Roger Dupouy, 1–12. Paris: Félix Alcan, 1912.

Régis, Louis. *Constantine: Voyages et séjours*. Paris: Calmann Lévy, 1880.

Rekand, Tiina. "Absinthe, the Nervous System and Painting." *International Review of Neurobiology* 74 (2006): 271–8.

Remlinger, Paul. "Les progrès de l'alcoolisme au Maroc." *Bulletin de la Société de pathologie exotique* 5 (1912): 747–52.

Rémy, Jules. *Lettres d'un voyageur à M. L.G.-G.* Châlons: Imprimerie de T. Martin, 1858.

Rénon, Louis. *Les maladies populaires: Maladies vénériennes, alcoolisme, tuberculose. Leçons faites à la faculté de médecine de Paris*. Paris: Masson et Cie, 1905.

"Report on: Macé. Vœu de MM. Carles et Macé, tendant à ce que la vente de l'anisette à 40° soit autorisée dans les débits de l'Algérie." *Délégations financières algériennes* 3 (May–June 1920): 1069–77.

Reynolds, Siân. "Vélo-Métro-Auto: Women's Mobility in Belle Epoque Paris." In *A 'Belle Epoque'? Women in French Society and Culture 1890–1914*, edited by Diana Holmes and Carrie Tarr, 81–94. New York/Oxford: Berghahn Books, 2007.

Riant, Aimé. *L'alcool et le tabac*. Paris: Librairie Hachette et Cie, 1876.

Ribouleau, Ch. *À travers l'hygiène: Guide précieux de la santé, causeries variées, littéraires et scientifiques sur l'hygiène physique, morale et sociale*. Reims: published by the author, 1901.

Richardot, Henri. *Sept semaines en Tunisie et en Algérie: Avec itinéraire et les dépenses du voyage*. Paris: Combet & Cie, 1905.

Rivière, Ch. "Plantes à fécule et à sucre; leurs alcools." *Revue des Cultures Coloniales* 6 (20 May 1900): 289–93.

Rochard, Jules. "L'alcool. Son rôle dans les sociétés modernes." *Revue des Deux Mondes* 74 (March 1886): 871–900.

– *Traité d'hygiène publique et privée*. Paris: Octave Doin, 1897.

Rogers, G. Albert. *A Winter in Algeria: 1863–64*. London: S. Low, Son, and Marston, 1865.

Rohlfs, F. Gerhard. *Marokko und die Reise südlich vom Atlas durch die Oasen Draa und Tafilet. Reisebericht*. Bremen: J. Kühtmann's Buchhandlung, 1873.

Ross, Andrew Israel. "Serving Sex: Playing with Prostitution in the *Brasseries à femmes* of Late Nineteenth-Century Paris." *Journal of the History of Sexuality* 24, no. 2 (May 2015): 288–313.

Rossignol, Jacques-François-Rémy-Stanislas. *Traité élémentaire d'hygiène militaire*. Paris: Alexandre Johanneau & Garnier Frères, 1857.

Rouby, Pierre. "De l'alcoolisme en France et en Algérie." In *Congrès des médecins aliénistes et neurologistes de France et des pays de langue française*, 237–50. Paris: G. Masson, 1895.

Roux, Joseph. *Étude sur les rapports de l'alcoolisme et de la phthisie pulmonaire*. Paris: Alphonse Derenne, 1881.

Rude, Maxime. *Tout Paris au café*. Paris: Maurice Dreyfous, 1877.

Ruyssen, Théodore. "La tempérance." *Revue de métaphysique et de morale* 1 (1913): 132–49.

Saliège, Joseph. "Rapport." In *Procès-verbaux des délibérations. Conseil supérieur de gouvernement (Alger)*, 151–68. Algiers: no publishing house, 1911–12.

Salle, Georges-François-Sigisbert. *Gelures et insolations chez le soldat, en particulier sur les troupes d'infanterie en marche*. Paris: Henri Charles-Lavauzelle, 1898.

Santi, Louis de. *De l'entérite chronique paludéenne ou diarrhée de Cochinchine: Essai d'interprétation de la pathologie des régions paludéennes intertropicales*. Paris: Rueff & Cie, 1891.

Saxton, Lauren. "Before Addiction: The Medical History of Alcoholism in Nineteenth-Century France." PhD thesis, CUNY, 2015.

Schaffner, Margaret A. "Absinthe Prohibition in Switzerland." *American Political Science Review* 2, no. 4 (1908): 562.

Scheltema, Johann Friedrich. "The Opium Question." *American Journal of Sociology* 16, no. 2 (September 1910): 213–35.

Schneider, William. "Toward the Improvement of the Human Race: The History of Eugenics in France." *Journal of Modern History* 54, no. 2 (June 1982): 268–91.

Schultz, Gretchen. "Celebration and Censure: The Aperitif and the Art of the

Poster in Belle Époque France." *Art in Print* 7, no. 4 (November–December 2017): 19–24.

Schwarz, Gerhart S. "Society, Physicians, and the Corset." *Bulletin of the New York Academy of Medicine* 55, no. 6 (June 1979): 551–90.

Senn, Martin. "Wo Spott und Absinth blühen: Dorfgeschichten um Môtiers." *Heimatschutz* 82, no. 3 (1987): 12–14.

Shaker, Anthony F. "The Beginning and Historisation of Decline Theories." In *Niedergangsthesen auf dem Prüfstand*, edited by Merdan Güneş and Bacem Dziri, 51–78. Berlin: Peter Lang, 2020.

Sirven, Alfred. *Les abrutis*. Paris: F. Cournol, 1865.

Skibicki, Marcin. "Victimes de stéréotypes ou chantres de la modernité? L'ambiguïté de l'image de la femme dans l'affiche française de la Belle Époque." *Orbis Linguarum* 53 (2019): 221–30.

Smith, Philip E.M. "Absinthe Attacks." *Practical Neurology* 6 (2006): 376–81.

Solmon, F.-Jules. *Essai d'enseignement militaire antialcoolique. L'alcool et l'alcoolisme. Les aromates et l'aromatisme*. Dieppe: Imprimerie centrale et Delevoye réunies, 1903.

Souamaa, Najib. "La loi des huit heures: un projet d'Europe sociale? (1918–1932)." *Travail et Emploi* 110 (April–June 2007): 27–36.

Soubeiran, Jean-Léon. *Hygiène élémentaire*. Paris: Librairie Hachette et Cie, 1873.

Souguenet, Léon. *Route de Timmimoun: Heures religieuses*. Brussels: Oscar Lamberty, 1914.

Steeg, Jules. *Les dangers de l'alcoolisme*. Paris: Librairie Classique Fernand Nathan, 1896.

Steele, Valerie. *The Corset: A Cultural History*. New Haven: Yale University Press, 2005.

Stocker, Franz August. "Der Absinth." *Vom Jura zum Schwarzwald: Blätter für Heimatkunde und Heimatschutz* 2 (1885): 31–7.

Stoler, Ann Laura. *Carnal Knowledge and Imperial Power: Race and the Intimate in Colonial Rule*. Berkeley: University of California Press, 2002.

Strang, John, Wilfred Niels Arnold, and Timothy Peters. "Absinthe: What's Your Poison?" *British Medical Journal* 319 (1999): 1590–2.

Studer, Nina S. "Remembrance of Drinks Past: Wine and Absinthe in Nineteenth-century French Algeria." In *The Politics of Historical Memory and Commemoration in Africa*, edited by Cassandra Mark-Thiesen, Moritz A. Mihatsch, and Michelle M. Sikes, 169–91. Oldenbourg: De Gruyter, 2021.

– "The Green Fairy in the Maghreb: Absinthe, Guilt and Cultural Assimilation in French Colonial Medicine." *Maghreb Review* 40, no. 4 (2015): 493–508.

– "The Same Drink? Wine and Absinthe Consumption and Drinking Cultures Among French and Muslim Groups in Nineteenth Century Algeria." In *Alcohol Flows across Cultures: Drinking Cultures in Transnational and Comparative Perspective*, edited by Waltraud Ernst, 20–43. London/New York: Routledge, 2020.

– "Under the Influence." *History Today* 72 (7 July 2022): 60–71.

– "'Was trinkt der zivilisierte Mensch?' Teekonsum und morbide Normalität im kolonialen Maghreb." *Schweizerische Zeitschrift für Geschichte* 64, no. 3 (2014): 406–24.

– "'Without Coffee, Our Algeria Would Be Uninhabitable': Ambivalent Attitudes to Coffee Drinking in Medical Accounts on Nineteenth-Century Algeria." *Historische Anthropologie* 29, no. 1 (2021): 11–30.

"Suppression de l'absinthe en Belgique." *La Croix-Rouge suisse: Revue mensuelle des Samaritains suisses* 13, no. 5 (1905): 40.

Tailhade, Laurent. *La "Noire Idole": Étude sur la morphinomanie.* Paris: Librairie Léon Vanier, Éditeur, 1907.

Terril, Weldon Clark. "Dudes, Decadence, and Degeneracy: Criminalisation of Absinthe in the United States." *Cultural and Social History* (2022): 1–17.

Thévenot, Jean-Pierre-Ferdinand. *Traité des maladies des Européens dans les pays chauds, et spécialement au Sénégal, ou essai statistique médical et hygiénique, sur le sol, le climat et les maladies de cette partie de l'Afrique.* Paris: J.-B. Baillière, 1840.

Thierrin, Dominique. *Dangers de l'abus des boissons alcooliques: Manuel d'instruction populaire à l'usage des instituteurs.* Sion: Imprimerie Kleindienst & Schmid, 1896.

Thierry-Mieg, Charles. *Six semaines en Afrique: Souvenirs de voyage.* Paris: Michel Lévy Frères, 1861.

Tissandier, Gaston. *Les merveilles de la photographie.* Paris: Hachette et Cie, 1874.

Treille, Georges. *Principes d'hygiène coloniale.* Paris: Georges Carré et C. Naud, 1899.

Triboulet, Henri, and Félix Mathieu. *L'alcool et l'alcoolisme. Notions générales. Toxicologie et physiologie. Pathologie. Thérapeutique. Prophylaxie.* Paris: Georges Carré et C. Naud, 1900.

Tsikounas, Myriam. "Quand l'alcool fait sa pub: Les publicités en faveur de l'alcool dans la presse française, de la loi Roussel à la loi Évin (1873–1998)." *Le Temps des médias* 2 (2004): 99–114.

Varin, Paul. *L'Algérie deviendra-t-elle une colonie?* Paris: E. Dentu, 1861.

Vibert, Paul. *Les questions brûlantes, exemples d'hier et d'aujourd'hui: La philosophie de la colonisation.* Vol. 1. Paris: E. Cornély, 1906.

Vignon, Louis. *La France en Algérie.* Paris: Libraire Hachette et Cie, 1893.

Villacrose, A. *Vingt ans en Algérie: Ou tribulations d'un colon racontées par lui-même:*

la colonisation en 1874, le régime militaire et l'administration civile, mœurs, coutumes, institutions des indigènes, ce qui est fait, ce qui est à faire. Paris: Challamel Ainé, 1875.

Villon, A.-M. "L'Absinthe." *La Nature: Revue des sciences et de leurs applications aux arts et à l'industrie. Journal hebdomadaire illustré* 1105 (4 August 1894): 149–51.

Viré, Camille. *En Algérie. Une excursion dans le département d'Alger.* Paris: Charles Bayle, 1888.

Viry, Charles. "Hygiène militaire." In *Encyclopédie d'hygiène et de médecine publique,* edited by Jules Rochard, 1–402. Vol. 7. Paris: Lecrosnier et Babe, 1895.

– *Manuel d'hygiène militaire: Suivi d'un précis des premiers secours à donner en attendant l'arrivée du médecin.* Paris: A. Delahaye et É. Lecrosnier, 1886.

Vogt, Donald D. "Absinthium: A Nineteenth-Century Drug of Abuse." *Journal of Ethnopharmacology* 4 (1981): 337–42.

Vogt, Donald D., and Michael Montagne. "Absinthe: Behind the Emerald Mask." *International Journal of the Addictions* 17, no. 6 (1982): 1015–29.

Vuillaume, Dominique. "Entre toxicomanie et addiction, l'impossible assimilation de l'alcool à une drogue." *Sciences sociales et santé* 34, no. 1 (March 2006): 103–10.

Wade, Jenny. "Going Berserk, Running Amok, and the Extraordinary Capabilities and Invulnerability of Battle Trance." *International Journal of Transpersonal Studies* (2022): 1–30.

Wahl, Paul-Lucien. *Le crime devant la science.* Paris: V. Giard & E. Brière, 1910.

Waldthausen, Clara von. "Reflection on the Material History and Materiality of Photographic Gelatin." *Topics in Photographic Preservation* 16 (2015): 347–59.

Walker, Emma E. "The Effects of Absinthe." *Medical Record* (13 October 1906): 568–72.

Walker, Warren S. "Lost Liquor Lore: The Blue Flame of Intemperance." *Journal of Popular Culture* 16, no. 2 (Autumn 1982): 17–25.

Walmsley, Hugh Mulleneux. *Sketches of Algeria during the Kabyle War.* London: Chapman and Hall, 1858.

Wilson-Bareau, Juliet. "Manet's Absinthe Drinker." *Art in Print* 7, no. 5 (January–February 2018): 29–35.

Windham, W.G. *Notes in North Africa: Being a Guide to the Sportsman and Tourist in Algeria and Tunisia.* London: Ward and Lock, 1862.

Young, Marnin. "Heroic Indolence: Realism and the Politics of Time in Raffaëlli's *Absinthe Drinkers.*" *Art Bulletin* 90, no. 2 (June 2008): 235–59.

Znaien, Nessim. "Une généalogie coloniale des politiques prohibitives en France durant la première guerre mondiale?" *Le Mouvement social* 278 (2022): 41–53.

Index